Nikolai Zabolotsky (1903–1958) was one of the great poets of twentieth-century Russia. As the last link in the Russian Futurist tradition and the first significant poet to come of age in the Soviet period, Zabolotsky wrote poetry both highly experimental and classical. This is the first critical biography of Zabolotsky to appear in English. Goldstein examines not only Zabolotsky's poetic career but also his life, from his obscure origins in the Russian countryside to his arrest and imprisonment in the 1930s. At the same time, Goldstein highlights the deep ambiguity of Zabolotsky's era by exploring the ways in which the poet was influenced both by the avant-garde and by the Soviet scientific establishment.

CAMBRIDGE STUDIES IN RUSSIAN LITERATURE

NIKOLAI ZABOLOTSKY
Play for mortal stakes

NIKOLAI ZABOLOTSKY

Play for mortal stakes

DARRA GOLDSTEIN

Associate Professor of Russian, Williams College

CAMBRIDGE
UNIVERSITY PRESS

Published by the Press Syndicate of the University of Cambridge
The Pitt Building, Trumpington Street, Cambridge CB2 1RP
40 West 20th Street, New York, NY 10011–4211, USA
10 Stamford Road, Oakleigh, Melbourne 3166, Australia

First published 1993

Printed in Great Britain at the University Press, Cambridge

A catalogue record for this book is available from the British Library

Library of Congress cataloguing in publication data
Goldstein, Darra.
Nikolai Zabolotsky: Play for mortal stakes /
Darra Goldstein.
p.   cm.
Includes bibliographical references and index.
ISBN 0 521 41896 8
1. Zabolotskii, N. (Nikolai), 1903–1958 – Biography.
2. Poets, Russian – 20th century – Biography.   1. Title.
PG3476.Z2Z67   1993
891.71′42–dc20   92-46108   CIP
[B]

ISBN 0 521 41896 8 hardback

CE

To the memory of my brother, Jared Haft Goldstein,
who merged the scientific and the humane
in his work and his life

But yield who will to their separation,
My object in living is to unite
My avocation and my vocation
As my two eyes make one in sight.
Only where love and need are one,
And the work is play for mortal stakes,
Is the deed ever really done
For Heaven and the future's sakes.
            Robert Frost, "Two Tramps in Mud Time"

We must shatter the glass wall that
Socrates and Aristotle placed between
   nature and the sweet lechery of an
      inquiring mind.
                  Guy Davenport, "Tatlin!"

Contents

Illustrations

All photographs are from the Zabolotsky family archive, courtesy of Nikita Zabolotsky.

Acknowledgements

This book could not have been written without the generous help of many. I am indebted to Gregory Freidin, who first introduced me to Zabolotsky's poetry and shared his considerable knowledge with me. Other perceptive readers include John Bowlt, the late Edward J. Brown, Caryl Emerson, George Gibian, Irene Masing-Delic, Nina Perlina, Cathy Popkin, and William Mills Todd. Ilona Bell and Josephine Woll offered succor at critical times. Nils Åke Nilsson provided a haven at the Slavic Institute of Stockholm University, and Sally Kux was a model researcher. Thanks are also due my editor, Katharina Brett, who sensitively guided this book into its present form. Grants from the American Council of Learned Societies, the Fulbright-Hays Foundation, the International Research and Exchanges Board, the Kennan Institute for Advanced Russian Studies, and Williams College allowed me time for writing and research and opportunities to travel to Soviet archives.

In Russia, I benefited from the help of the staff at TsGALI, the Central Archives for Literature and Art. Nikita Zabolotsky opened the family archives to me, and his wife, Natalya, opened their home. Without their assistance this book would not be complete. Yekaterina Vasilyevna Zabolotskaya graciously provided personal information about her husband, and Asar Eppel guided me to some obscure sources. Natalya Roskina gladly shared her knowledge of Zabolotsky's late years, as did the poet Viktor Sosnora in St. Petersburg. Also in St. Petersburg, Anatoly Aleksandrov took the time to show me the places where Zabolotsky lived and worked as well as giving me material from his own archives. Igor Bakhterev shared lucid memories of his OBERIU days with Zabolotsky.

No acknowledgement would be complete without a word of thanks to my husband, Dean Crawford. For all the hours of skilled editing, writerly insight, and emotional support, I am especially grateful.

Parts of chapters one and three appeared in *Slavic Review* (Winter 1989) and *Russian Literature* (1983, 13).

Notes on transliteration and translation

The transliteration of Russian into English is always thorny. I have opted for a double standard to make this book useful to the widest possible audience. Thus, all Russian names in the text have been rendered phonetically in order to ease pronunciation for the general reader. For the specialist, however, all literary terms and quotations have been transliterated according to the modified Library of Congress system, as have all footnote and bibliographic references. It is my hope that any confusion arising from such variants as Mayakovsky and Maiakovskii, or Fyodorov and Fedorov, will be more than offset by the respective accessibility and precision afforded.

Unless otherwise noted, all translations from the Russian are mine. For the poetry, I have chosen to present literal, line-by-line translations rather than attempt poetic renderings which might mask Zabolotsky's intended meanings. Those able to read Zabolotsky's poetry in the original are encouraged to do so to experience his marvelous word plays and rhythms.

Introduction

The lives of Russian poets are like the lives of saints, legendary but unenviable. Too many gifted voices have been silenced; too many altered through censorship, criticism, and imprisonment. Faced with this historical injustice, scholars have set out to resurrect work which might otherwise have been lost, and now a number of poets have a broader readership than they enjoyed in their lifetimes. Some have been hailed as martyrs, others cast as prophets. Yet one of the great literary figures of this century, Nikolai Zabolotsky, is still hardly known beyond the circles of the Russian intelligentsia.

If the most important reason for our interest in poets is the quality of their work, then in Zabolotsky's case there exists a secondary reason for our concern: in certain ways, he embodies the conflicts of twentieth-century Russian society. Zabolotsky's poetry suggests the deep ambiguity of his age. Straddling as it does the worlds of both Russian and Soviet experience, his art resists easy classification. Zabolotsky was both the last link in the Russian Futurist tradition[1] and the first significant poet to come of age in the Soviet period.

Zabolotsky never fitted easily into any literary grouping. In the cultural circles of Petrograd, he appeared as a parvenu, a country boy who might well have languished in the provinces had the Revolution not occurred. Zabolotsky was grateful for all the Revolution had provided him. Even so, he never performed the rôle of political mouthpiece, unlike others similarly obliged. Nor did he turn dissident when the same mechanism that once had buoyed him sought to drown him. Less for reasons of calculation than because of his nature,

I

Zabolotsky pursued poetry according to his own, highly personal lights.

Zabolotsky's name should be familiar for his ordeals alone. Instead, his reputation has suffered because he lacked the historical good fortune to die young. Though Zabolotsky did die prematurely, at age fifty-five, his death was caused neither by his own hand nor at the hands of the security organs. Rather he died of a heart attack, and this prosaic demise did nothing to enhance his reputation as a poet either in the West or in the Soviet Union. No matter that he had been officially castigated for his poem on collectivization, "The Triumph of Agriculture." No matter that he had spent eight years in labor camps and exile. The fact remains that Zabolotsky ended his life as a poet in good standing with the State, a fact that left him vulnerable to attack from another quarter – those readers who judge the merit of a poet not by his verse, but solely the circumstances of his life. This is a tradition of sorts in Russian literature; we seek, for example, to recreate and savor the brief romantic lives of the nineteenth-century poets Aleksandr Pushkin and Mikhail Lermontov, who may loom larger in our imaginations for their tragic deaths in duels than they would had they died in their sleep. Writing of the nineteenth-century poet Dmitri Venevitinov, the critic Yury Tynyanov commented that "Venevitinov, a complex and curious poet, died at twenty-two, and ever since, he has been remembered for one thing only – that he died at twenty-two."[2] Far too often it is the voice of the martyr, not that of the poet, that speaks, and so the poet comes to be revered for his biography, not for his verse. This has been the unfortunate case even with such dazzling poets as Osip Mandelstam, Marina Tsvetaeva, Anna Akhmatova, and Boris Pasternak.[3]

Particularly in the case of Zabolotsky, the apparently simple facts of the poet's life do not begin to reveal the complexity of experience. The truth of Zabolotsky's art, as of his biography, lies behind his publicly perceived personae. We must then ask, can a modern Russian poet who has not been martyred hope to be known purely for his or her verse? Can the poet's voice ever be heard over the din of such times?

Largely because Zabolotsky chose to conceal his fundamental self, he suffers from detractors on both the right and the left, both here and in his native land. Some critics chastise him for accepting honors from a government that persecuted his peers; others quibble not with his status at the end of his life but with the unconventional poetry of his youth. Either way, the essential poet is lost, even as the critics bolster their arguments by citing his work. Such polemic arises, in part, from the admittedly striking difference in style and tone between Zabolotsky's early and late verse. Critics persistently have felt the need to place themselves in one camp or another, favoring either the young or the mature Zabolotsky, and they seem reluctant to accept the evidence of a highly complex poet whose work does not yield to ready labelling. Because Zabolotsky's verse comprises no single lyric voice, it defies easy characterization. Indeed, the lofty, philosophical lyrics of his declining years may seem to contradict his early, modernist experiments.

Zabolotsky's work may be divided into three distinct periods: the daring experiments of his early work (1926–28); the visionary poems of his middle period (1929–1938); and the more conventionally philosophic verse of his post-imprisonment years (1946–1958). The relationships between these phases of his career are intricate but not obvious. Zabolotsky's 1929 volume of verse, *Stolbtsy (Scrolls)*, a series of urban grotesques reflecting life in Leningrad of the NEP era, typifies his early phase. But after a period of transition, the later Zabolotsky abandoned the city for meditations upon the natural world and man's rôle in it. If Zabolotsky's early poems are Gogolian in sentiment, then his later verses recall a contemplative Tyutchev or Boratynsky. Precisely this discrepancy between the stages of Zabolotsky's career has led critics to speak of "the two Zabolotskys,"[4] labelling him both a "modernist" and a "classicist," a "progressive" and a "conservative." The assumption is that, like two opposing ideologies, Zabolotsky's poetic periods can never be reconciled. And because the gap between Zabolotsky's middle and late periods indicates the eight years he spent in labor camp and exile, critics of all stripes have found useful ammunition in this biographical fact. At least one staunch Soviet scholar has concluded that Zabolotsky's years in the labor camps helped him to overcome the errors of his youthful ways,[5] while Western researchers have tended to concentrate almost exclusively on Zabolotsky's early verse, contending that his internment forced him subsequently to compromise by resorting to more traditional verse. Neither view, however, satisfactorily explains Zabolotsky's stance or his place in Russian literature. While the historical events occurring during Zabolotsky's lifetime should not be excluded from consideration – after all, the Revolution provided opportunity for Zabolotsky, and his era shaped his poetic vision – the hard evidence of his poetry shows that despite the personal upheavals and the external changes in his verse, Zabolotsky's artistic consciousness remained consistent throughout his life.

There exist not two Zabolotskys, but one. Rather than simply attributing Zabolotsky's abandonment of modernism for classicism to the shock of years spent in the labor camps, we may perceive the development of Zabolotsky's poetry as a natural progression, the result of internal experience rather than external pressure. Zabolotsky's evolution as a poet was intrinsic, and even in his most mature poems one can still discern the whimsical futurist, just as the brooding classicist is already hovering over his early grotesques. The changes in Zabolotsky's verse signal his vitality as an artist, and if, as Tsvetaeva has written, the only way finally to comprehend a poet is to take his or her work in its entirety, for "creative work is continuity and gradualness,"[6] then certainly Zabolotsky, perhaps more than others, needs to be read *in toto*. When Zabolotsky's *œuvre* is taken as a whole, the forms he chose to work in recede in importance as the overall integrity of his poetic vision becomes clear.

The poems Zabolotsky wrote in his middle or transitional period are especially useful for illuminating the entire body of his work. In particular, his three long dramatic poems of the thirties serve as a microcosm of his poetic world, encompassing the problems that interested him throughout his career. These poems, "Torzhestvo zemledeliia" ("The Triumph of Agriculture," 1929–1930), "Bezumnyi volk" ("The Mad Wolf," 1931), and "Derev'ia" ("The Trees," 1933), demonstrate how Zabolotsky's developing philosophy of man's rôle in nature begins to enrich lyrics still marked by striking verbal experimentation. Ideas and styles clash head-on as a thematic battle is waged between the civilization imposed by man and the natural cycles of the universe. In a different sense, though, these poems represent a battleground where Zabolotsky's own poetic struggles were waged; and they must be recognized as the turning-point between his early and later verses, the point where the "progressive" and the "conservative" meet. These poems provide a necessary link between all of Zabolotsky's works, testifying to the existence of a single – though evolving – poetic consciousness.

What are the attributes of this consciousness? More than his contemporaries, Zabolotsky aimed at creating not simply a body of poems, but rather an entire poetic universe. While a single consciousness prevails in his poetry, it consists of many voices. The poet's desire to perceive the world so intensely as to encompass it, in all of its varied manifestations, gives his verse an extraordinary vigor. Zabolotsky attempts to express the nature of the entire universe, to show the vital connections among all things, those both seen and merely felt. In effect, Zabolotsky seeks to map the universe, and his verse becomes a writing of the world, its poetic representation. In this way his vision constitutes a kind of cosmography.

Zabolotsky was fascinated by the variety of the universe, and he sought to merge his own consciousness with creation by putting all that he perceived into his verse. Thus his cosmography embraces many different eras and traditions, ranging from Antiquity into the future, from Russian folklore to Eastern religious beliefs. Zabolotsky perceived the matrix of the universe as protean, and the world he creates is fluid, in continual motion, as expressed by his metaphor of metamorphosis. This unified view of existence reflects not only the poet's own cosmic orientation, but also the tendency of his age.

In the wake of Einstein's discoveries, scientists were rethinking their conceptions of the universe; and the avant-garde artists in Russia, to whose ideas Zabolotsky's are linked, were quick to respond with their own creative imaginings. Like other visionaries, Zabolotsky looked beyond his own narrow ken as a provincial Russian to try to embrace the totality of experience.

In doing so, Zabolotsky drew from sources as diverse as literature and science, history and art. His poetry is informed by an awareness of varying modes of thought and expression. In this respect Zabolotsky's long poems take on particular importance, for their very form indicates the poet's attempt to find a vehicle large enough to encompass his new cosmography, one that would allow for its heterogeneity and complexity. Filtered through Zabolotsky's artistic consciousness, different eras and ideas reverberate throughout his verse. Here the attentive reader will find philosophers (Grigory Skovoroda and Nikolai Fyodorov), scientists (Konstantin Tsiolkovsky and Vladimir Vernadsky), poets (Gavriil Derzhavin, Aleksandr Pushkin, and Velimir Khlebnikov), and painters (Pavel Filonov and Kazimir Malevich), whose plangent voices ultimately come together to form, in Zabolotsky's words, "a single harmonious chorus." Yet the multivoiced chorus echoing throughout Zabolotsky's poetry in no way diminishes the power of the poet's own voice, which remains distinct.

To explore the formation and evolution of the poet's voice, this book takes as its model Zabolotsky's own plastic approach. Thus, textual analysis is not the sole criterion for determining the characteristics of Zabolotsky's verse. Instead, the many sources that inspired Zabolotsky will be explored in order to demonstrate just how far Zabolotsky's ambitions extend. This book offers an open approach to Zabolotsky's texts, one which will reveal the comprehensive nature of the poet's vision without losing sight of the principal consciousness at the heart of all his work.

Finally, the extraordinary circumstances of Zabolotsky's life – his singular experience as a poet who actually survived the labor camps to make a comeback in a hostile environment –

compel us to place this analysis against the background of his biography, without distracting us from the primary pursuit of his poetry. His biography reveals both the intellectual and emotional encounters that he syncretized in his verse. Zabolotsky's poetic universe embraces numerous systems of thought, like planets revolving around a sun that represents the core of his poetic vision. The many satellites of his system can help us to understand not only the poet, but also the epoch in which he lived.

CHAPTER I

Emergence

Motion and moment always in process of renewal.

Ovid, *Metamorphoses*

When Nikolai Zabolotsky arrived in Petrograd in August, 1921, he found the city in a state of famine, just barely alive. Severe cold and the deprivations of the Civil War years had taken their toll, and the streets were deserted. Attrition from disease, starvation and exhaustion added to the wartime casualties.[1] Yet in this austere environment of privation and despair, beauty could be discerned, a certain purity of thought attained. The habitual eye was challenged by the city's desolation. The air itself seemed rarefied: objects stood out vividly and sharply defined. No blurred edges softened the scene. The city was stark, and its starkness freed the imagination from the confines of accustomed perception. Commonplace objects suddenly appeared as things in themselves, no longer defined primarily by their use or by the observer's expectations. These new perceptions, fresh and original, seemed full of sudden beauty and, potentially, truth.[2] But they also carried the risk of delusion. The Petrograd atmosphere was ripe for hallucination, but, as demonstrated by Zabolotsky's first volume of verse, *Stolbtsy* (*Scrolls*, 1929), "hallucinations"[3] (like dreams) may reveal underlying truths.

When Zabolotsky arrived in Petrograd, his individual idiom was just beginning to develop. He had been drawn to the city because of its close ties with Russian literature: the urban grotesques of Dostoyevsky, Bely, and especially Gogol moved him and contributed to his own, later forms of grotesque. Petrograd's image as a center of science attracted him, too;

innovations in science often seemed to spur innovations in artistic life. Petrograd commanded Zabolotsky's attention, engaging his talent as never before, and Zabolotsky adopted this city of heightened sensations as his own.

Like the great Futurist poets Khlebnikov and Mayakovsky before him, Zabolotsky came to urban life unschooled in cosmopolitan ways and distant from the cultural traditions of the Acmeists or Symbolists. He had only just begun to read Blok, Balmont, and Akhmatova and was provoked by the literary debates of the previous decade, when the Acmeists, with their demand for a new poetic realism expressed in concrete images and well-defined lines, opposed the dominant Symbolist aesthetic of the word as a vessel of mystical experience. On Petrograd's half-deserted streets, Zabolotsky felt the surge of literary activity around him. Numerous groups were springing up throughout the city, each claiming ascendancy over the rest in representing true revolutionary literature. Serious discussions were held on the importance of literature in the new society.[4] The intensity of the Petrograd intellectual life, heightened by the harsh living conditions, exhilarated Zabolotsky and impelled him to devote himself once and for all to poetry, relinquishing earlier impulses toward a career in science. In the barrenness of a student dormitory, Zabolotsky began to write in earnest, "imitating now Mayakovsky, now Blok, now Yesenin."[5] Outside the dormitory walls lay the great city of Petrograd which had become "so fantastic, so gruesomely unreal ... that the borderline between the real and the unreal seemed to be obliterated ... life had indeed become 'stranger than fiction.'"[6] It was this fantastic world which Zabolotsky had to experience before he could find his own poetic voice. And perhaps only as a provincial outsider, a newcomer to the city, could Zabolotsky see the reality behind the majestic mask of Petrograd.

EARLY YEARS

Nikolai Alekseyevich Zabolotsky was born on a farm outside the city of Kazan on May 7, 1903 (April 24, old style), the first

1   Zabolotsky with his parents, Lidiya Andreyevna and
Aleksei Agafonovich, 1904

of six children. His mother, Lidiya Andreyevna Dyakonova, a
former schoolteacher, harbored revolutionary sympathies and
was frustrated by her lot as mother and housewife in a tiny
provincial town, "fated to die a slow spiritual death."[7] She

would often tell her children about revolutionary figures and took pride in her sister, who had served a term in prison for her activities. Zabolotsky's father, Aleksei Agafonovich, stood "halfway between the peasant and the *intelligent* of the time"[8] and was given to dressing in peasant garb and wearing his beard in two symmetrical wedges. Aleksei Agafonovich seems to have taken after his father, Zabolotsky's grandfather, in his peasant good looks and strength. The grandfather was extraordinary, capable of bending brass coins with his fist. Both father and grandfather worked the land, the former an agronomist, the latter a forest warden. The Zabolotsky[9] clan stemmed from the village of Krasnaya Gora in the Urzhum region of Vyatka province. These origins stirred Zabolotsky's imagination, for the village, located on the banks of the Vyatka River, was the legendary settlement of river pirates who had come downstream from Novgorod and Pskov. Zabolotsky was proud of the native democratic traditions of his Novgorodian forbears and liked to muse about the possibility of pirate blood in his veins.

Zabolotsky's family remained on the farm until he was six, at which time they moved to the remote village of Kukmor, and later to the village of Sernur. This period was a difficult one, since Aleksei Agafonovich was at times compelled to work as an insurance agent and was at other times unemployed. A distant relative of Zabolotsky, Leonid Dyakonov, provides a gossipy tale of the Zabolotsky family life,[10] in which he implies that vodka played a large rôle. Still, some interesting biographical details may be gleaned from his account. We learn, for example, of the fortitude of Zabolotsky's mother, Lidiya Andreyevna, who was orphaned at an early age when her mother died in childbirth (according to Dyakonov, the father had long since abandoned the family, making only periodic visits home). Her elder sister, Olga, brought up the five younger children, and all four daughters managed to graduate from the Vyatka *gimnazium*, where Lidiya Andreyevna won a silver medal for her studies. She went on to earn a teaching diploma and taught school for a few years in the small town of Nolinsk, until she was afflicted with a throat ailment which

2 Zabolotsky as a child, *c.* 1906

caused her to lose both her voice and her job. She then moved
to a farm outside of Kazan where her brother was working;
there she met Zabolotsky's father, Aleksei Agafonovich. Their
marriage was not a happy one. Dyakonov claims that in the
early years of their marriage Lidiya Andreyevna called her
husband by the formal "Aleksei Agafonovich," while to him
she was always "Lida" or "Lidochka." This inequality had to
do not only with the nearly twenty-year difference in their
ages, but also with a consciousness of Lidiya Andreyevna's
poverty *vis-à-vis* Aleksei Agafonovich's relative prosperity at

the time of their wedding – a discrepancy constantly assailed by Aleksei Agafonovich's sisters, if one is to believe Dyakonov. Though the details of domestic life in the Zabolotsky household remain obscure, we do know that the family's financial situation eased following their move to Sernur, where Aleksei Agafonovich again found work as an agronomist. Sernur was little more than a crossroads, with two intersecting main streets, a school, and a hospital. But if the village itself had little to offer, the surrounding countryside more than compensated for its meagerness. In his autobiographical sketch Zabolotsky wrote:

The countryside in and around Sernur was marvelous! I remember the Epifaniev farm – the estate of a wealthy old-fashioned priest – a decrepit house built of hundred-year-old logs blackened with age, a huge, majestic garden, ponds overgrown with willows, and endless lands: fields and groves. My first indelible impressions of nature are tied to this landscape. There, to my heart's content, I listened to nightingales and gazed at sunsets and all of the chaste charm of the vegetable kingdom. I have lived nearly all of my conscious life in big cities, but the wonderful nature of Sernur has never died in my heart and is reflected in many of my poems.[11]

Zabolotsky's early enthusiasm for country life was not solely passive, however. Each spring he eagerly participated in experiments in his father's makeshift laboratory, where they examined and cultivated various seeds of forage plants.[12]

Despite his love for the Sernur landscape, Zabolotsky was delighted to be accepted into the Urzhum Practical High School[13] at the age of ten. Not only did he glimpse a larger world, but he finally was able to extricate himself from an unhappy family life characterized by frequent dissension between his parents. Urzhum, a provincial town 180 kilometers from the nearest railroad, seemed to the young Zabolotsky a great metropolis. In Urzhum he first heard the strains of a piano and first encountered the charms of young schoolgirls in their brown frocks and white aprons. Zabolotsky soon began writing poems dedicated to these girls. The high school was apparently a good one (better than many Zabolotsky later saw in Leningrad), particularly in the fields of history and art. Zabolotsky began to draw and to paint, demonstrating noticeable talent.

A certain gratitude toward the school comes across in Zabolotsky's memoirs, as does gratitude toward his father, who instilled in his son a reverence for books. Not a great reader himself, Aleksei Agafonovich nevertheless assiduously collected the fiction supplements from the popular magazine *Niva* (*Grainfield*) and carefully bound them.[14] The supplements were kept behind the glass door of a bookcase, which carried this admonition: "Dear friend! Love and respect books. Books are the fruit of the human mind. Take care of them. Don't soil or tear them. It's not easy to write a book. For many people, books are the same as bread."[15] Zabolotsky spent long hours at the family bookcase, loath to play outdoors, preferring instead to dream over books. He wrote: "I would sit alone in silence, and I was not the least bit bored. My mind was obviously occupied with some important thoughts."[16] This ability to lose himself in meditation served Zabolotsky well later in his life, when he was compelled to give up literary activity and work as a laborer. We may imagine that seated in front of his father's bookcase and "occupied with some important thoughts," Zabolotsky was first inspired to produce handwritten journals for his family, copying out poems by Pushkin and Lermontov from their collected works and reading them to his sisters, who naively assumed that they were hearing their precocious brother's own verse. Soon Zabolotsky did add poems of his own to these "journals," including one long one (*poema*) in which the mythical serpent Zmei Gorynych descends upon Sernur and devours everyone but the poem's young author.[17]

At the very least, Zabolotsky's school years in Urzhum provided him with pleasant memories and a good, basic education. No doubt he was also influenced by the inhabitants of the town itself. Although provincial, Urzhum boasted an interesting population, since the area around Vyatka was a favorite place of exile under the tsars. The future Soviet Commissar of Education, Anatoly Lunacharsky, spent a year in Vyatka;[18] and the ill-fated political leader Sergei Kirov began his revolutionary activity in Urzhum, where he was born. Activism continued after the 1917 Revolution, when the students of Urzhum eagerly organized into groups to carry out cultural work. It is not unlikely that Zabolotsky participated in such groups, since one of his friends at the time was Pyotr Shchelkanov, a prominent Komsomol (Communist Youth League) worker and head of the Vyatka section of the State Publishing House.[19] Zabolotsky's interests already lay in literary production; by the time of the Revolution he had been dabbling in verse for several years. One early attempt, "Na smert' Koshkina" ("On Koshkin's Death"), was written on the death of a school graduate at the front in World War I. Zabolotsky wrote this ode in the grand eighteenth-century style of Lomonosov and Derzhavin, and for many years he considered it his most elegant verse. But not all of his poems were serious in intent. The 1918 "Urzhumiada" ("The Ur-zhumiad"), for example, featured his classmates and their antics.[20] Unfortunately, few of Zabolotsky's early works have survived.

In the years following the Revolution, urban intellectuals flocked to the provincial towns to escape the growing hunger of the cities. These new acquaintances encouraged Zabolotsky to go to the "center" (i.e., Moscow) and develop his talent. Spurred on by the sense of new beginnings engendered by the Revolution, Zabolotsky determined to leave behind his provincial past, a determination soon heightened by the chance appearance in Urzhum of a book of poems including "Dvenadtsat'" ("The Twelve") and "Skify" ("The Scythians") by Aleksandr Blok and a poem by Andrei Bely.[21] In the spring of 1920, Zabolotsky graduated from the Urzhum Practical High School, and that autumn he left for Moscow, where he enrolled in the Faculty of History and Philology at the First University of Moscow.

The trip was not an easy one. Even preparations were complicated. In a letter to his aunt in Vyatka, Zabolotsky requested that she buy him a spool of 40- or 50-weight thread, so that he could sew himself a suit appropriate for Moscow from some material he had been issued.[22] There was no thread at all in Urzhum at the time. Zabolotsky set out with a friend, Misha Kasyanov, by steamer up the Vyatka River to Kotelnich, where they changed for a train. Kasyanov describes their further adventures: "Boarding the train was awful. Crushed and nearly trampled, we managed with difficulty to take root on the platform, dragging our three sacks of rusks up behind us. On this platform and later, in the narrow corridor next to the toilet, we travelled for four days to Moscow, suffering extremes of heat, stuffiness, and confinement."[23]

Arriving in Moscow from the countryside where food was adequate if not abundant, Zabolotsky was unprepared for the severe shortages he encountered. Within a very short time he had consumed all the provisions brought from home; then he began to go hungry. Unwilling to give in to the demands of his stomach and thereby forego his chances at education, Zabolotsky decided to enrol simultaneously in the Medical School, where the students were given extra rations. He hoped to continue parallel study in the humanities, but the medical curriculum proved too demanding, and Zabolotsky found himself devoting all of his time to medicine. This stratagem carried Zabolotsky through his first autumn in Moscow, but shortly after the new year the food situation worsened, and the special rations for medical students were withdrawn. Faced again with hunger as well as an undesirable course of study, Zabolotsky left Moscow in February or March of 1921 to return to his family and the relative plenty of Urzhum. Nothing is known of that time spent in the countryside, but by August, 1921, Zabolotsky was once again *en route*, this time to Petrograd, where his life as a poet was to begin.

PETROGRAD/LENINGRAD

Zabolotsky travelled 1,700 kilometers to reach Petrograd from Urzhum; in a way, he travelled even further. Petrograd was an imposing city, more so than Moscow of the time, a city not only of Russian culture, but of Western culture too: the uneasy confluence of East and West, as characterized by Andrei Bely in his novel *Petersburg*. Petrograd represented worldly affairs,

Western art and architecture. It was known also as the city of Maxim Gorky's benevolence toward young writers. But Zabolotsky arrived in Petrograd without the protection of a benefactor. He was unable to set himself up in Gorky's House of the Arts (*Dom iskusstv*), a haven for needy artists during the Civil War years. Nor did he enrol at Petrograd University or the Institute of the History of the Arts, both of which offered excellent courses in literature, and where he might have come into contact with such luminaries as Viktor Zhirmunsky, Viktor Shklovsky, Yury Tynyanov, Boris Eikhenbaum, and Grigory Gukovsky. No doubt feeling inadequate in his knowledge of modern and ancient languages, prerequisite for a university course of study, Zabolotsky entered the lesser Herzen Pedagogical Institute, Department of Language and Literature, even though he professed no real interest in a teaching career. Basically he sought a sound background in literature, without which he felt he could never be a successful writer. Throughout his years at the Institute (1921–1925), Zabolotsky wrote a great number of poems, imitating each new poet he discovered.[24]

The Herzen Pedagogical Institute was an orthodox Marxist institution, in contrast to the Institute of the History of the Arts, which was dominated by the Formalist school of criticism and comprised the Petrograd cultural elite. But Zabolotsky did study under one professor who exerted a profound influence upon him, Vasily Alekseyevich Desnitsky, a literary critic and model Marxist who had been a close friend of Lenin. Zabolotsky was drawn to this man of wide-ranging interests who collected unusual pebbles from the beach at Koktebel just as avidly as he collected books, and who affirmed Zabolotsky's own interest in both science and art.[25]

Zabolotsky spent his years at the Institute in a student dormitory, subsisting mainly on black bread and boiled water, as his stipend was exceptionally meager. Letters to friends reveal that his main preoccupation, in spite of himself, was finding nourishment for his weakening body. To this end, Zabolotsky worked variously as a longshoreman and a lumberman to earn some money during his first months of study.[26] Still, the hardships of Petrograd life did not deter him; in fact, they may have served as a kind of inspiration. The poet Mandelstam's description of the Civil War years is equally apt as it relates to the circumstances of Zabolotsky's student life: "Culture has become a church. Church-culture has become separate from the state. Worldly life no longer concerns us, we don't have food, but a refection, not a room, but a cell, not clothing, but vestments. We finally have attained inner freedom, genuine inner joy."[27]

Zabolotsky succumbed to this special inspiration of Petrograd, turning increasingly to the writing of poetry. The image of a strict, yet visionary young man is confirmed by the literary critic Dmitri Maksimov, who recalled Zabolotsky in those years, when he would drop in at Maksimov's literary circle, "Octopus," and read his latest poems. On first appearance, Zabolotsky did not strike his listeners as a poet, resembling rather a bookkeeper, controlled and precise. But once he began to read, this first impression vanished.[28]

Right from the beginning of his studies at the Institute, Zabolotsky was involved in producing a student journal, *Mysl'* (*Thought*), sponsored by the literary group "Workshop of the Word" (*Masterskaia slova*). In addition to Zabolotsky, members of this group included the poets Nikolai Braun and Mariya Komissarova. *Thought* published poetry, prose, satire, and theoretical articles, as well as commentary on student life. It was distributed in typed, hand-bound copies. Fairly recently, the journal's first issue was discovered in the archives of the Pedagogical Institute, having languished there for fifty years. Listed among the editors at the back of the twenty-two-page booklet is Nikolai Zabolotsky, his name spelled in the old style. This first issue included three of his poems: "Nebesnaia Sevil'ia" ("Seville in the Sky"), "Prosvistel sizyi ibis s papirusa" ("From the Papyrus the Grey Ibis Whistled"), and "Serdtse-pustyr'" ("The Desolate Heart"). Zabolotsky also published his first theoretical article in *Thought*: "O sushchnosti simvolizma" ("On the Essence of Symbolism"). In this brief treatise, Zabolotsky assesses Symbolism quite positively, making his imminent evolution into the author of the grotesquely realistic *Scrolls* seem all the more striking. Even so, one can detect Zabolotsky's incipient interest in the grotesque in his analysis of the Symbolist vision:

In poetry the realist is a simple observer, but the symbolist is always a thinker. Observing street life, the realist sees distinct figures and experiences them in [their] apparent, obvious simplicity ... A street ... A decrepit old man begs for alms ... A painted woman approaches, her fake stones glittering ... The symbolist, experiencing the obvious simplicity of the action, mentally and creatively penetrates into its hidden meaning, its hidden abstraction. "No, that's no beggar, no woman of the *demi-monde* – that's Need and Debauchery, that's the children of the Colossus-City, the death of its stony embraces ..."[29]

Zabolotsky finished the Pedagogical Institute in 1925 and was able to devote himself completely to poetry until called into the army late in 1926. At this time a mood of optimism prevailed in the literary world. Writers met at cafés, clubs, and private apartments to debate the direction Soviet art should take. The fervidness of their discussions, coupled with the still unsettled state of literature, encouraged variety, and hundreds of publishing houses existed to broadcast their work.[30] For Zabolotsky, the dream of a real career as a poet seemed entirely within reach, even though he was an unknown. Despite his literary aspirations, after five years in Leningrad he had not been taken up by any group. Neither had he frequented the House of the Arts or the House of Literati where he might have forged helpful connections. So it was without recommendation, and very much on his own, that Zabolotsky entered the literary world in 1925.

During this period of emergence Zabolotsky was fortunate to come into contact with two remarkable poets, Daniil Kharms[31] and Aleksandr Vvedensky, who helped to bring him out of obscurity. Zabolotsky met Kharms and Vvedensky in the spring of 1926, and an immediate affinity drew the young poets together. They gathered almost daily to discuss their ideas and ambitions at the home of Leonid Lipavsky,[32] a philosopher who served as the intellectual stimulus of the group. Lipavsky's philosophical inquiries revolved around the issue of man's place in nature, a question Zabolotsky was soon to address in his poetry. Lipavsky found many of the conversations so provocative that he jotted them down. Thus we are able to learn something more about Zabolotsky at the beginning of his career. Particularly telling is Zabolotsky's response to the question of what interested him:

Architecture, designs for large buildings. Symbolism. The depiction of thoughts in the representational arrangement of objects and their parts. The practice of religion according to enumerated things. Poetry. Various simple things – a fight, dinner, dances. Meat and pastry. Vodka and beer. Folk astrology. Folk numerology. Sleep. Situations and figures of the revolution. Northern peoples. Music, its architecture, fugues. The structure of pictures of nature. Domestic animals. Beasts and insects. The figures and situations in military maneuvers. Death. A book, how to create one. Letters, signs, numbers. Cymbals, ships.[33]

Encouraged by the participants in Lipavsky's impromptu gatherings, Zabolotsky wrote his first poems on urban themes, startling in the originality of their vision. (These early poems [1926–1928] were collected in the 1929 volume of *Scrolls*.) Zabolotsky himself marks 1926 as the beginning of his poetic career, when he suddenly freed himself from the derivative styles that had characterized his earlier verse.

During 1927 Zabolotsky served in the Red Army in a detachment of "short-termers" in Leningrad. His fellow recruits were mainly from the Leningrad intelligentsia, and Zabolotsky soon found an appreciative audience for his humor and his poetry. The troop medic was particularly friendly to Zabolotsky and more than once signed him into the dispensary where he could "recuperate" by writing poems for several days.[34] Zabolotsky edited and contributed to his division's wall newspaper, considered the best around, and his poems already held the attention of the Leningrad literary *cognoscenti*, who circulated them in manuscript form. After passing an examination for platoon commander, Zabolotsky was discharged into the reserves and once again found himself caught up in the life of the late NEP period[35] in Leningrad.

Shortly after his discharge, Zabolotsky was offered a job in the Children's Section of the State Publishing House. For want of more suitable attire, he continued to wear his army greatcoat, which metonymically came to represent him. The critic Lidiya Ginzburg recalls the impression Zabolotsky's appearance made on her housekeeper Nyusha, newly arrived from the countryside: "Lidiya Yakovlevna! Some soldier's come to see you!"[36] Ginzburg recounts this episode as an anecdote, but the memoirs of another acquaintance of Zabolotsky more accurately reflect the poet's penurious condition at the time. Zabolotsky apparently dreamed of owning a black suit, something beyond his means. He felt that no other color would do for a serious poet.[37] (In contrast, his poetic cohort Kharms favored outlandish clothing.)

At the Children's Section, Zabolotsky was fortunate to work not only with Kharms and Vvedensky, but also with Samuil Marshak, Yevgeny Shvarts, and Nikolai Oleinikov. Together these writers produced some of the best and most innovative children's literature in the Soviet Union.[38] As independent literary life grew increasingly difficult in the late 1920s, children's literature provided an excellent outlet for the writers' talents, as well as income when they could no longer easily expect to publish their adult work. Between 1929 and 1931 Zabolotsky channelled much of his energy into writing poems and stories for the popular children's journals *Ezh* (*The Hedgehog*) and *Chizh* (*The Siskin*).[39] He continued to work professionally in children's literature until 1937, contributing to the journals *Pioner* (*Pioneer*) and *Koster* (*Campfire*)[40] as well as publishing separate books.

The first pieces Zabolotsky wrote exclusively for children appeared in 1928: *Khoroshie sapogi* (*Good Boots*), a tale in verse about Karlusha, whose feet won't obey him until he puts them in boots; and *Krasnye i sinie* (*The Reds and the Blues*), the story of Misha's adventures as he helps the Reds in their struggle against the enemy Blues. These first two published works of juvenilia underscore Zabolotsky's conflict in his early attempts to achieve success in the contracting literary world. While one hand created a charming entertainment for children, the other felt compelled to propagate current ideology. During the late twenties, the fanciful continued to vie with the hortatory. By 1930, Zabolotsky's didactic tales in both verse and prose were predominating, and he chose to sign his works with the pen name "Ya. Miller,"[41] hoping to disassociate the serious poet Zabolotsky from the likes of *Grazhdanskaia voina* (*The Civil War*), *Kak my otbili Iudenicha* (*How We Beat Yudenich*), and *Pervomai* (*The First of May*). Even this disavowal did not seem sufficient, however, and the further progression of Zabolotsky's career as a children's writer indicates his discomfort with the kinds of books he was producing. By the mid-1930s he abandoned writing original works for children and turned instead to translation. Here, at least, he could have a greater margin of choice. Among Zabolotsky's most notable publications are juvenile versions of *Gargantua and Pantagruel* (1935) and *Till Eulenspiegel* (1936), prepared from existing translations. Zabolotsky was particularly proud of the fanfare with which *Gargantua and Pantagruel* was produced, with illustrations by Gustave Doré.

Zabolotsky's decision to concentrate on translation was correct. With some exceptions, his original works for children were never as spontaneous or successful as the more nonsensical verses of Kharms and Vvedensky; too often Zabolotsky betrayed didacticism. Lidiya Chukovskaya explains the predicament of the "adult" poets who worked for the State Publishing House: "It was necessary to discipline the young poets to ensure that their capriciousness took on meaning. In their literature for adults [they] worked toward shock and parody, but now, for the first time, educational tasks were set before them."[42] Zabolotsky approached these tasks too assiduously, perhaps. In his case, the oppressiveness of his assignments and the ever more threatening political reality combined to squelch the capriciousness and liveliness that mark his work for adults. The pressures even children's writers felt are evident from such journalistic attacks as "Against Hackwork in Children's Literature"[43] and "One Must Speak Seriously with Children,"[44] where the author rebukes the editors of *Ezh* for the "defective literature" they are producing.

The ponderousness of much of Zabolotsky's juvenilia seems

all the more striking when compared to the spontaneous nonsense verse he liked to compose throughout his life.[45] These humorous rhymes or *stishki*, as he called them,[46] were never commissioned; they represent Zabolotsky's own irrepressible sense of humor, his instinctive responses to various situations. Zabolotsky's *stishki* are often highly irreverent, as in the following verse:

> Однаждый некий агроном
> В штанишки сделал каки ком
> И этот ком, упав на луг,
> Всеобщий вызвал там испуг.
> Сказали пастуху коровы:
> – Пастух мы, верно, нездоровы,
> Увидев эту каку, мы
> Ввели в смятение умы.
> – Дурашки! – им пастух в ответ, –
> Что это кака – спору нет, –
> Но кто ее здесь обронил?
> Агроном, окончивший академию
>   имени Тимирязева![47]

One day a certain agronomist
Made a lump of kaka in his pants
And, falling on the field, this lump
Caused universal panic.
The cows said to the shepherd:
– Shepherd, really, we're not well,
Seeing this kaka has
Brought us to confusion.
– Fools! – the shepherd answered them –
That this is kaka, there's no question –
But who dropped it here?
An agronomist from Timiryazev's academy!

In spite of his highly developed sense of play and his love of witticisms, Zabolotsky – in contrast to Kharms and Vvedensky – never more than dabbled in the absurd. And he was never as wholeheartedly involved as his fellow poets in children's literature. As he himself put it, children's literature did not "exhaust [his] interests,"[48] and he persevered in writing poetry for adults. Zabolotsky did derive one important

benefit from his work in children's literature, however: he was
able to collaborate with members of the artistic avant-garde.
Two of his verse tales were illustrated by Vera Yermolayeva, a
talented student of Suprematism.[49] Alisa Poret, who belonged
to Pavel Filonov's Collective of Analytical Art, made the
drawings for *Civil War*; and Tatyana Glebova, also a student of
Filonov, illustrated *How We Beat Yudenich*. Through his close
contact with these artists, Zabolotsky could maintain a valued
connection with the innovative, if increasingly stifled, art
world.

This artistic connection intensified around 1927, when
Zabolotsky began making public appearances with Kharms,
Vvedensky and some other young Leningrad poets. They held
readings in dormitories and military sections, at the Union of
Poets and the Institute of the History of the Arts. Their
favorite reading place was the House of the Press (*Dom pechati*),
which soon provided them a regular stage for performances.
The House of the Press had been founded in 1920 on the same
pattern as the House of the Arts, the House of Literati, and the
House of Scholars, all of which served as cultural magnets for
the Petrograd populace. Each of these professional clubs had
its own focus, sponsoring appropriate exhibitions, lectures,
films, discussions, and readings. The House of the Press in
particular provided a forum for writers, artists and performers
who had not yet gained wide acceptance among the public
at large.

The foyer and auditorium of the House of the Press were
decorated with marvelous frescoes commissioned from the
painter Pavel Filonov:

Pink and lilac cows and people, whose skin coverings seemed to have
been removed by some miraculous surgery, were depicted in gentle,
transparent shades. Veins, arteries and internal organs shone
through distinctly. Shoots of bright green grass and trees grew
through the figures. The lengthened proportions and strict dimensions of the compositions recalled the frescoes of ancient masters,
inspired and void of physical density. But the pictures were not
morbid. The tenderly drawn pale blue and pink veins reminded one
of the rainbow coloring of the human eye, and the emerald shoots
growing through them implied the invariable rebirth of life.[50]

These frescoes provided a fitting visual correlative to Zabolotsky's startling verse.

While the readings at the House of the Press always caused a sensation, the result was more shock than scandal for a public long ago inured to the antics of the Futurists. Only Kharms persisted in playing the part of an eccentric, dressing in a long plaid frock-coat with a tiny cap on his head, out from under which his red hair protruded in all directions. More often than not a green dog or similar figure was painted on his cheek.[51] Vvedensky was generally unkempt. Zabolotsky always wore his army greatcoat. Blond and clean-shaven, he had the rosy cheeks and immaculate hair part of a schoolboy, and he suffered from this typecast. While he had successfully rid himself of his provincial Vyatka accent, he could do nothing about his "seemingly intentional pink, blond and almost unnaturally spanking-clean looks."[52] Zabolotsky jokingly accounted for his rosy cheeks by claiming that his father had forced him as a child to drink the blood of freshly slaughtered sheep, considering it good for his health. "And I really can't complain about my health. A poet should be healthy."[53]

Veniamin Kaverin recalls a reading by Zabolotsky, Kharms and Vvedensky in the Red Parlor of the Institute of the History of the Arts. The year was 1927. Zabolotsky appeared first, reading the poem "Poprishchin,"[54] which revealed his considerable and unusual talent. Kharms performed next with excerpts from his dramatic poem "Elizaveta Bam," after which Zabolotsky's difficult verse seemed like the "model of classical poetry" to Kaverin. Vvedensky's verse in turn made Kharms' seem highly comprehensible.[55] The audience did not know how to react to this poetry. Was it to be taken seriously or not? Since Kharms often advertised these readings by riding wildly dressed through Leningrad on a tricycle,[56] it was hard to be sure. One contemporary of his states with certainty: "Kharms was made up entirely of jokes."[57] The young performers' poetry seemed either brilliant or nonsensical – but did one attribute necessarily preclude the other? At least from Zabolotsky's verse some sense could be made, even if the

imagery was startling and strange. To the audience, Zabolotsky's poetry sounded the most accessible of the three.

THE ASSOCIATION FOR REAL ART

Before meeting Zabolotsky, Kharms and Vvedensky had been
allied in an informal group called the "Chinari," a name
Kharms had coined from the verb *chinit'*, "to cause or perpe-
trate."[58] Based on one review of a "Chinari" performance, his
neologism was apt. Following the performance in question, a
group of students protested to the Leningrad Union of Poets,
demanding Kharms' exclusion from that organization: "... in
a legal Soviet organization there is no room for those who, at a
highly attended meeting, dare to compare a Soviet institution
of higher learning with a whorehouse and stables."[59] At the
same time, Kharms and Vvedensky referred to themselves as
the "Left Classics" (*Levye klassiki*) or "Left Flank" (*Levyi flang*)
of the Union of Poets, names associating them with the poetic
theorist Aleksandr Tufanov. In 1925 and 1926 Kharms had
performed publicly with Tufanov, who worked at the "Priboi"
publishing house and was a great proponent of *zaum*, the
trans-rational language practiced by several Futurists. (After
Velimir Khlebnikov's death, Tufanov alternately proclaimed
himself "Velimir the Second" and "Chairman of the *Zaum*
Globe.") Although Kharms was influenced by Tufanov's
affinity for "fragments [and] poetic shards as antipodes to that
which is complete, fixed and logical,"[60] and although he
learned from Tufanov's experiments with "phonic music" or
sounds, he and Vvedensky soon came to repudiate Tufanov's
poetic ideology, believing instead that art could concern itself
with daily life and still remain art. While the word remained
the foundation of their aesthetic, it was not the word as such
that concerned them now, but its effect on the reader, how it
was used and manipulated. Thus their poetry frequently
employed such techniques as *sdvig* "displacement" and *ostrane-
nie* "estrangement."
    The two poets continued to call themselves *chinari* until the
autumn of 1927, when along with Zabolotsky and several

other poets they formed the OBERIU[61] or "Association for Real Art" (*Ob"edinenie real'nogo iskusstva*).[62] Its nucleus was composed of Zabolotsky, Kharms, Vvedensky, Konstantin Vaginov, Igor Bakhterev, and Boris Levin, although at various times other writers were associated with the group.[63] For instance, Nikolai Oleinikov, Zabolotsky's friend from the publishing house, had close ties to the Oberiuty, as they were called. It was not necessarily easy to become allied with the group: Kharms and Zabolotsky would test the creative potential of candidates by having them answer questions like "Where is your nose?" and "What is your favorite dish?"[64]

Even before their formal alliance, the OBERIU poets had met regularly to discuss their artistic theories and goals. Their poetic platform came to the attention of Mayakovsky, who was intrigued enough to commission an article on the group for his journal *Novyi LEF* (*New LEF*).[65] The article was duly written by Vasily Klyuikov and edited by Zabolotsky, but Osip Brik, the editor in charge, opposed its publication. Because the piece never appeared, exactly how the poets characterized themselves early on is not certain.

The Oberiuty performed regularly at the House of the Press in presentations memorable for their bravura. The theatricality of these evenings eventually led to some friction within the group, for while Kharms was a master magician and juggler, Zabolotsky did not entirely enjoy such calculated dazzle. Still, theater as an art form (especially as a carryover from the *balagan* or popular drama) was important to the group's aesthetic notions, and on January 24, 1928, their performance of "Tri levykh chasa" ("Three Left Hours") at the House of the Press earned them notoriety.

The evening's first hour included an announcement of the OBERIU Declaration and readings by the OBERIU poets, throughout which the "master of ceremonies [rode] a tricycle in unbelievable lines and figures."[66] (Such antics seem less surprising if one believes Igor Bakhterev's claim that the group used to drink [*vypivat'*] before performances "to muster courage.")[67] The second hour was devoted to a presentation of Kharms' dramatic extravaganza, "Elizaveta Bam." During the third hour a film by Aleksandr Razumovsky, "Miaso-rubka" ("The Meat Grinder"), was shown. The performance was accompanied by jazz and followed by a lively dispute. The following day a rather dumbfounded review appeared in *Krasnaia gazeta* (*The Red Gazette*), entitled "Ytuerebo" – Oberiuty (mis)spelled backwards. The author contended that "something unprintable took place in the House of the Press yesterday" and declared the entire performance "incomprehensible."[68] By all accounts, the evening was rowdy, with the audience playing its part by whistling, hissing and booing. Thus the OBERIU's fame was born. The group lasted until 1930, when a particularly critical review in the orthodox RAPP (proletarian) style appeared in the newspaper *Smena*[69] and caused the group to think better of its union and disband. Zabolotsky, however, had left the OBERIU earlier, due to irreconcilable differences with Vvedensky. Fragments from Kharms' notebook imply that Zabolotsky broke with the group as early as the autumn of 1928: "We mustn't fear a small number of people ... Three people completely bound to each other are better than ..."[70]

The OBERIU is of particular interest because, arising as it did late in 1927 when Soviet literature was already heading toward disaster, its brief and flashy appearance on the brink may be perceived as a last burst of individualism in an increasingly restrictive environment. When Kharms and Vvedensky first announced their participation in the "Left Flank" of literature, various factions were still vying for supremacy as the true voice of the new socialist state. Indeed, at the Communist Party meeting of June, 1925, it was resolved to allow the warring factions to war in peace. This relative leniency encouraged much experimentation in literature and the arts. As one observer commented: "In the poetry of the twenties there was a sense of eternal youth, as if everything had only just begun ..."[71] New discoveries in science inspired the arts, and a rash of scientific and utopian literature began to appear. Even such anti-utopias as Mayakovsky's *Bedbug* and Mikhail Bulgakov's *Fatal Eggs* and *Heart of a Dog* were inspired by the new emphasis on technology and the universality presaged by the Revolution. Of the numerous visionary groups that sprang up in the early twenties, the Biocosmists (*Biokosmisty*) believed in the possibility of conquering not only time and space but death as well; the Freeformists (*Form-libristy*) used geometrical concepts to test the soundness of their art; and "See-Know" (*Zorved*) sought to depict in painting a world without boundaries or divisions.[72] As the various groups scrambled for attention, their interests often coincided. Thus the Biocosmists, as members of the Proletkult (Proletarian Cultural and Educational Organization), propounded industrial themes, only their visions of factories were portrayed on a cosmic scale.

In addition to their visionary sense, many of the works of the twenties also evinced a feeling for the grotesque. This characteristic is hardly surprising, for the grotesque was apparent in the daily life of the post-revolutionary years. The aura of catastrophe still in the air heightened ordinary occurrences, distorting them into events simultaneously risible and tragic. Olga Forsh recalls a typical rhymed poster of the War Communism era, advocating cremation as part of the government's campaign against religion. It read: "Kazhdyi grazhdanin imeet pravo byt' sozhzhennym" ("Every citizen has the right to be cremated"). This poster appeared throughout the city at a time when there was not enough fuel available to keep people alive, let alone burn them after they had frozen to death.[73] The clash of life's routine with the incongruous conditions of the city, against its eerie backdrop, created an atmosphere of confusion and ambivalence. A metamorphosis was taking place: the death of the old order, the birth of the new.

These changes were reflected in literature. For the first time since the late nineteenth century, prose was gaining over poetry.[74] By 1925, the new Soviet novel had made its debut, touted by favorably-disposed critics as equal to, if not surpassing, the great classics of the nineteenth century. It was in this climate of fading interest in poetry that Kharms and Vvendensky first appeared on the literary scene. Limited artistic freedom still prevailed (although ominous undertones were never long absent), and Kharms and Vvedensky were not thwarted in their experimentation. But by the time of the

OBERIU's inception late in 1927, this freedom had begun to wane. With the advent of the First Five-Year Plan in 1928, the situation worsened; and by 1929 the Proletarian Writers' Association (RAPP) was already exerting pressure on all "neobourgeois" and fellow traveller writers to conform. The great explosion of artistic excitement and diversity was coming to an end. Thus the OBERIU, arriving as it did in the footsteps of more restrictive measures toward literature, may be seen as the last heir of Futurism, with Zabolotsky, whose first book of poems was published in 1929, as the last Russian modernist.[75]

THE OBERIU DECLARATION

Highly aware of the prevailing political atmosphere, the Oberiuty were careful to state their case in favor of the social usefulness of poetry. Art was not to stand above the masses, but to be accessible to them, transforming them by affording a new and revolutionary perception of the world. The Oberiuty were fond of reciting the slogan "Iskusstvo kak shkap" ("Art as a Cupboard") to emphasize the inseparability of art and more prosaic aspects of life. (Then, too, their formulation represents a conscious mimicry of Viktor Shklovsky's Formalist description of "Iskusstvo kak priem" ["Art as Device"].[76]) By hauling an actual cupboard onto stage during their performances,[77] the Oberiuty proclaimed the concretization of abstract concepts, their objectification. The image of the cupboard also suggests the ability of art to store impressions until they are released by the reader's imagination, ultimately leading him to an understanding of the object beyond its purely relative aspect.[78] With such provocative slogans, the OBERIU attracted considerable attention, with good and bad consequences.

Their official group declaration was published in January, 1928, in the short-lived journal *Afishi doma pechati* (*Posters of the House of the Press*) (no. 2, 1928).[79] Yury Vladimirov, a sometime member of the group, described the declaration as having been "written on flannel" ("zapisan na flaneli").[80] By this he presumably meant that the various members of the OBERIU, each highly individualistic in his approach to art, were united under a single, solid covering, a blanket or "flannel" which afforded them a sort of refuge or complicity in their individuality. The OBERIU Declaration set forth the scope of the group and the characteristics of its members, as well as the OBERIU theories about film and the theater. The first two parts of the declaration, "The Social Role of OBERIU" and "The Poetry of the Oberiuty," were drafted by Zabolotsky.

Basically, the OBERIU manifesto declared that art should become a part of people's lives, that its function is primarily practical although its aesthetic element should not be ignored. The Oberiuty professed an entirely new approach to art, and their declaration is peppered with the words "new" and "universal," as if to emphasize the transformation they hoped to effect in society: theirs was a "universal method, universal will"; they were the "poets of a new perception of the world and a new art, builders of a new poetic language, creators of a new perception of life and its objects." But exactly how new their approach was is arguable. The idea of art grounded in reality may be traced to the Acmeists and their reaction against Symbolist transcendence, as can the idea of the word as the foundation of their art. The Futurists, too, placed great emphasis on the word and stressed the "object" or *veshch'*[81] – formulated by the Oberiuty as the *predmet*. This *predmet*, not unlike Khlebnikov's *goloe slovo* ("naked word") free of extraneous attributes, was regarded with *golye glaza* ("naked eyes") in order to discern its essence. The Oberiuty also took up the Futurist concept of *sdvig* (displacement), terming it *stolknovenie slovesnykh smyslov* ("clash of verbal meanings"). And like the Constructivists they believed in the use of functional, everyday objects as valid components of art. As self-proclaimed "honest workers of our art," the Oberiuty shared common ground with the proletarian writers; and as individuals, each "with his own artistic personality," the Oberiuty agreed with a basic tenet of the Serapion Brotherhood.

What *was* new about the OBERIU was the amalgamation of these various principles into a single artistic outlook, under a single covering or "flannel." The OBERIU goal was to create a "new proletarian and artistic culture" where writers were not caught in abstractions but had their feet planted firmly in the reality of the new socialist state. Like other modernists, they wanted to transform the world through the word. Thus they sought to "sink their teeth deep into the pith of the word" and thereby reveal the object behind it. But the word for them was not an end in itself as it was for the Futurists; rather, the Oberiuty sought to unite the word and the object it represented in such a way that not only was the object seen afresh, but the word itself became new and elementary again. This collision of word and object they called *predmetnost'* ("concreteness") and it constitutes a basic principle of OBERIU aesthetics. In coining this term, the OBERIU reacted against the *bespredmetnost'* (non-objectivity or lack of concreteness) of much of avant-garde art. They used *predmetnost'* to emphasize the objective nature of their art, its distance from abstraction. Their idea must also be distinguished from the *veshchizm* of the Constructivists, which focussed on the "consciously made object,"[82] its material formulation. The OBERIU stressed neither the primacy of the word nor of the object, but rather the interrelation of the two, especially insofar as it could serve to distort customary perception.

The OBERIU Declaration further expounded the group's artistic approach: after transforming people's sensibilities, art must equip the people with the ability to live according to their new perceptions. People should be cleansed of the "mire of sufferings and emotions" to which they have grown accustomed, finding themselves surrounded instead by "pure, steadfast, and concrete" forms. It is precisely these concrete, simple forms of everyday life, the things that readily can be perceived by all, that concerned the Oberiuty and their art. Because art is not distinct from reality (it *is* reality), OBERIU art stressed the tangibility of this reality by emphasizing the object or *predmet*. Zabolotsky concluded the second section of the declaration with the following statement:

People of the concrete world, object, and word – we see our social significance in this direction. To touch the world with the toiling movement of the hand, to cleanse from the object the dirt of ancient, decayed cultures – is this not a real demand of our time? For this reason our association bears the name OBERIU – The Association for Real Art.

The Oberiuty sought not to destroy the meaning of the object and the word, but to cleanse them, to expand and intensify them. Theirs was a positive attitude toward the word, and a therapeutic one. The OBERIU aim in society was admittedly therapeutic as well, for they hoped to heal tainted perceptions through the medium of the word as object. The new Soviet citizen, caught in a confusing and rapidly-changing society, would learn to cope by changing his attitudes and perception of reality. While the rest of Soviet society was beginning to concentrate on rebuilding the world, the Oberiuty were trying to rebuild man's attitude toward it.

Although individual experience and impressions remained at the basis of OBERIU art, the scope of the group's work was both universal and impersonal. In its attempts to generalize and to create new myths for the new Soviet culture, OBERIU art may be perceived as a form of folk literature. Relying greatly on the element of play in their work – an element commonly associated with folk art – the Oberiuty tried to instill in people new patterns of perception. Like the dramas of Khlebnikov[83] and the productions of Nikolai Yevreinov, the OBERIU theatrical evenings were based on carnival pranks and linguistic patterns derived from folk theater. The group's predilection for play is revealed, too, in their common love for the fictitious nineteenth-century sage Kozma Prutkov and his absurdities,[84] as well as in the doggerel they constantly composed for one another. While some critics rightly consider the OBERIU the heir of Prutkov,[85] others have likened Zabolotsky and friends to the fictional Captain Lebyadkin of Dostoyevsky's *The Possessed*, a scribbler of light album verse and a bumbler who wildly, though wittily, distorts well-known poetry.[86] Although this comparison is not inappropriate, Zabolotsky's poetic distortions were always conscious, not accidental, his choice of words always motivated. The alleged awkwardness, incoherence and absurdity of his poetry is merely a faked ineptitude; his "primitivism," a conscious imitation of those who came before. Indeed, the themes Zabolotsky treats in his serious work often reappear in his humorous verse: his *stishki* are remarkable not so much for their silliness as for their content.

Although the writings of the Oberiuty seem childish, even simplistic, at times (as does much of folk literature), the poets were more concerned with the effect of their work on the reader than with the child's vision *per se*. In order to elicit the desired response, the Oberiuty felt there was a proper way for their works to be read. In his self-characterization in the declaration, Zabolotsky explained what this approach must be:

N. Zabolotsky is a poet of bare, concrete figures moved right up to the eyes of the observer. He should be heard and read more with the eyes and the fingers than with the ears. The object does not fracture, on the contrary it fuses and substantializes to the extreme, as if ready to meet the observer's groping hand. The unfolding of action and the milieu play a secondary rôle to this major task.

Each of the OBERIU poets is introduced in terms of his relation to the object, and for himself, Zabolotsky takes pains to stress the tactile nature of his art. His emphasis on the tangibility of the word is remarkably similar to the Constructivist Vladimir Tatlin's idea of "tactile" or plastic space where the eye (or, in Zabolotsky's case, the ear as well) is put "under the control of touch."[87] Through Zabolotsky's perspective the word takes on a new dimension, a spatial existence where a keen visual and tactile sensibility leads to greater cognition on the reader's part.[88]

For instance, in "Shkola zhukov" ("The School of Beetles," 1931) Zabolotsky reveals to the reader the intrinsic properties of nine different trees – ash, larch, pear, lime, moa, thuya, nut, rosewood, and ebony. The characteristics of each tree suggest the most appropriate uses for its wood. Here Zabolotsky's poetic process mirrors Tatlin's manipulation of materials in his visual medium. In both cases the *faktura* or texture of the woods is shown to the reader or viewer in fresh perspective:

Черные полосы лиственниц
Научат строительству рельсов . . .
Дерево моа похоже на мед –
Пчеловодов учитель . . .

The black strips of larch
Will teach the laying of rails . . .
The moa tree resembles honey –
The counsellor of beekeepers.

Zabolotsky's "moa tree" is probably the moabi or African pearwood. In the early thirties he had a collection of polished wood samples, which he carefully kept in a wooden trunk and frequently examined.[89] It may be supposed that Zabolotsky's comparison of the moabi tree to honey is a reflection of the wood tone; but he deepens the comparison by coining the word "moa," similar in sound to the Russian *myod* or "honey." Zabolotsky's close examination of wood also recalls the experiments of the artist Pavel Mansurov at Leningrad's Museum of Artistic Culture in the early twenties. Mansurov studied objects from nature to discern the "intrinsic, natural laws of color and form," from which he believed man could learn.[90]

FILONOV'S ANALYTICAL ART

Zabolotsky recognized the affinity of his poetry with the visual arts, and his description in the OBERIU Declaration affirms their common ground, where concrete figures frequently confront the observer "as if ready to meet his groping hand." In the chaotic aftermath of revolution, the need for tangibility seemed particularly acute. As the German critic Walter Benjamin observed, ". . . everywhere, even in advertisements, the people characteristically demand[ed] that some tangible action be represented."[91] But Zabolotsky's choice to align his literal art with the visual was not prompted merely by external considerations; rather, he believed that poetry has more in common with painting and architecture than with the medium of prose.[92] The affinity between poetry and art was felt particularly strongly by the Futurist poets, many of whom had begun their artistic careers as painters.[93] Zabolotsky likewise tried his hand at drawing.[94] In his brief autobiography he troubles to mention the art classes he so greatly enjoyed at the Urzhum Practical High School, and his interest in drawing apparently did not wane even after his move to Petrograd, for the walls of his room on Horse Street were covered with his own colored-ink drawings of all sorts of freaks.[95]

Zabolotsky designed bright covers for his manuscripts of poems, considering their external appearance to be nearly as important as their content, and he always recopied his rough drafts in fine calligraphy. Like the Futurists, he believed that handwriting expresses a "poetic impulse" and provides an "auxiliary graphic source of expression that intensifies the poetic image."[96] With this concept in mind, Zabolotsky encouraged the production of a striking poster for the OBERIU evening of "Three Left Hours." This poster was designed by Vera Yermolayeva and Lev Yudin, who had studied with Malevich.[97] The artists mixed letters of various styles and sizes and placed them on the page at diverging angles, even upside down and backwards. Zabolotsky himself contributed to the overall effect of the announcement. Following his suggestion, the posters were placed not singly throughout Leningrad, but in pairs, one right side up, the other inverted.[98]

Zabolotsky was so pleased by this poster that he asked Yudin to design the book cover for *Scrolls*: "It seems to me that the lettering you used for the large poster for '3 Oberiut Hours' would suit the book very well ... The word STOLBTSY should be done in your script, it dominates. Your script is distinctive, but controlled and complete. It expresses the whole point. On first glance – nothing special, but when you look closely, something entirely new opens up. Two colors: white and black ..."[99] And later: "What's new and good in your work? [Make the] cover as austere as possible, but with spirit – you know."[100] Zabolotsky's widow recalls Yudin's finished design: "On the cover from the top in black on a white background was written: STOLBTSY. Lush letters of different sizes were tightly spaced and appeared as a unified whole."[101] Zabo-

3 Poster for the OBERIU presentation of "Three Left Hours" at
Leningrad's House of the Press, 1928

lotsky was greatly disappointed by the functional cover his
publisher chose over Yudin's design.[102]

Zabolotsky admired the work of several artists, whose techniques he would apply to his poetry, transforming a visual
picture into a verbal image. He particularly delighted in the
works of Bruegel, Le Douanier Rousseau, and the Georgian
naif Pirosmani (Niko Pirosmanashvili), three painters who
share a boldness of color and expression, two a primitiveness
of form. But the painter whose work most deeply affected

Zabolotsky and his poetry was Pavel Nikolayevich Filonov, founder of the school of "Analytical Art."

While the various links between Futurist poets and artists have been well documented,[103] the relationship between the OBERIU and the artistic avant-garde has not been given much attention, perhaps because alliances never developed fully. The connections are pertinent, however.[104] One contemporary critic considered the early OBERIU poetry a kind of Suprematism of the word, similar to Malevich's Suprematism of form.[105] And because the Oberiuty all had artistic interests beyond poetry, the influential critic Nikolai Punin conceived a plan to ally the group with the artists Malevich, Leonid Chupyatov, Nikolai Tyrsa, and Vladimir Lebedev. Although Malevich himself participated in the negotiations, nothing ever came of them.

Like Malevich, Filonov had close ties to the OBERIU throughout its brief existence. In fact, the opening of the OBERIU Declaration expresses the group's opposition to Filonov's expulsion from the Academy: "We don't understand why the Filonov School has been forced out of the Academy, why Malevich cannot develop his architectural work in the USSR, why Terentyev's "The Inspector General" was so foolishly catcalled."[106] While Kharms and Vvedensky were closer to Malevich, Zabolotsky, of all the Oberiuty, was most drawn to Filonov and his art. He reportedly took lessons from the painter[107] and even liked to draw in imitation of his style.[108]

Filonov was born into a poor family in Moscow in 1883 and as a child was forced to cross-stitch towels and tablecloths for money. Orphaned at the age of thirteen, he left Moscow for Petersburg to study art. Filonov's dream was to enter the Academy of Arts, but he had to try four times before finally being accepted as an auditor. He studied at the Academy from 1908 to 1910 and was once suspended for "corrupting [his] classmates with [his] work."[109] In 1910 he joined "The Union of Youth" (*Soiuz molodezhi*), an early Futurist group that boasted such articulate and talented members as Malevich, Mikhail Matyushin and Elena Guro. Filonov participated in

4 Zabolotsky's self-portrait, executed in the style of Filonov, 1925

their exhibitions, and his painting "The Adoration of the Magi" (*Poklonenie volkhvov*) was first reproduced in the Union of Youth collection of 1912 (no. 2).[110] By 1912, Filonov was already speaking out against Cubism and what he termed its "mechanics," proposing instead the "organics" of his new method of art. Of his affiliation with the Union of Youth, he is best known for the stage designs he prepared for the first performance of Mayakovsky's tragedy, "Vladimir Mayakovsky" (1913).

When in that same year the Union of Youth merged with the avant-garde group "Hylaea" (*Gileia*), Filonov met the poet

Khlebnikov, and their friendship proved dynamic. Filonov
undertook to illustrate many of Khlebnikov's poems, and
under the poet's influence published a volume of his own
strangely lyrical verse, *Propeven' o prorosli mirovoi* (*Hymn of
Universal Flowering*, 1915). Although this collaboration
between poet and painter may seem remote from Zabolotsky –
who at the time was only a twelve-year-old boy living in the
provinces – in fact the cross-pollination of influences so con-
sequential to him began long before he arrived on the scene.

In designing the illustrations for Khlebnikov's poetry,
Filonov sought to make the words speak for themselves, to
concretize and materialize them, thus intensifying Khlebnikov's poetic images. For example, for the poem "Perunu"
("To Perun"), Filonov formed both the "P" and the "n" as
zigzag arrows of lightning, affording the reader an immediate
visual image of Perun as the heathen Slavic god of thunder,
beyond the mere semantic connotation of his name.[111] Such a
visual depiction, akin to the Chinese ideogram, was very likely
inspired by the Oriental scholar Vladimir Markov, who along
with Filonov belonged to the Union of Youth.[112] Besides
creating evocative symbols for key letters, Filonov often accen-
ted them by enlargement or shading, thus creating a kind of
zvukopis' or sound painting for the reader. Under Filonov's
masterful hand, Khlebnikov's verse was augmented by a
visual dimension; and Filonov's printing of the poetic text
added a new, graphic interpretation.

Filonov also illustrated his own poem. One drawing from it,
entitled "The Principle of Pure Active Form," depicts horses
in motion. Given Zabolotsky's attraction to Filonov's art, one
can propose the poet's inspiration for his 1927 "Dvizhenie"
("Motion"), for which Filonov's drawing provides a striking
representation:[113]

> Сидит извозчик как на троне,
> Из ваты сделана броня,
> И борода, как на иконе,
> Лежит, монетами звеня.
>
> А бедный конь руками машет,
> То вытянется, как налим,

То снова восемь ног сверкают
В его блестящем животе.

The coachman sits as on a throne,
His armour is of cotton wadding,
And his beard, as on an icon,
Lies jingling with coins.

And the poor horse waves his arms,
Now he stretches like a burbot,
Now his eight legs flash anew
In his shining belly.

Of course, the urge to depict motion was common to many modernists, who followed the Italian Futurists in their desire to "render the prolongation of objects in space" and "synthesize the unique forms of continuity in space."[114] Zabolotsky's "Motion" represents a poetic attempt to fix movement on the page,[115] just as the Futurist painters sought to capture motion on canvas.[116] As for Filonov, his depiction of movement had to do with his conception of time, which he believed "materialize[d] in the many-layered, vibrating, mobile surface of the canvas."[117] The closely-worked *faktura* or texture of his paintings was an attempt to express "the self-movement, the flowing of real time."[118] The painter's desire to materialize time is portrayed fictionally in Khlebnikov's story "KA," where the writer describes an encounter with an artist:

I met a certain artist and asked him whether he was going to war. He answered:
"I too am waging a war, only it's not for space, it's for time. I sit in a trench and take a small scrap of time from the past. My duty is just as difficult as that of the troops [fighting] for space."[119]

The artistic interchange between painter and poet appears particularly intricate when one considers Khlebnikov's poem "Zhut' lesnaia" ("Sylvan Terror," 1914). One stanza of this poem describes Filonov's painting of a horse that was shown at the last Union of Youth exhibition in 1914.[120] But because Khlebnikov's poetic persona identifies with this horse, in writing about Filonov's painting, the poet is actually writing about himself. Thus, through Khlebnikov's description of

Filonov's horse, we can actually conjure up an image of the
man as Filonov's brush might have captured him.[121] And
when we consider Khlebnikov's etymological system, where
the words *kon'* (steed) and *ikona* (icon) are integrally related,[122]
the poem stands as an iconic representation bearing spiritual
significance:

Я со стены письма Филонова
Смотрю, как конь усталый, до конца.
И много муки в письме у оного,
В глазах у конского лица.
Свирепый конь белком желтеет,
И мрак залит [ый] [им] густеет,
С нечеловеческою мукой
На полотне тяжелом грубом
Согбенный будущей наукой
Дает привет тяжелый губам.

From the wall of Filonov's painting
I eternally look out, like a tired steed.
One sees great torment in that painting,
In the eyes of the horse's face.
The whites of the fierce steed show yellow,
And the gloom that he casts congeals.
With inhuman torment,
On the coarse, thick canvas,
Bent by the weight of future science,
He forms a heavy greeting on his lips.

Animal faces with human eyes, gazing out at the viewer with
ineffable suffering, are characteristic of Filonov's paintings. In
the context of Khlebnikov's poetic response to Filonov's art, it
is also interesting to note that in Zabolotsky's 1926 "Litso
konia" ("The Face of the Horse"), horses' eyes similarly
mirror suffering.

Like Filonov, Zabolotsky strove to grasp the infinite
through his art, whether expressed in the inexorable passage of
time, eternal suffering, or endless movement. What specifically appealed to Zabolotsky was the firm grounding of Filonov's art in *thought*, his analytical premise. Filonov had first
expounded the principles of his analytical art in the 1914
manifesto "Sdelannye kartiny" ("Made Paintings").[123] The

outbreak of World War I, during which he served on the Rumanian Front, interrupted his work, but his return to Petrograd after the Revolution marks a period of great artistic activity. For a while Filonov taught at the Institute of Artistic Culture (INKhUK) as head of the ideological section, working to perfect his theories. In 1925 he officially opened a workshop whose participants were known as the "Masters of Analytical Art" (MAI).

Filonov's style of pedagogy was intense. His students would draw for hours at a time,[124] not stopping for meals, and as they drew, Filonov would proclaim his artistic ideology. Even those students who did not always agree with Filonov's theories fell under his sway: "Listening to Filonov's adamant arguments, I felt the pressure of his will on me, it overwhelmed me, even though I consciously continued to oppose and doubt the rightness of his words."[125] Those who knew Filonov well imagined him as made up less of vital fluids than of "burning coals, smoldering logs, the heart of a tree scorched by lightning."[126] At the least, pedagogy was for Filonov a crucial weapon in his struggle with the Academy.[127] He intended to imbue his students with the ideology he himself lived and breathed, and his methods soon came to be recognized as a distinct school of art. His followers, informally known as *filonovtsy*, frequently exhibited at the House of the Press where the OBERIU performed, and thus the artist's ties with that group were strengthened.

In 1923 Filonov had issued a declaration of his methods, in which he set forth the principle of "madeness" as the basis of Analytical Art. In the "Declaration of Universal Flowering," he explained his precepts as follows:

Because I know, analyze, see, and intuit that in any object there exist not just two predicates – form and color – but a whole world of seen and unseen phenomena, along with their emanations, reactions, inclusions, geneses, and separate realities, as well as their known or unknown properties which sometimes contain infinite predicates of their own; because of this I categorically denounce as unscientific and moribund the dogma of the contemporary realism of "two predicates" together with all of its right- and left-wing sects. In its place I propose a scientific, analytical, and intuitive naturalism; the researcher's initiative into all of the object's predicates, the phenomena of the entire world, and the phenomena of human processes, both seen and unseen by the naked eye; I propose persistence on the part of the master-inventor; and I propose the principle of a "biologically made painting."[128]

Through analysis of the object and its phenomena, understanding takes place, and the artist is then able to synthesize what he sees into a harmonious vision. Filonov posits a distinction between the "seeing" eye and the "knowing" eye. The seeing eye is able to perceive only two attributes of an object – color and form – but the knowing eye, on the basis of intuition, can capture the many hidden processes in the object and thus understand it more completely.[129] The observer's eye, as much as the artist's, is expected to be "knowing" in order to see as much in the depiction of the object as the artist saw in the object itself.[130] Filonov firmly believed that the impact of any object or depiction of it lay as much in the intuited as in the apparent. In his strictly-organized paintings he sought to convey not only the essence of things but also the larger metaphysical questions they implied. The intuitive observer can feel in each element of Filonov's paintings an intense energy which is communicated on a psychic, as well as an intellectual, level. Even though many of Filonov's paintings depict only a certain aspect of the universe, a particular "microworld," the intuition informing them leads to a sense of universality in the paintings, a convergence of all the phenomena of nature, seen and unseen, known and merely felt. Like Bruegel, Filonov expresses a "sense of imminent, universal transformation" in his art;[131] and precisely this visionary impression attracted Zabolotsky to both painters as he sought to convey the intuited in his own work.

The universal, even cosmic,[132] impact of Filonov's art is all the more startling because his technique is concerned primarily with analysis of the most minute parts of the universe: atoms, not masses. Filonov's work depicts myriad small worlds, moments of existence, which are whole and complete unto themselves. His concerns lay first in the part; only through the part could one hope to consider the whole. Often Filonov began to paint from one corner of the canvas, believing that a painting should grow and evolve in the same way as plants do in nature, and that the growth should be just as orderly and organic – atom by atom, cell by cell.[133] In a letter to one of his students, Filonov admonished: "Think persistently and accurately about each atom of a thing being made. Draw each atom persistently and accurately."[134] Filonov's idea of a "biologically-made painting" is to be taken literally. His belief in organic growth and gradual transformation led to "tattooing," for example, flowering shoots on human faces to represent pictorially the "intermediate step between the plant and animal worlds."[135] Through the depiction of "vital, internal processes,"[136] Filonov gradually brought his paintings to a state of *sdelannost'* or "madeness."

BIOLOGICAL GROTESQUE

It was not until several years after Filonov had publicized his theory of *sdelannost'* that the OBERIU appeared on the scene with the notion of *predmetnost'*. The two ideas have much in common. Indeed, as early as 1916 Mikhail Matyushin had characterized Filonov's art in terms of its *predmetnost'*: "In Filonov's paintings man and his face are always tightly bound with nature and with concreteness."[137] Like Filonov, the Oberiuty were interested in the analytical possibilities of art; they appreciated Filonov's painting as a science in which each detail was given over to close scrutiny. Filonov's technique had the greatest impact on Zabolotsky, whose 1933 "Ptitsy" ("Birds") demonstrates a poetic analysis relying, like Filonov's paintings, on a sort of biological grotesque:[138]

> Если строение голубя хочешь узнать ты – какие
> жилы в нем есть, как крылья устроены, ноги,
> Как расположены органы в нем и, подвешены чудно,
> Между костей образуют они тройную фигурку, –
> Надобно прежде доску найти . . .

> If you want to discover the structure of a dove – what
> Veins it has, how its wings are constructed, its legs,

How its organs are arranged and how, magically suspended,
They form a three-fold figure among its bones, –
You must first of all find a plank ...

In Filonov's paintings, veins, tendons and muscles are all
revealed; nor does Zabolotsky spare his reader physiological
detail. And just as the painter often depicted the close borders
between disparate realms,[139] so too did the poet seek to
identify the relationship between animate and inanimate
objects. Zabolotsky saw man's constructions as an attempt to
imitate existing forms in nature:

...

Далее – скальпелем сделай надрез посредине
Маленькой грудки, где киль возвышается длинный.
Славен киль в кораблях, острый могуч в пароходах,
Крепко устроил его человек себе на потребу.
Как же, подумай, должны мы прославить легчайший,
Маленький голубя киль – прообраз людского строенья!

Next – with your scalpel make an incision along
Its small breast, where the long keel-bone rises up.
The keel in ships is renowned, keen and mighty in steamers,
Man made it sturdy for his own needs.
How then, imagine, shall we praise this most light,
This smallest keel of the dove – the prototype of human construction!

In "Birds," Zabolotsky has a classful of fowl dissect a dove to
reveal its innermost parts. Filonov similarly breaks apart his
object into its component parts – a technique not unlike
dissection. Indeed, his term *razlozhenie*[140] denotes both structural and biological de-composition.

Filonov's interest in anatomy can be traced to his formal
studies at the Academy; Zabolotsky's fascination with the
biological sciences goes back even further, to his childhood,
when his agronomist father encouraged his elementary laboratory experiments. Recognizing his aptitude for analysis, Zabolotsky at one time considered "devoting [himself] exclusively
to science";[141] and even after he had decided on a literary
career, he continued to peruse scientific texts.[142] Indeed, many
of Zabolotsky's deepest poetic visions may be seen as conversations with science.

Through their art, both Filonov and Zabolotsky sought to discern the underlying structures of objects – the inner fabric that determines outer form – and in this respect both painter and poet participated in the Neovitalist movement in Russia. Neither artist considered the mere identification of an object's inner structure sufficient, however; the knowledge achieved had to be put to greater purpose.[143] Thus Filonov, having once decomposed the object, reconstructed it "biologically" in order to form a more concrete and (he believed) harmonious whole. Zabolotsky likewise perceived the world in terms of its progressions to ever more perfect natural forms:

> ... Даже в потемках науки
> Что-то мне и сейчас говорит о могучем составе
> Мира, где все перемены направлены мудро
> Только к тому, чтобы старые, дряхлые формы
> В новые отлиты были, лучшего вида сосуды.

> ... Even in the darkness of science
> Even now something speaks to me of the powerful composition
> Of the world, where all changes are wisely directed
> Toward one thing only: that old, decrepit forms
> Might flow into the very best kind of new vessels.

Numerous paintings by Filonov, particularly those bearing the title "Formula," depict the process of evolution. Under the influence of this art, Zabolotsky conceived of his own "formula," meant to reveal the underlying patterns in nature. His long poem "Derev'ia" ("The Trees," 1933) begins as a penned counterpoint to Filonov's brush technique, evoking the process of organic growth through the union of individual parts into an integrated whole:

> Бомбеев
> – Кто вы, кивающие маленькой головкой,
> Играете с жуком и божией коровкой?
>
> Голоса
> – Я листьев солнечная сила.
> – Желудок я цветка.
> – Я пестика паникадило.
> – Я тонкий стебелек смиренного левкоя.
> – Я корешок судьбы.

– А я лопух покоя.
– Все вместе мы – изображение цветка,
Его росток и направленье завитка.

Bombeev
Who are you, nodding tiny head,
Playing with the beetle and ladybug?

Voices
– I am the sun's energy of the leaves.
– I am the flower's stomach.
– I am the chandelier of the pistil.
– I am the slender stem of the humble gillyflower.
– I am the small root of fate.
– And I am the burdock of rest.
– All together we are the image of a flower,
Its shoot and the direction of its tendril.

This recitation continues throughout the Prologue as the individual parts of a stormy sky and then of the genesis of life itself speak up.

Бомбеев
– А вы, укромные, как шишечки и нити,
Кто вы, которые под кустиком сидите?

Голоса
– Мы глазки жуковы.
– Я гусеницын нос.
– Я возникающий из семени овес.
– Я дудочка души, оформленной слегка.
– Мы не облекшиеся телом потроха.
– Я то, что будет органом дыханья.
– Я сон грибка.
– Я свечки колыханье.
– Возникновенье глаза я на кончике земли.
– А мы нули.
– Все вместе мы – чудесное рожденье,
Откуда ты свое ведешь происхожденье.

Bombeev
– And you, sheltered ones, like cones and filaments,
Who are you, sitting underneath the bush?

Voices
– We are beetles' eyes.

– I am the caterpillar's nose.
– I am the oats sprouting from a seed.
– I am the small pipe of the soul, barely formed.
– We are the guts not yet wrapped in a body.
– I am that which will be the organ of breathing.
– I am the dream of a microorganism.
– I am the flickering of a candle.
– I am the incipience of an eye on the edge of the earth.
– And we are the ciphers.
– All together we are miraculous birth,
  Whence you trace your origins.

Here Zabolotsky has enumerated the parts, then affirmed the whole. His early characterization in the OBERIU Declaration ("the object does not fracture; on the contrary, it fuses and substantializes to the extreme ...") would seem to apply for "The Trees" as well, in that things are assembled and constructed, rather than broken apart. Yet these lines may be regarded from the opposite point of view, as a dissection, rather than construction, of the object: "Zabolotsky's poetry professes to show ... construction as opposed to dissection, but it amounts to the same thing."[144] The point is that like Filonov, Zabolotsky emphasized not just the visible composite of any given phenomenon, but its unseen, intuited parts, that place "on the borderline/of life and death, of the conscious and the unconscious,/[where] the small faces of plants grow" ("The Trees"). Notably, at the very start of his career Filonov was already incorporating this concept of intuited parts into his paintings.[145] By 1928, twenty years later, his approach had hardly changed:

... the knowing eye of the researcher-inventor-master of Analytical Art aspires towards a maximum, exhaustive vision as far as this is humanly possible. He looks with his analysis, with his brain and sees [things] that escape the artist's eye. For example, while seeing only the trunk, branches, leaves and flowers of, say, an apple-tree, it's possible at the same time to know (or to attempt to know by analysis) how the tendrils of the roots take and absorb the juices of the earth, how these juices flow upwards through the cells of the wood, how they distribute themselves as they respond continuously to light and heat, how they are transformed, distilled and converted into the atomistic structure of the trunk and branches, into green leaves, red

and white flowers, green, yellow and pink apples, and the rough bark
of the tree. This is what should interest the master and not the
external aspect of the apple-tree.[146]

Filonov sought to reveal higher truths in the minute analyses of his paintings; Zabolotsky's poetry also may be construed
as visionary. It is indicative of both the originality and the
unconventionality of these artists' visions that their earliest
works were labelled "unhealthy" and "grotesque"; certain
critics even accused painter and poet of something close to
sexual abnormality.[147] What Filonov and Zabolotsky *do* reflect
in their work is a sense of alienation experienced in reaction to
the city; and in both cases this alienation contributed to their
startling and neoteric approaches to art. In this respect, the
critics were not incorrect to use the term "grotesque," for a
grotesque perspective certainly is one consequence of alienation. As Wolfgang Kayser writes, "the grotesque world is –
and is not – our own world. The ambiguous way in which we
are affected by it results from our awareness that the familiar
and apparently harmonious world is alienated under the
impact of abysmal forces, which break it up and shatter its
coherence."[148]

Although elements of the grotesque figure in the works of
both artists, rarely is the depicted world left as shattered as
Kayser suggests. In his pictorial analyses Filonov revealed the
grotesque aspect of life: exposed arteries and veins;[149] humans,
plants, animals, and buildings all enmeshed. But once having
fractured the world, he strove to reconstruct it and synthesize
it, in order that the made painting might portray the harmony
of all the universe, of its many parts. Filonov meant for his
paintings to express the diversity of life and the interrelationships of its many facets. Thus sprouts of plants poke through
human skin; human faces are superimposed on buildings
while skyscrapers peer out from human eyes;[150] and men with
horses' faces or horses with the demeanors of men stare incon-
solably out at the viewer. Only when Filonov failed to achieve
synthesis in his paintings did they suffer from a lack of unity
among his many "small worlds" and from too great
abstraction.

It was precisely Filonov's ability to bring the disparate worlds of his canvas together into one harmonious whole that appealed so much to Zabolotsky, whose poetic quest throughout his career may be seen as the pursuit of a rational harmony in nature. Both Zabolotsky and Filonov saw man as an integral part of nature and sought to express the unity of the universe by juxtaposing its many microworlds. Thus Zabolotsky could write in "The Trees":

> Да, человек есть башня птиц,
> Зверей вместилище лохматых,
> В его лице – миллионы лиц
> Четвероногих и крылатых.
>
> И много в нем живет зверей,
> И много рыб со дна морей,
> Но все они в лучах сознанья
> Большого мозга строят зданье.

> Yes, man is a tower of birds,
> A receptacle of shaggy beasts,
> In his face are millions of faces
> Of four-legged and winged animals.
> And many beasts reside in him,
> And many fish from the depths of the seas,
> But all of them, in the rays of consciousness
> Of his great brain construct a building.

Zabolotsky and Filonov investigated the kinship between man and nature, rather than portraying man as purely dominant. Such a stance increased their vulnerability in a political atmosphere that stressed more and more the concept of rebuilding in nature and demanded the exploitation of nature's resources. In 1929 a large retrospective of Filonov's work was scheduled to open at Leningrad's Russian Museum, but after a vitriolic controversy over his art appeared in the press, the exhibition was cancelled, despite the fact that a catalogue had already been printed and the paintings hung.[151] By the mid-1930s, the tenets of Socialist Realism dictated that nature be portrayed as man's opponent in his great struggle to conquer the elements; it was no longer politically safe to depict nature as harmonious or as an environment within which man could live. Whoever did not see man as beyond nature was considered heretical. Thus, Filonov's paintings were for decades relegated to the basements of State museums. His works were not shown again until 1967, when an exhibition opened in remote Novosibirsk.[152]

Throughout the 1930s Filonov continued to work unobtrusively at home. Although he needed money, he refused to sell his paintings, believing that art should be in the public domain, not privately held. Filonov died in 1941, neglected and destitute, during the blockade of Leningrad. He had exhausted his strength trying to protect his paintings.[153] By 1941, Zabolotsky's strength was also nearly depleted from incarceration in a Siberian labor camp; but the decade between Zabolotsky's association with the OBERIU and his internment in the camps had seen his maturation as a poet and the development of his remarkable artistic philosophy.

CHAPTER 2

The last Russian modernist

> Man should believe in immortality ... If I work on
> unceasingly till my death, nature is bound to give me
> another form of being when the present one can no longer
> sustain my spirit.
>
> Goethe, *Conversations with Eckermann*

Zabolotsky saw Filonov not only as a gifted painter but also as
a visionary whose artistic technique yielded a sense of the
infinite. His attraction to precisely this quality of Filonov's art
anticipated the enthusiasm he would soon demonstrate for the
scientist Konstantin Tsiolkovsky's theories of microworlds and
cosmic harmony. What appealed to Zabolotsky in both
Filonov and Tsiolkovsky was their will to look beyond the
known dimensions. In his early poetry, in fact, Zabolotsky
transcended spatial and temporal planes, allowing his characters to move freely throughout the universe among different
eras and worlds. In this dissection of the universally-
recognized planes – a necessary step leading to the ultimate
unity of his poetic world – Zabolotsky's poetry is most closely
aligned to the spirit of Filonov's art. Anatoly Aleksandrov has
termed such dissection "fragmentation," and he considers this
technique crucial to Zabolotsky's art: "Fragmentation
becomes a basic principle of the composition, and the dynamics of 'displacement' become its nerve, reflecting the spiritual
shock of the poet."[1]

Proceeding from this idea of fragmentation, Zabolotsky's
early poems may be likened to the shards of a ceramic vessel:
when assembled, the shards create a unified piece, but the
outlines of their individual shapes remain apparent, like a bowl

repaired with glue, each shard constituting an integral part of the whole. These "shards" in Zabolotsky's poetry may be interpreted on two levels. First, they are the fragmentary moments in any given poem which add up to a unified composition. Second, and more broadly, the shards are the individual poems in the collection *Scrolls*,[2] each of which represents a certain small part of the larger picture of urban life depicted in the volume. Zabolotsky's poetic "fragmentation" may also be compared to the cinematic technique of montage developed around that time by Sergei Eisenstein, whereby quick and heterogeneous shots of life are rapidly juxtaposed upon the screen. Taken *in toto*, the scenes jar the viewer into perceiving the world in a new way by creating an integrated picture that is all the more vivid for having been dissected before him. Zabolotsky's technique in *Scrolls* often approaches montage in its use of abrupt juxtapositions and dissolves. Furthermore, such displacements challenge the reader to participate in the poetic process.

SCROLLS

When published in 1929, *Scrolls* created a *succès de scandale*, and the edition of 1200 sold out almost immediately. In the volume Zabolotsky included twenty-two poems written between 1926 and 1928. These poems carry the reader on a strange circuit of Leningrad, a city caught in the vulgarities and confusion of the NEP period. The tour begins at a bar called the "Krasnaia Bavariia" ("Red Bavaria"), a "paradise of bottles" where the windows float in goblets and a pale "siren" behind the bar regales her guests with beer. From there the reader goes out into the "Belaia noch'" ("White Night") of a Leningrad summer:

> Гляди: не бал, не маскарад,
> Здесь ночи ходят невпопад,
> Здесь, от вина неузнаваем,
> Летает хохот попугаем;
> Раздвинулись мосты и кручи,
> Бегут любовники толпой,

5 Manuscript page of Zabolotsky's poem "Disciplina clericalis," copied in calligraphy

Один – горяч, другой – измучен,
А третий – книзу головой . . .
Любовь стенает под листами,
Она меняется местами,
То подойдет, то отойдет . . .
А музы любят круглый год.

Look: it's no ball, no masquerade,
Here night irrelevantly follows night,
Here a laugh, from wine distorted,
Soars up like a parrot.
The bridges and cliffs have moved apart,
Lovers run past in a crowd,
One is hot, another bushed,
A third one hangs his head ...
Love moans under the leaves,
It keeps on changing places,
First it approaches, then backs off ...
But muses love all year round.

The summer night looms large in its unsettling paleness, only then to fade away, creating an impression of delirium.[3] Fully in the Petersburg tradition, Zabolotsky's White Night is stripped of its romantic aura as the realities of furtive and frivolous lovemaking are described. The poem's final stanza demonstrates Zabolotsky's feel for the uncanny that pervades all of *Scrolls*:

И всюду сумасшедший бред,
И белый воздух липнет к крышам,
А ночь уже на ладан дышит,
Качается как на весах.
Так недоносок или ангел,
Открыв молочные глаза
Качается в спиртовой банке
И просится на небеса.

And all around lies mad delirium,
The white air sticks to the roofs,
And night, with one foot in the grave already,
Sways as if on scales,
Just as a premature infant or angel,
Having opened its milky eyes,
Sways in a jar of spirits
And begs for heaven.

The discomfiting nature of these lines is accentuated by their conservative form. Written in a highly regular iambic tetrameter, and with an established pattern of rhyme (admitting, however, both truncated and oblique forms), the stanza is grounded in tradition even as it breaks with it. The resulting tension is reflected in the frequency of words expressing instability: *sumasshedshii* "mad"; *bred* "delirium"; *kachaetsia* "sways" (repeated twice). At the same time, the reader experiences a sense of suffocation as the night "sticks" to the roofs and takes its last, difficult breaths. (The metaphor *dyshit na ladan*, literally, "to breathe incense," refers to the incense-filled censer swung by the priest during funeral rites. A censer "sways"; here Zabolotsky has displaced the verb and applied it associatively to the scales in the following line.) Death does seem imminent: no longer is the city festive and lit by fireworks, as at the beginning of the poem; now it is drained of color, and even the eyes of the spirits inhabiting it are colorless, "milky."

Yet despite its heavy haze of unreality, Leningrad is still concretely evoked in Zabolotsky's allusion to the Kunstkammer, Peter the Great's famed scientific chamber, where he preserved medical curiosities such as premature babies, cyclopes, and Siamese twins in bottles. Zabolotsky invests his grotesque image with several layers of meaning. The Kunstkammer, a city landmark, suggests the idea of *Peter's* city, which alludes in turn to the Petersburg literary tradition. This literary reference, at first perceived generally, becomes specific as Zabolotsky echoes Boratynsky's "Nedonosok" ("The Premature Child"), an 1835 poem in which the spirit of a premature child hovers disconsolately between heaven and earth. Thus Zabolotsky challenges his reader to a wide range of associations that carry him beyond the confines of the stifling White Night.

Proceeding through the city, the reader sees a soccer game ("Futbol'"), a marketplace ("Na rynke"), and a bakery ("Pekarnia"). The world portrayed in all of these poems seems to exist outside of time and space:

> . . . Приходит ночь.
> Бренча алмазною заслонкой
> Она вставляет черный ключ
> В атмосферическую лунку –
> Открылся госпитал.
> Увы!

Здесь форвард спит
                                без головы.
                "Футбол"

                ... Night comes.
Jingling its oven doors of diamond,
It places a black key
In the atmospheric hole –
The hospital has opened.
                                Alas!
The forward sleeps here
                                without a head.
                                "Soccer"

Waking and dream states, the real and the unreal, merge into one. Zabolotsky surpasses habitual barriers by continually jarring his reader out of one level of consciousness and into the next. The result is a verbal grotesque, not unlike that described by the avant-garde theater director Vsevolod Meyerhold: "The main thing in the grotesque is the artist's constant striving to lead the viewer out of the plane he has only just reached and onto another which he didn't expect."[4] Yet even as Zabolotsky shifts planes, startling his reader from accustomed perceptions, he fixes the images in the reader's mind by making them concrete: the loud laughter in "White Night" flies fleetingly through the air, but Zabolotsky makes it visible and very nearly palpable by likening it to a parrot.

At times Zabolotsky's concretization serves to make objects that are not fixed in time seem eternal; this is the effect in "Ivanovy" ("The Ivanovs"). The Ivanovs are generic;[5] they represent the philistine inhabitants of the city who are reproduced millions of times each day:

Но вот – все двери растворились,
Повсюду шепот пробежал:
На службу вышли Ивановы
В своих штанах и башмаках.
Пустые гладкие трамваи
Им подают свои скамейки;
Герои входят, покупают
Билетов хрупкие дощечки,

Сидят и держат их перед собой,
Не увлекаясь быстрою ездой.

Suddenly all the doors swing open,
A whisper rushes through the air:
The Ivanovs are off to work
In their trousers and their shoes.
The tramcars, standing smooth and empty
Offer up to them their benches;
The heroes enter, and they buy
Their fragile pasteboard books of tickets.
They sit and hold them out in front,
They don't enjoy the rapid ride.

In the repetition of their passage to and from work the Ivanovs become infinite, never-ending. Their reproductions seem kaleidoscopic, each a slight distortion from the preceding one. But something sinister lies behind the Ivanovs' normality, as suggested by Zabolotsky's tone. His poem seems a verbal counterpart to Salvador Dali's 1929 painting "Illuminated Pleasures," where identical men bicycle mechanically in all directions, each crowned with an embryonic form and appearing dangerously capable of reproduction. The Ivanovs represent a threat to Zabolotsky, and he uses images of enclosure to stress the inescapability, the monotony, of bourgeois life:

Стоят чиновные деревья,
Почти влезая в каждый дом;
Давно их кончено кочевье –
Они в решетках, под замком.
Шумит бульваров теснота,
Домами плотно заперта.

Here stand bureaucratic trees,
Nearly climbing into every house;
Their wanderings ceased long ago –
They're now in grates and under lock.
The crowded boulevards roar,
Shut densely in by houses.

The world beyond the street is likewise compressed: "mir, zazhatyi ploskimi domami" ("the world, compressed by flat houses"). With the grates, the locks, and the serried streets, the world seems cramped indeed. The sense of confinement is heightened by the masculine rhyme endings of *zamkom* and *zaperta*, which linguistically simulate a lock snapping shut. The poet craves some chaos in this overly controlled and ordered environment, where even the trees seem like social climbers. He wonders whether he will ever find a place for himself in this society:

> Ужели там найти мне место,
> Где ждет меня моя невеста,
> Где стулья выстроились в ряд ...

> Will I really find a place there,
> Where my bride awaits me,
> Where chairs are set out in a row ...

The Ivanovs represent the most common human denominator of Zabolotsky's world, and it is clear that the poet feels an aversion to them and to the philistine values of the NEP society they cherish. Even so, he follows the denizens of this world in their passage from bar to brothel, guiding the reader through their haunts. We pass the flea markets near Leningrad's Circular Canal ("Obvodnyi kanal") and stop to listen to the street musicians who perform in the courtyards ("Brodiachie muzykanty"). One of the most raucous visits is to a wedding ("Svad'ba"), where preparations for the wedding feast and celebration are described:

> ... проклинает детство
> Цыпленок, синий от мытья –
> Он глазки детские закрыл
> Наморщил разноцветный лобик
> И тельце сонное сложил
> В фаянсовый столовый гробик.
> Над ним не поп ревел обедню,
> Махая по́-ветру крестом,
> Ему кукушка не певала
> Коварной песенки своей –
> Он был закован в звон капусты,
> Он был томатами одет,
> Над ним, как крестик, опускался

На тонкой ножке сельдерей.
Так он почил в расцвете дней –
Ничтожный карлик средь людей.

Часы гремят. Настала ночь.
В столовой пир горяч и пылок,
Бокалу винному невмочь
Расправить огненный затылок.
Мясистых баб большая стая
Сидит вокруг, пером блистая,
И лысый венчик горностая
Венчает груди, ожирев
В поту столетних королей.
Они едят густые сласти,
Хрипят в неутоленной страсти,
И, распуская животы,
В тарелки жмутся и цветы.
Прямые лысые мужья
Сидят как выстрел из ружья,
Но крепость их воротников
До крови вырезала шеи,
А на столе – гремит вино,
И мяса жирные траншеи
И в перспективе гордых харь
Багровых, чопорных и скучных –
Как сон земли благополучной,
Парит на крылышках мораль.

     ... A chicken, blue from washing,
Cursed its childhood,
Closed its infant eyes,
Knit its motley brow,
And lay down its small, sleepy body
In an earthenware table grave.
No priest howled mass over it,
Waving a cross in the wind,
No cuckoo sang to it
A crafty little song –
The chicken was fettered in chimes of cabbage
And clad in tomatoes;
Over it, like a cross,
Celery lowered a slender leg.
Thus it passed away in its prime –
A mere dwarf among men.

The clock rings out. Night has come.
The feast in the hall is hot and fervent,
It's too much for a goblet of wine
To smooth out a fiery head.
A pack of meaty women
Sits around with feathers shining,
A worn halo of ermine
Wreathes their breasts, grown fat
In the sweat of centennial queens.
They eat dense sweets,
Wheeze with insatiable passion,
And spread their bellies
So that even the flowers on the plates shrink away.
Erect, bald husbands
Sit like a gunshot,
The stiffness of their collars
Has engorged their necks with blood.
On the table wine resounds,
And greasy slabs of meat,
And in a vista of proud faces
Purple, prim and dull,
Like the dream of a prosperous earth
Hover morals on small wings.

Zabolotsky's wedding scene rivals Mayakovsky's in *The Bedbug*, and like Mayakovsky, Zabolotsky is not entirely tongue-in-cheek when he mocks NEP values. The repugnance he felt toward the rude life portrayed in *Scrolls* is borne out by the story of how "The Wedding" came to be written.[6] In 1928 Zabolotsky attended the wedding of his friend K. Bogolyubov, a graduate student under Desnitsky. As soon as Zabolotsky returned home from the celebration, he sat down and wrote the poem. The next day he went to see Bogolyubov and handed him the poem in an envelope without even stepping over the threshold. Bogolyubov found Zabolotsky's wedding description "so grotesque and generally so unlike reality" that he did not take offense. No doubt missing its irony, he even praised the poem and read it to the guests still assembled at his house. But Zabolotsky was troubled enough by the vulgarity of the wedding that he broke off his friendship with Bogolyubov.

While the unity of art and life was very much a part of the modernist credo, in his strictness Zabolotsky risked confusing

the two. The seriousness with which he approached all aspects
of his life suggests that he did not hold his being entirely
distinct from his art. As an idealist, he was disappointed to find
that in contemporary society a moral laziness had replaced the
lofty aspirations of the Revolution, and such poems as "Tsirk"
("Circus") and "Narodnyi dom" ("The People's House")
reflect his perception of the era as fun-seeking, carnivalistic. In
fact, Zabolotsky's circuit of the city in *Scrolls* ends at "The
People's House" with its amusement-park attractions. This
final poem of the collection would seem to express the poet's
ultimate view of a country skewed by bourgeois values: "Ves'
mir oboiami okleen" ("The whole world is covered in wall-
paper").

The episodes Zabolotsky depicts in *Scrolls* are the small
worlds comprising the larger world of NEP Leningrad, fragments of life that metonymically represent the city itself. If, as
has been said of Filonov's painting, "each piece of the picture is
an hour of life passing,"[7] then each poem in *Scrolls* mirrors a
larger chunk of life – distorted though the glass may be. This
element of distortion in Zabolotsky's early poetry has caused
some critics to term his verse "surrealistic."[8] However, if we
apply Wallace Stevens' gnomic critique of surrealism ("the
fault of surrealism is that it invents without discovering"), we
find that Zabolotsky's poetry is not at all surrealistic; indeed,
one of its essential characteristics is discovery – seeing the
object anew with the naked eye (*golymi glazami*). To this end
Zabolotsky uses displacement, odd metaphors, and irregular
syntax to liberate the object from the fetters of habitual
perception. Once freed, the object can then be rediscovered.
Significantly, Zabolotsky's focus on the object always reveals
the essential truth behind it, never an invented (or surrealistic)
fantasy; thus his craft might better be termed "hyperrealistic."
"At the Market" presents the marketplace in an unexpected
way, causing the reader to enter into an uncomfortable,
heightened reality:

> . . .
> Здесь бабы толсты словно кадки,
> Их шаль – невиданной красы,
> И огурцы, как великаны,

Прилежно плавают в воде.
Сверкают саблями селедки,
Их глазки маленькие кротки,
Но вот – разрезаны ножом –
Они свиваются ужом;
И мясо властью топора
Лежит как красная дыра;
И колбаса кишкой кровавой
В жаровне плавает корявой . . .

. . .

Here women are as fat as tubs,
Their shawls are of rare beauty,
And pickles, like giants,
Swim diligently through the brine.
Herrings flash like sabers,
Their tiny eyes are meek
But suddenly – cut with a knife –
They coil up like snakes.
And by the power of the axe, meat
Lies like a red hole;
And sausage with its bloody guts
Floats in the crude brazier . . .

Countering the common cliché of the marketplace as a
wonderland of luscious vegetables and fruits, Zabolotsky's
marketplace presents its real essence to the reader, its blood
and guts, so to speak. Yet the element of wonderland is not
entirely lost in the poem, since it is reflected – perversely – in
such words as "rare beauty, "giant," and "sabers," all part of
the lexicon of fairy and heroic tales. By their very nature these
words carry the reader into another realm, if only through
subconscious association. Yet the words are paired not with
the expected "maidens" (*devy*) or "vessels" (*sosudy*), but with
the coarse and prosaic "peasant women" (*baby*) and "tubs"
(*kadki*).

"At the Market" further provides a good example of what
the OBERIU meant by *predmetnost'*. The women in the first line
are concretized through their comparison to tubs. This comparison is likely enough, as both peasant women and tubs are
sturdy and fat. But through their association, the distinctions

between the two fade, and the women are objectified into the things they resemble: like the tubs, they become so many more goods at the marketplace open to public scrutiny. Like melons, Zabolotsky's women can be "felt with the fingers" (*oshchupyvat' pal'tsami*). Zabolotsky's purpose is not merely to objectify, however; he seeks also to explore the interrelationships among the objects of the universe. Thus, in the first three comparisons alone, animate women are likened to inanimate tubs; pickles are likened to giants; herrings to sabers. The associations are unexpected. Zabolotsky confuses categories and the distinctions between them, and this clash of genera gives the poem power. If, as Mandelstam wrote of the 1920s in Petrograd, the word had become flesh,[9] then Zabolotsky took it one step further, transmuting the flesh into a tangible object.

VOICE IN THE CHORUS

Just as each poem in *Scrolls* depicts one aspect of the greater world of Leningrad, so *Scrolls* itself portrays only a fragment of the universe, which Zabolotsky conceived of as multifold. Zabolotsky envisioned the time when the world's many microcosms, while remaining distinct, would nevertheless be united into a single, concordant whole, when flora and fauna would rate equally with human life. The cosmos he dramatizes is highly complex, and he mediates his conception of it, as well as his perceptions, through his poetic voice.

The question of voice in Zabolotsky's poetry is complicated, however, by the coexistence of many different ones; indeed, one of the hallmarks of Zabolotsky's cosmography is its plethora of distinguishable voices. Zabolotsky creates a chorus, but one that allows for a solo even as background voices continue to sing. Much of Zabolotsky's verse may be perceived as polyphony from precursor texts – the background voices – but Zabolotsky never fails to orchestrate them. He filters these voices through his own playful consciousness, allowing them to reverberate while still maintaining control, so that in the end his own voice predominates even as others are heard.

The effect is a spiralling one: at the very center lies Zabolotsky's core vision which, as the spiral widens, is expressed by
other voices that soar with his initial idea, expanding it.
Zabolotsky encompasses the spiral and conforms the voices to
his own. In this way the voices merge into Zabolotsky's, but
paradoxically, they do not lose their individuality. In a process
analogous to Filonov's concept of analytical art, separate parts
merge into a unified whole without relinquishing their identi-
ties. Reading Zabolotsky is, at times, almost like reading
several poets simultaneously: from a single poem we can take
pleasure in them all.[10]

Zabolotsky's 1927 "Ofort" ("An Etching") from *Scrolls*
serves as a good example of a poem that echoes the voices of
others. It describes a corpse that comes to life and appears in
the city, a theme immediately evoking Nikolai Gogol and the
whole Petersburg tradition of Russian literature:

И грянул на весь оглушительный зал:
– Покойник из царского дома бежал!

Покойник по улицам гордо идет,
Его постояльцы ведут под уздцы;
Он голосом трубным молитву поет
И руки ломает наверх.
Он – в медных очках, перепончатых рамах,
Переполнен до горла подземной водой,
Над ним деревянные птицы со стуком
Смыкают на створках крыла.
А кругом – громобой, цилиндров бряцанье
И курчавое небо, а тут –
Городская коробка с расстегнутой дверью
И за стеклышком – розмарин.

And there burst out across the whole deafening hall:
"The deceased has run from the royal home!"

The deceased goes proudly through the streets,
The lodgers lead him by the bridle,
In a trumpet voice he sings a prayer
And wrings his hands above his head.
He wears copper glasses, membranous frames,
He's filled to bursting with underground water,
Above him wooden birds, with a thud,

Fold their wings on the shutters.
All around's a thundering din, a clanging of cylinders
And a curly sky, but here –
A city box with its door yawning wide
And behind the glass – rosemary.

This enigmatic poem becomes clearer once we recognize that Zabolotsky's motivation for "An Etching" is Aleksei Tolstoy's poem "Vasilii Shibanov,"[11] which opens with the line, "Kniaz' Kurbskii ot tsarskogo gneva bezhal" ("Prince Kurbsky ran from the royal [i.e., the tsar's] anger"). Certainly Zabolotsky has written his poem in amphibrachs to associate it with Tolstoy's work, since he otherwise rarely used this meter. Yet even as Zabolotsky acknowledges his debt to Tolstoy's poem, he mocks its heroic posture by making his own poetic hero not a nobleman, but a corpse. Here we find Zabolotsky's grotesque irony at its sharpest – neither the corpse's bloated condition nor his membranous eyesockets are spared us. Zabolotsky's semantics also serve to further his parodic intentions. In line 4, for instance, we find a familiar Zabolotskian displacement. Traditionally mourners lead horses that carry the coffin. But through Zabolotsky's semantic shifts the deceased himself comes to be led by the bridle. Such use of *sdvig* often signals a subtext, and here Zabolotsky nods to two highly different sources:[12] Valery Bryusov's poem "Kon' bled" ("Pale Horse"), with its lofty, apocalyptic imagery; and the absurd locution of "peshii po-konnomu" ("equinely pedestrian") from Kozma Prutkov. From this initial displacement, Zabolotsky proceeds to transfer not only the bridle to the corpse, but all of the funeral activities, from the priest intoning to the mourners wailing. He calls attention to the absurdity of a dead man as hero by suddenly breaking from a tetrameter into a trimeter as the corpse wrings his own hands in lament.

True to his title, Zabolotsky etches his images deeply, and the poem leaves a palpable sense of its depth and dimensions. Moving from the huge hall out into the streets and under an open sky, we gain an actual sense of space, and a feeling of freedom follows. But this impression quickly fades as the corpse is confined to his coffin, where we, too, sense confinement – the ultimate confinement of the grave. Zabolotsky goes on to enhance this spatial dimension with a visual one, making the traditional carved wooden birds on house shutters so concrete as to bring them alive. Using spare, taut lines, Zabolotsky nevertheless creates a lush sensory environment. We even hear this strange world where corpses are heroes – its "deafening hall," the "thud" of its birds, the "trumpet voice," the overall din.

An even more extensive layering of voices can be found in Zabolotsky's long poems. At the heart of "The Mad Wolf," for instance, lies Zabolotsky's own vision of society transformed, yet he turns to external sources to express his idea. From Russian poetry, Pushkin's voice is most clearly heard, but Gavriil Derzhavin and Mikhail Lomonosov also echo in Zabolotsky's lines. From the prose tradition, Gogol speaks. Then Zabolotsky broadens his conception and makes it more universal by drawing from Goethe and *Faust*. He enriches his text further from folkloric and scientific sources (Mari legends and the writings of Konstantin Tsiolkovsky), so that the complete poem represents an amalgam not only of different voices but also of different genres and traditions. Yet "The Mad Wolf" is immediately recognizable as a Zabolotsky poem. Zabolotsky internalizes and ultimately transforms what was once external to his poetic consciousness; the borrowings serve as the mechanism for initiating a process of syncretization that yields Zabolotsky's own distinctive voice.

In this way Zabolotsky is able to extend his poetic personality, for the *alloglossai* of his verse are like masks[13] behind which he always stands. Vladimir Nabokov has written that "a fondness for the mask is an essential trait of the true poet,"[14] and Zabolotsky revels in masquerade. His many masks allow him the freedom to make daring associations and play with odd ideas, since he can don or remove them at will. Yet unlike lesser poets, Zabolotsky does not attempt to cover his tracks as he uses the voices of others: they always remain recognizable. Nor does he become captive to them, unlike, say, his contemporary Mikhail Zoshchenko, who "is always seemingly confined in a shell of others' . . . words."[15] Instead, Zabolotsky turns the words of others to his own purpose.

The diversity of voices in Zabolotsky's verse is an aspect of what may be termed his syncretistic approach to his material: he unites various systems of thought under the umbrella of his own superseding consciousness. This consciousness is marked by a lively skepticism that causes Zabolotsky to treat voices and ideas in a playful, ironic manner, particularly in his early and middle periods. He takes the big ideas and dallies with them. On first reading Zabolotsky may seem deadly serious about his subject – and to a certain extent he is. But he cannot repress a puckish impulse to twist meanings and subvert ideas.[16] For instance, in "Iskushenie" ("Temptation," 1929), Zabolotsky makes use of the time-honored lyric *topos* of a dead maiden as he describes her untimely demise. Yet even as the poem explores the very serious implications of death and transformation, Zabolotsky turns his poor maiden into cabbage soup (*"byla deva, stala shchi"*). He may make discriminating use of important ideas, but he just as readily parodies them with a childlike glee. Writing about the real problems of old age and sexual desire, Zabolotsky underscores their absurdities through his syntax and semantics, as in "Mechty o zhenit'be" ("Dreams of Marriage," 1928). The profundity of the ideas within his poems is never undercut, however. In this way Zabolotsky is both sophisticated and ingenuous in his approach to his subject.[17]

Zabolotsky's playfulness involves not only the ideas in his poetry, but his language as well, and this interplay of earnestness and mockery is distinctively Zabolotskian. Take, for instance, the poem "Obed" ("Dinner," 1929):

Мы разогнем усталые тела.
Прекрасный вечер тает за окошком.
Приготовленье пищи так приятно –
Кровавое искусство жить!

Картофелины мечутся в кастрюльке,
Головками младенческими шевеля,
Багровым слизняком повисло мясо,
Тяжелое и липкое, едва
Его глотает бледная вода –
Полощет медленно и тихо розовеет,
А мясо расправляется в длину

И – обнаженное – идет ко дну.
Вот луковицы выбегают,
Скрипят прозрачной скорлупой
И вдруг, вывертываясь из нее,
Прекрасной наготой блистают;
Тут шевелится толстая морковь,
Кружками падая на блюдо,
Там прячется лукавый сельдерей
В коронки тонкие кудрей,
И репа твердой выструганной грудью
Качается атланта тяжелей.

Прекрасный вечер тает за окном,
Но овощи блистают, словно днем.
Их соберем спокойными руками,
Омоем бледною водой,
Они согреются в ладонях
И медленно опустятся ко дну.
И вспыхнет примус венчиком звенящим –
Коротконогий карлик домовой.

И это – смерть. Когда б видали мы
Не эти площади, не эти стены,
А недра тепловатые земель,
Согретые весеннею истомой;
Когда б мы видели в сиянии лучей
Блаженное младенчество растений, –
Мы, верно б, опустились на колени
Перед кипящею кастрюлькой овощей.

We will dispel our weary bodies.
A fine evening wanes outside the window.
Preparing food is so pleasant –
The bloody art of living!

Potatoes toss in the kettle,
Moving their infant heads,
Meat hangs awhile like a crimson slug,
Heavy and sticky,
The pale water barely swallows it –
It gurgles slowly and quietly pinkens,
While the meat extends lengthwise
And – naked – dives for the bottom.

Now the onions scamper out,
Their translucent shells squeak

And suddenly, slipping free of them,
They shine, lovely in their nudity;
Here a fat carrot stirs,
Tumbling in circles on a plate,
There crafty celery hides
In fine crowns of curls,
And a turnip with firm, shaven breast
Staggers more heavily than Atlas.

A fine evening wanes outside the window,
But the vegetables shine like the daylight.
We will gather them up with calm hands,
Wash them with pale water,
They will warm themselves in our palms
And slowly sink to the bottom.
And the primus will flare up in a ringing halo,
A shortlegged household dwarf.

And this is death. If we could see
Not these squares or these walls,
But the warm bowels of earths,
Warmed by the languor of spring;
If we could see in the radiance of the rays
The blessed infancy of plants, –
Surely we would fall onto our knees
Before this simmering kettle of vegetables.

"Dinner" opens with the standard attributes of nineteenth-century romantic poetry – a beautiful sunset somehow heightened by the sense of bodily fatigue. But from the very start Zabolotsky overturns this tradition by displacing the object of the verb "dispel." Instead of the logical "We will dispel the weariness of our bodies," the bodies themselves are dispelled. And Zabolotsky toys further with his readers' expectations. Because the first stanza is written from the first person, we anticipate that the poem will continue from the same personal point of view – as it does, even though the middle stanzas express not a human perspective but a vegetable one. Zabolotsky produces this effect by using highly active verbs for the vegetables to contrast the human lassitude of the first line. He describes the vegetables' experience in the stockpot as they "toss, move, extend, dive, scamper, slip out, stir, tumble, hide, stagger, and sink"; and the reader comes to regard them less as generic soup vegetables than as individuals, with whom we identify more readily than we do with the undifferentiated members of our own species. In fact, compared to the indeterminate human "bodies," the vegetables seem more akin to us and more sympathetic: they have "infant heads," "crowns of curls," a "breast." Zabolotsky further piques our interest by presenting the vegetables in frankly sexual terms: we see their helpless "nudity," their "naked" condition. These allusions, coupled with the gradually bloodying water, create a violent picture of soupmaking (no less disturbing for being cartoon), and Zabolotsky's imagery – fanciful and horrifying at the same time – jolts the reader into regarding his daily soup in quite a new fashion, even as the poem itself parodies the idea of a pleasant, languorous meal at sundown.[18] Zabolotsky wrote "Dinner" neither entirely *v shutku* (jokingly) nor *vser'ez* (in earnest), and for those unfamiliar with his art, it is often difficult to determine his intentions. Although Zabolotsky does poke fun at dinner preparations, he also takes the idea of "the bloody art of living" altogether seriously. The final image of the poem is a solemn one. Through a series of subtle perspectival shifts, Zabolotsky moves from a description of human fatigue to a depiction of rapture as he opens himself – and his readers – to a vision of life worth revering.

The ambiguity of tone that results from this sort of equivocating confounded Zabolotsky's critics, who failed to understand the essential irony of his vision, which often turns on the grotesque. Reading Zabolotsky can be like re-experiencing the old Halloween prank where a bowl of skinned grapes is set out, and the blindfolded victims who put their hands into the bowl are told the grapes are eyeballs. Even though the victims know that these "eyeballs" are actually grapes, they can't free themselves of the disturbing image. Zabolotsky creates the same sort of dislocating sensory impressions through his powerful imagery. And this is as true of his late poetry as it is of his early.

Zabolotsky's language can encompass so many different echoes and tones that it appears by turns sprightly and ponderous, dazzling and plodding. As in "An Etching," Zabolotsky can evoke a surreal world even as he remains earthbound. The poet's mischievous urge tussles with his contemplative one, resulting in verse both offbeat and tender. This variability in no way reflects inexperience on the poet's part; rather, his use of language represents a calculated attempt to evince the multiformity of the universe and the density of experience. Zabolotsky's language expresses the range of the universe through its fluidity, its ability to slip from one voice into another, combining with his themes to represent a universe that is not fixed in time or space, but ever-changing.

CRITICAL RECEPTION

The elite reading public of Leningrad avidly discussed Zabolotsky's poetry, which it found new and exciting, and when *Scrolls* appeared, an uproar ensued. The implied order of "columns" Zabolotsky had imposed on his volume did little to quell the riotousness of the poetry inside, and the critical response – whether laudatory or not – was strong. Favorable reviews appeared in the weekly *Literary Gazette*, as well as in the journals *Oktiabr'* (*October*), *Novyi mir* (*New World*) and *Zvezda* (*The Star*), where the critic Nikolai Stepanov likened Zabolotsky's verbal art to the visual: "A compulsiveness, an almost *lubok* [woodblock] vividness of the word is one of the principles of his poetic method."[19] Stepanov's enthusiasm for Zabolotsky's verse and his insight in relating it to folk art were lost on other critics, however, who responded to Zabolotsky's work with vituperation. Four reviewers in leading publications censured Zabolotsky for what they perceived as his depiction of a timeless vulgarity from which there was no escape.[20] Zabolotsky should have been using his considerable talent – which they conceded – to extol the rebuilding of society, the great theme of the turn of the decade in Soviet Russia. Instead, he offered no solutions, only an appalling and offensive reality. At times these negative reviews bordered on the absurd. The same critic who wrote that "... [Zabolotsky] is not a poet, but some sort of sexual psychopath"[21] also faulted the frequent mention of alcohol in Zabolotsky's poetry: in a society where the "working class strides from plenum to plenum," Zabolotsky's heroes go merely "from bottle to bottle."

His sudden notoriety gave Zabolotsky confidence, and for the first time he felt like a public man in his chosen profession. He was so proud of *Scrolls* that he sent a copy to Pasternak (who responded with a polite, if restrained, note of thanks).[22] While troubled by the nature of the attacks against him, Zabolotsky shrugged them off with humor. He would copy out the worst statements to read aloud to friends and did not take the criticism entirely seriously.[23] Along with his new confidence Zabolotsky acquired a certain sense of self-importance, and acquaintances from this time remember him as totally devoted to his craft, leading an "ascetic" and even "valiant" life.[24] Lidiya Ginzburg saw Zabolotsky as a living example of the kind of "made art" he so greatly admired in Filonov.[25]

The negative response to *Scrolls* from certain quarters was indicative of the deteriorating literary situation. At about the same time as Zabolotsky's book appeared, the Association of Proletarian Writers (RAPP) attacked Boris Pilnyak, Yevgeny Zamyatin and Mikhail Zoshchenko for not carrying out the Party line in their work. Attacks against Zabolotsky, too, began to appear sporadically in the press, although he remained fairly oblivious to them. He was absorbed by his major new poem, "The Triumph of Agriculture," two sections of which (the Prologue and Part 7) he published late in 1929.[26] By the time Zabolotsky completed the poem around April, 1930, however, his status in the Soviet literary hierarchy was already so questionable that he was unable to find a publisher for several years. When the poem finally did appear in its entirety in 1933 (*Zvezda*, no. 2–3), it was immediately assailed.

For one thing, "The Triumph of Agriculture" is a long dramatic poem, and the times were notably anti-epic.[27] For another, the critics were simply unable to understand Zabolotsky's complex irony. Almost unanimously they denounced "The Triumph of Agriculture" as a mockery of collectivization, calling it a "lampoon,"[28] an "attempt to ridicule the reality of our collective farms ... and class-hostile slander against socialism."[29] They censured not only Zabolotsky, but *Zvezda* as well. Six months after Zabolotsky's poem appeared, *Pravda* took the journal to task for its choice of contributors:

Remnants of the Petersburg period of literature, fragments of old classes and literary schools continue to live. V. Shklovsky, O. Mandelstam, Vaginov, Zabolotsky. No matter that some have come directly from the past and that others, who are younger, perpetuate the traditions of the past. ... *Pravda* has already written about Zabolotsky. His idiotic [*iurodstvuiushchaia*] poetry has a definite kulak character. The roots of Zabolotsky's poetry lie in the verses of the Klyuevs and Klychkovs – strong "muzhiks" who were recruited into Russian literature by the decadents and the mystics; those "people of the folk," by means of whom the hysterical intelligentsia of Merezhkovskys, Berdyaevs and Filosofovs tried to obscure the approaching revolution.[30]

This officially sanctioned review marked the beginning of a press campaign against Zabolotsky, and over the next years he was repeatedly attacked for the alleged mockery and idiocy of his verse. Some of the attacks were sophisticated, like the review that appeared in *Red Virgin Soil*.[31] Its author, Anatoly Tarasenkov, rightly praised Zabolotsky for his verbal masquerade, for the way he draws on the rich tradition of Russian poetry to create his own, original idiom. But then Tarasenkov craftily turned this feature of Zabolotsky's verse against him, using masquerade as a poisoned metaphor (a favorite literary slogan of the era was "For the Removal of Any and All Masks"):

Yes, Zabolotsky is an enormous, original, genuine poet and innovator. A manifold sense of the world combined with a most original vocabulary, rhythms, and other artistic accessories make for the uniqueness of his verse ...
However ... let us end this lively masquerade. Let's turn up the lights. All the lights. Let's tear off the masks and wash away the rouge and dye ...
And you see: here he stands on the stage – the chief mechanic and director of the farce that's just been performed, a little man who looks like a monk from a Nesterov painting ... The little man stands on the empty stage and smiles. He slowly twiddles his thumbs.
Do we need special arguments to prove the simple and obvious

truth that the hand of this little man pulled the ropes to make the
dolls of this foolish farce jump? He pretended to be a fool, an infantile
storyteller, and in front of us he enacted a crafty and vile lampoon on
collectivization.

He presented the greatest human struggle in the world as a
senseless and foolish pastime. He danced, clowned, stuck out his
tongue, let loose scabrous jokes ...

"The Triumph of Agriculture" is a kulak poem ...

It is natural that the remnants of the last capitalist class would use
foolishness, farcical shamanism and affectation as one of its new
masks. The kulak dons this mask because the cause of his class has
been decisively compromised in the eyes of the many-million masses
of workers, because according to the immutable laws of history, a
dying class turns to foolishness and idiocy for help. This mask is their
last self-defense and their last attempt at a counterattack on independent sectors of the front.

This mask must be torn away.

Largely because of such negative reviews of "The Triumph
of Agriculture" (which often included *Scrolls* in their
indictments), Zabolotsky's second book of poems was suppressed, even though it already existed in galley proofs and had
been scheduled for publication.[32] This volume, entitled simply
Stikhotvoreniia 1926–1932 (Poems 1926–1932), is important for the
poet's organization of his verse into two distinct groups: the
urban-grotesque or *stolbtsy*; and the lyrical-philosophical or
derev'ia. But the book never went to press, and Zabolotsky
subsequently abandoned this formal classification.

Despite increasing pressures, Zabolotsky remained very
much his own poet, and politically naive. He still could count
among his admirers such important literary figures as Boris
Eikhenbaum, Veniamin Kaverin, and Yury Tynyanov. But for
the most part he was reserved in his relationships. He had long
ago broken off all contacts with the OBERIU poets, and while
he was friendly with such writers as Yevgeny Shvarts and
Nikolai Oleinikov, the only person he considered a close friend
was Nikolai Stepanov. Zabolotsky trusted Stepanov implicitly.
He could relax with him, since Stepanov was not given to
posturing,[33] and importantly, Stepanov enjoyed Zabolotsky's
stishki.

As for his private life in the early thirties, Zabolotsky was content. In 1930 he married Yekaterina Vasilyevna Klykova,[34] whom he had met during his fourth year at the Pedagogical Institute when a mutual acquaintance introduced him to her as a poet. Yekaterina Vasilyevna's first impression of this poet was hardly dignified: Zabolotsky was limping around the Institute with a cane, suffering from scurvy brought on by a poor diet. Klykova shared Zabolotsky's provincial background, although her family belonged neither to the intelligentsia nor to the peasantry, her father being a none-too-successful shopkeeper in the town of Lyubim, Yaroslavl province. Shortly after their marriage, Zabolotsky asked Yekaterina Vasilyevna not to work, considering employment unbecoming for the wife of a poet. The Zabolotskys lived comfortably in the writers' house on Griboyedov Canal, just down the street from the editorial offices of *Ezh*. Their first child, Nikita, was born in 1932; their daughter, Natalya, in 1937.

If Zabolotsky's personal life was happy, his public life was becoming more of a struggle. In 1934 the *Literary Gazette* reported that Zabolotsky's choices for poetic survival lay either in "creative internal suicide or a radical switch (*perekliuchenie*)."[35] But Zabolotsky still hoped to remain viable as a public (i.e., Soviet) poet without having to compromise his art. He sought an alternative approach to survival by retreating more and more deeply into his own world, although to support himself and his family he continued to work in children's literature and began a second career as a translator – the traditional exiles of Russian writers.

Lidiya Ginzburg recalls a changed Zabolotsky in the years of his tenure at *Ezh*:

Zabolotsky sits in [the editorial offices of] *Ezh*. He's respectably dressed. He has become completely sleek, rosy and stout (without, however, being pudgy). Unpleasant in manner. We talked for about fifteen minutes. He obviously does not want to talk about literature and does not want to read his poetry. I was struck by the combination of physiologically golden and rosy well-being with [such] internal remoteness and depression. He goes to work, sits home with his wife,

6 Zabolotsky in Leningrad, 1933

doesn't even meet with Kharms and Vvedensky, and seems to be studying chemistry and math.[36]

Ginzburg had not seen Zabolotsky for several years and remembered the vivacious young Oberiut of the twenties. But in fact the remoteness she describes had always been characteristic of Zabolotsky, who was never entirely comfortable in any group. Zabolotsky's remoteness and self-imposed isolation make it difficult to place him among other writers in the early thirties. Unlike, say, Mandelstam, Akhmatova, and Pasternak, who were in frequent communication and whose writings each help to place the others in context, Zabolotsky did not actively share his artistic life with others. Though he took part in social activities, particularly after the Leningrad Writers' Union was formed, he kept largely to himself, except for his friendship with Stepanov. He did, however, have a small but devoted following in Leningrad, organized by the poet Aleksandr Gitovich. This group, including Gleb Chaikin, Anatoly Chivilikhin, Vladimir Livshits, Boris Semyonov, and Vadim Shefner,[37] gathered frequently to discuss Zabolotsky's poetry and learn from it. They knew all of his work by heart. Based on this following, Zabolotsky dreamed of founding his own school, one that would have official status.

Zabolotsky never defined what the precepts of this school would be, and it did not materialize. Between his poetry and domestic pursuits he had little time – or patience – for other distractions. In a way Zabolotsky was quite narrowly focussed; his daily life did not parallel the diversity of experience evinced by his poetry. For the most part, he kept his head down during the thirties, and the apparently circumscribed life he led indicates his determination to pursue poetry. His career was just beginning, and official hounding had not yet reached a serious peak. But as the decade progressed, the artistic climate grew increasingly arid. The pall caused by Mayakovsky's suicide in 1930 still hung in the air. A poem Mandelstam wrote in 1931 bespeaks more than his own situation:

> Помоги, Господь, эту ночь прожить:
> Я за жизнь боюсь – за Твою рабу –

В Петербурге жить – словно спать в гробу.
                    "Помоги, Господь, эту ночь прожить"

Help me, Lord, to live through this night:
I'm afraid for my life – for Your slave –
Living in Petersburg is like sleeping in a grave.
                    "Help me, Lord, to live through this night"

Despite the constraints and fear of repression, Zabolotsky –
however naively – still believed it possible not only to be a poet,
but to gain recognition. In this respect he differed from other
important poets of his time who had already experienced the
limelight; they knew better. Pasternak, for one, was fully aware
of the menacing political situation, and wary. Akhmatova,
having already experienced trouble, was prepared for the
worst. As for Mandelstam, he was "ready for death."[38] Zabolotsky was not. His naiveté reflects not only his credulity, but
also his stubbornness. He wanted to write poetry and get on
with his life. He was determined that nothing should stop him.
    Zabolotsky's independent cast of mind was not in keeping
with the times. In 1932 all independent literary organizations
had been abolished and a new Union of Soviet Writers formed.
Many writers initially were pleased with this measure, which
they took as a sign of democratization: now all literary groups
would have equal standing. But it soon became clear that as an
arm of the Communist Party, the Writers' Union aimed to
promote a new tendentiousness in literature, whereby all
heroes were to be "active builders of a new life,"[39] full of
enthusiasm, courage, and optimism for a "radiant future."
Since by definition the new literature was meant to represent
the ruling proletariat, it was expected to be political.[40] Zabolotsky was accepted into the Writers' Union in 1934, along
with such diverse figures as Zoshchenko, Tynyanov, Aleksei
Tolstoy, and Eikhenbaum.[41] Shortly thereafter, in August, the
First Congress of Soviet Writers was held in Moscow. Zabolotsky was not invited to participate.[42]
    At the Congress the discussion of poetry centered around a
long speech by Nikolai Bukharin, since early 1934 the editor-
in-chief of the Party newspaper *Izvestiya*. Bukharin had praise
for such poets as Pasternak and the Constructivist Ilya

Selvinsky but criticized the popular proletarian poets Demyan Bedny and Aleksandr Bezymensky for their overzealousness in promoting Komsomol-spirited verse. Bedny criticized Pasternak for remaining nothing more than a "lyric nightingale" in politicized times, but Bezymensky came up with the worst epithets. Perhaps in response to Bukharin's targeting of him, Bezymensky lashed out at others, and Zabolotsky – unmasked as a "hidden enemy" – bore the brunt of his invective:

Much more dangerous [than Gumilev's "imperialist romanticism" or Yesenin's "kulak bohemianism"] is the mask of nonsense that our enemy puts on. This kind of work is represented by the poetry of Zabolotsky, a much underrated enemy ... In the guise of "infantilism" and deliberate nonsense Zabolotsky mocks us, and the genre corresponds exactly to the content of his verses and their ideas, while it is the "kingdom of emotions" that is disguised.[43]

Thus Zabolotsky publicly was branded an enemy of socialism, dangerous to the cultural and literary life of the Soviet Union. He was fortunate, however, to have Bukharin as a supporter, and so he benefited from a period of relative grace for several years to come.

INTO THE WHIRLWIND

Under Bukharin, *Izvestiya* was the most popular and highly read of all Soviet newspapers in 1934.[44] The paper promoted the cult of Stalin and was decisively anti-Fascist in its politics.[45] Bukharin was powerful enough to protect numerous writers who had fallen into disfavor, and he helped them by publishing their work in *Izvestiya*. Between 1934 and 1937 Zabolotsky published nine poems there, ironically gaining a wider readership than ever before despite the aspersions against him. Of these poems, two were written for obvious political ends ("Predateli" ["Traitors," 27 January 1937]; and "Voina – voine" ["War to the War," 23 February 1937]). Zabolotsky later felt ashamed of these poems, and neither was ever reprinted. But even in these distasteful verses one can find a typically Zabolotskian reliance on grotesque imagery. Here is how Zabolotsky describes the Germans:

Откуда эта гнусная порода?
Какие матери взрастили их? Какой
Кровавой пищею питала их природа?
Кто дал им право в жизни трудовой
Вершить без страха эти преступленья?
Известны нам в природе извращенья:
По темным норам ядовитый гад
Ползет, хватая пищу, наугад;
Вонючка брызжет ядовитым соком;
Могильный ворон на дубу высоком
Сидит вблизи, почуя мертвеца;
В чужие гнезда два иль три яйца
Кладет кукушка; от очей сокрыты,
Живут в телах животных паразиты.
Но что они в сравнении с людьми?
Их только обогрей да накорми –
Они и сыты. Человечий гад
Гнуснее их и мерзостней стократ.

Whence came this vile race?
What mothers nurtured them? What
Bloody food did nature feed them?
Who gave them the right in a life of labor
To commit these crimes without fear?
Perversions in nature are known to us:
Through dark burrows the poisonous reptile
Crawls, seizing food at random;
The skunk sprays its poisonous juice;
The sepulchral raven sits in a tall oak
Nearby, sniffing a corpse;
The cuckoo puts two or three eggs
Into other birds' nests; hidden from sight,
Parasites live in the bodies of animals.
But what are they compared to people?
Just warm them and feed them –
And they're sated. The human reptile
Is a hundred times more vile and loathsome.

As such rhetoric indicates, Zabolotsky was not necessarily ideologically opposed to Soviet rule, at least not in its early years. But he was opposed aesthetically. As a poet, he struggled to preserve his independence while still accepting the political reality. If he was not given to rebellion, neither did he sell out. He sought instead to find a way out of the menacing situation, one which entailed neither "internal suicide" nor "a radical switch." Standing unsteadily between these two poles, Zabolotsky was frightened enough to agree to a public recantation of his earlier "mistakes." During the height of the 1936 campaign against "formalism" in literature, Zabolotsky made a difficult speech at the Leningrad Writers' Union, which was subsequently published in *Literary Leningrad*:[46]

As I understand it now, the very conception of the poem ["The Triumph of Agriculture"] was mistaken in the sense that it united realistic and utopian elements. The result was that the utopian element destroyed all real proportions in my poem. Because of this, the depiction of the class struggle in particular was blurred to some degree. Underestimating the realistic truth of art led to an idyllic and pastoral poem which went contrary to reality. For this reason my readers, or at least some of my readers, interpreted the poem as ironic, parodic. The formalistic devices still present in the poem encouraged this interpretation.

Zabolotsky's self-criticism was not without self-justification, however. In the speech he originally prepared, he railed against the critics who had failed to support him. Only at Stepanov's insistence – and through his careful editing – did Zabolotsky soften his charge:

And the criticism? Did it help the author? Did it articulately and clearly explain to him how he had sinned before his reader? Two short quotes will suffice to answer this question. [There follow two passages, including the one where Tarasenkov depicts Zabolotsky as a monk on the stage.]

It seems that the critics have not mocked a single Soviet poet as they have mocked me. And no matter what my literary sins, such articles and public speeches do the new criticism no honor. Even more, they disorient the author and alienate him from art. That's their entire significance. What use are they?

Apart from this feisty rejoinder, Zabolotsky's speech was acquiescent, and apparently it worked. Where earlier he had been damned, he now was praised for his perspicacity. His situation was further eased by *Izvestiya*'s publication of "Goriiskaia Simfoniia" ("Gori Symphony") in 1936. This poem, a paean to Stalin, was likely written at Bukharin's urging,[47] just as Bukharin had encouraged Pasternak to publish his dutiful "Ia ponial: vse zhivo" ("I understood: everything is alive") in the 1936 New Year's edition of *Izvestiya*.[48] Its toadyish inspiration aside, "Gori Symphony" stands as a skillful poem in its own right. In typically controlled yet exultant fashion, Zabolotsky treats the theme of man in nature, investing the Georgian landscape with such potency that Stalin's birth seems a pantheistic parallel to the Immaculate Conception. Here is how Zabolotsky describes Stalin's birthplace:

> Как широка, как сладостна долина,
> Теченье рек как чисто и легко,
> Как цепи гор, слагаясь воедино,
> Преображенные, сияют далеко!
> Здесь центр мира. Живой язык природы
> Здесь учит нас основам языка,
> И своды слов стоят, как башен своды,
> И мысль течет, как горная река.

> How wide, how sweet the valley,
> The river currents so pure and light,
> How the mountain ranges, heaped together,
> Shine, transformed, in the distance!
> Here is the center of the earth.
> The living language of nature
> Teaches us the language basics,
> And vaults of words stand like vaults of towers,
> And thought flows like a mountain river.

Zabolotsky never renounced "Gori Symphony," as he had his other politically-inspired poems; in fact he rather liked it, despite its spurious basis.[49] He also was astute enough to recognize that this poem was necessary for survival. In a letter to a friend he candidly acknowledged its value: "If you read my 'Gori Symphony' in *Izvestiya*, you probably understood that this poem will play a significant rôle in my literary fate. Signs of this are already at hand. On November 16 there will be a [literary] evening devoted to me at the Writers' House – the first since 1929. A number of journals are requesting my poems. What happens next – we shall see."[50] As Nadezhda

Mandelstam has commented regarding her husband's own ode to Stalin, "Leading a double life was an absolute fact of our age, and nobody was exempt."[51]
Zabolotsky's "double life" stemmed in part from his desire for official recognition. While he did not seek acceptance at any price, he was ambitious and hoped for public acknowledgement on his own terms – a desperately naive hope. According to Yekaterina Vasilyevna, some of Zabolotsky's writings reflect his social aspirations: "Nikolai Alekseyevich strove to establish himself as an official poet while still pursuing his own course. His articles in *Izvestiya* were written around this time – they're so unpleasant. Later he never mentioned them."[52] The articles she refers to both appeared in *Izvestiya* in 1937: "Iazyk Pushkina i sovetskaia poeziia" ("Pushkin's Language and Soviet Poetry," 25 January); and "Glashatai pravdy" ("The Herald of Truth," 27 July [on Mikhail Lermontov]).

In his article on Pushkin, Zabolotsky criticized Pasternak's language, calling it "alogical, murky"; later he stated that "the ship of Soviet poetry will not take its bearings from Pasternak's poetry. The ship of Soviet poetry has charted a course toward the art of the people, a high-quality art comprehensible and close to the masses. 'Salon' art will remain on the sidelines."[53] Sadly, Zabolotsky's metaphor is not even original; he takes it from the famous caricature of Pasternak in a skiff being overtaken by the cruiser of Soviet poetry. His comments about Pasternak are troubling, as much for what they represent as for their uninspired content. They are the closest Zabolotsky ever came to political accommodation, and as Yekaterina Vasilyevna writes, he was rightly ashamed of them. But it must be pointed out that however distasteful Zabolotsky's judgements, they were not hypocritical. He greatly respected Pasternak but felt an aversion to some of his poetry. As early as 1928 he mentioned his annoyance at Pasternak's "musicality,"[54] and his ambivalence toward Pasternak's verse continued into the thirties.[55] To his credit, Pasternak did not censure Zabolotsky for this public criticism. He later graciously said that "I very much value [Zabolotsky's] response to my poems, [though] he didn't accept everything I wrote up to 'On Early Trains.'"[56]

As for the criticism of Zabolotsky's verse, the vitriolic campaign against him was, for the time being, in abeyance. His poems "Sever" ("The North," 1936) and "Sedov" ("Sedov," 1937)[57] were acclaimed as hallmarks of the "new" Zabolotsky, a poet who had laid city themes to rest along with the "formalistic excesses" of *Scrolls* and was now contemplating man's purpose in nature. *The Literary Contemporary* published a number of poems written in this "new" lyrical vein, and their positive reception enabled Zabolotsky, after a long eight years, to publish a second volume of verse, *Vtoraia kniga* (*The Second Book*, 1937). *The Second Book* contained seventeen poems of a natural-philosophical bent, written between 1929 and 1937. Some of these poems, such as "Metamorfozy" ("Metamorphoses"), "Vchera, o smerti razmyshliaia" ("Yesterday, Pondering Death"), and "Vse, chto bylo v dushe" ("All that was in my Soul"), number among Zabolotsky's best; and considering the poet's precarious position in the years they were written, their exaltation of life is particularly poignant. *The Second Book* received far less critical attention than *Scrolls*, however. Even those critics who favored Zabolotsky were timid in their praise, fearing to give too much approbation to a poet whose status was so uncertain.

For the moment, Zabolotsky seemed to have eluded the fate of so many other writers. As a mark of his acceptance, "Gori Symphony" was being set to music for the twentieth anniversary of the October Revolution.[58] But Zabolotsky should have been more cognizant of the political reality. When his fortunes shifted again suddenly, he was caught unawares. His powerful supporter, Bukharin, was arrested in February, 1937, and executed on March 13, 1938. Six days later, in the housecleaning that followed Bukharin's demise, the NKVD came for Zabolotsky.

THE ARREST[59]

Zabolotsky was working at a writers' retreat in Yelizavetino, outside of Leningrad, when he was summoned back to the city to report to the Party Committee of the Writers' Union – an

unusual summons, since he was not a Party member and had
no dealings with the committee. When he arrived, promptly at
eleven a.m. on March 19, 1938, he was unceremoniously
handed a search warrant. Two plainclothes policemen,
Lupandin and Merkuryev (whose "sad eyes" the poet's widow
still recalls), accompanied Zabolotsky to his apartment, where
they remained until evening. Although in those years the
threat of detention was never remote, Zabolotsky was caught
off guard by this daytime arrest, since the NKVD usually
carried out its malefactions at night. Following a thorough
search in which his books and manuscripts were confiscated,
Zabolotsky was taken to Leningrad's Remand Prison where he
faced immediate interrogation. In his own account of his first
days in prison, Zabolotsky describes the ways in which he was
tortured[60] and the delirium that ensued:

I remember that once I was sitting before a whole conclave of
investigators. I was no longer the least afraid of them and held them
in contempt. Before my eyes the pages of some huge imaginary book
were being turned, and I saw different illustrations on every page.
Paying no attention to anything else, I was expounding the contents
of these illustrations to my investigators. It is hard now to define the
condition I was in, but I recollect experiencing a sense of inner relief
and exaltation that these people had not succeeded in making a
dishonourable man of me.

   Zabolotsky's bizarre response to interrogation seems to have
worked his examiners into a frenzy: they used not only brute
force on him, but also high-pressure hoses and iron restraints.
These beatings and psychological torments caused Zabolotsky
to lose his mind for a period of time, a condition he understates
as "grave." He was placed in the prison's psychiatric ward for
ten days, where "a glimmer of consciousness still flickered
within me or returned from time to time. Thus I well remember how appalled the nurse was as she took my clothes away:
her hands and lips were trembling." (Zabolotsky's wife saw
him shortly after his transfer from this ward; and six years
later, travelling to Kazakhstan to join him in exile, she
remembered with horror how he had looked then and prayed
that she would not again see the same face.) The authorities

returned Zabolotsky to a common cell jammed with seventy or eighty prisoners in a space intended for only twelve to fifteen. Then, in August, 1938, he was transferred to Leningrad's notorious Kresty prison:

I remember the boiling hot day when, dressed in a thick woolen coat and carrying a roll of underclothing, I was brought to a small cell in Kresty intended for two people. Ten bare human figures, running with sweat and exhausted from the heat, squatted like Indian gods all round the edge of the cell. I greeted them, stripped off and sat down as the eleventh in their midst. Soon there appeared beneath me a great damp patch on the stone floor. So began my life at Kresty.

On September 2, Zabolotsky was accused of participating in a subversive writers' organization allegedly headed by Nikolai Tikhonov and was sentenced without trial to five years in a labor camp for "Trotskyite counter-revolutionary activity." He was allowed to meet only once with his wife. Like the wives of so many other prisoners, Yekaterina Vasilyevna had spent the long months of Zabolotsky's preliminary detention relentlessly trying to gain access to the Prosecutor's office to demand a review of her husband's case. Not only was she not granted an audience with the Prosecutor, but she could inquire about her husband only after he had been transferred to Kresty, and then only three times a month, on the 5th, 15th and 25th, the days designated for the letter "Z."

On October 25 Yekaterina Vasilyevna learned that she could see her husband on November 5 and give him a parcel before his deportation from Leningrad. Two days after their meeting, she herself, with their two small children, was deported from Leningrad to the distant Vyatka region where Zabolotsky had grown up. The next day, November 8, Zabolotsky was shipped to the Sverdlovsk transit prison, where he languished for nearly a month. On December 5 (ironically, Soviet Constitution Day) his gruelling journey to Siberia began; it dragged on for over two months. Often the prisoners were not even given water to drink, and in the barely heated freight cars, with inadequate rations, many of them died. Zabolotsky recalls the New Year's feast that ushered in 1939: the starving and thirsty denizens of his freight car licked the "black sooty icicles that had formed on the walls of the wagon from [their] own exhalations."

Although Zabolotsky wrote these memoirs in 1956, his highly pictorial descriptions betray him as still very much the author of *Scrolls*, a poet ever cognizant of the grotesque:

From time to time the authorities appeared in the wagon to carry out a check. So as to verify the numbers they made us all go on to one ledge of planks. At a special command we had to crawl across a board to the other ledge, and they counted us as we did so. The picture is as vivid before me as if it were happening now: black with soot, beards sprouting, we crawl one after the other on all fours like monkeys across the board, lit by the dim glow of lanterns, while a semi-literate guard holds us at rifle point and counts and counts away, getting muddled in his tricky calculations.

Zabolotsky was lucky to survive the transport. According to one account, while detained at a remote railroad siding he was virtually saved by a group of arrested prostitutes, who somehow singled him out from the crowds of men and fed, warmed him, and even laundered his meager belongings.[61] Perhaps he still retained the look of country innocence he had tried in vain to shed during his early Leningrad years.

In February the transport finally reached Komsomolsk-on-Amur, a brand-new city built to promote development in the Soviet Far East. Zabolotsky's group had been designated for the far northern reaches of Kolyma, but a last-minute order shifted them to Komsomolsk, a change that probably saved Zabolotsky's life.[62] His first three weeks in the Far East were spent in a transit camp, where all of his possessions were stolen. He slept on poles in place of planks. And as if to compound his despair, by some remote chance a copy of *Pravda* found its way into the camp. In the February 2, 1939, issue Zabolotsky read that Tikhonov, the alleged head of the alleged counter-revolutionary writers' organization, had been honored with a high governmental award.[63]

Early in March, Zabolotsky was ordered to begin hard labor deep in the taiga near a settlement called "Start," where a huge sign proclaiming "Death to the Enemies of the People" greeted him at the entrance to his new compound. The poet's first job was to fell trees. Each tree had to be cut down to a stump no more than ten centimeters high. Then the branches had to be removed and the trunk sawed into lengths. The norm was seven cubic meters a day. It was hard enough to avoid the crashing trees, let alone saw the wood. If the prisoners did not fulfill the norm, they received only three hundred grams of bread per day, plus a dipper of gruel.

Zabolotsky's next task was to dig holes, which entailed standing for hours in cold water that seeped up from underground. Somehow, he didn't fall ill: he was too keyed up to allow it. Then, early in April, a project bureau was organized for the construction of oil pipelines from Sakhalin Island to Komsomolsk-on-Amur. Counting on his early art training in the Urzhum high school, Zabolotsky recklessly claimed he was a draftsman. Because his hands were too wounded and swollen for him to set to work immediately, he was able to learn draftsmanship while they healed. Zabolotsky's transfer to the relative luxury of an indoor workplace ensured his survival, at least temporarily.

Zabolotsky's son has suggested that "after interrogation, prison, the psychiatric ward and the transport through Siberia, camp life didn't seem so unbearable" to the poet. Despite the harshness of its climate, the spectacular Far Eastern landscape provided an immediate source of wonder and beauty for Zabolotsky. Additionally, he was so convinced (if naively) of the injustice of his sentence that he tenaciously fought for a successful review of his case. While his efforts did not result in a reversal of his verdict, they probably did expedite his release once his initial term expired.

Zabolotsky sent his first appeal to the People's Commissariat on February 18, 1939. Several months later, in July, 1939, he managed to enclose in a letter to his wife an appeal to the Public Prosecutor of the Soviet Union, which he asked her to forward to the Moscow Writers' Union. He requested that

the best men of letters give their evaluation of my literary work and its artistic and political significance, and that the administration of the Writers' Union intercede on my behalf, on the basis of my literary work. Regarding my attitude toward "The Triumph of

Agriculture," it is easy to find the speech I gave at the discussion on Formalism at the House of the Press, which was published in *Literary Leningrad* under the title "A New Path."[64]

This note from her husband was the first indication Yekaterina Vasilyevna had as to the reason for Zabolotsky's arrest. Amazed that his appeal had arrived intact, she did not want to risk mailing it to Moscow, so with great difficulty she obtained permission to travel to Leningrad for medical help for her children. Once in Leningrad, she began making the rounds of writers' offices, acquainting them with Zabolotsky's appeal and seeking their support. Because Zabolotsky's document is of such historic interest, it bears reproduction in full, in English here for the first time:[65]

To the Public Prosecutor of the Union of Soviet Socialist Republics
From Prisoner Zabolotsky, Nikolai Alekseyevich
(Komsomolsk-on-Amur, NKVD Eastern Camp 27th column)

Application

I, the poet N. Zabolotsky, former member of the Union of Soviet Writers, author of two books of poetry and translator of Rustaveli's poem "The Knight in the Panther's Skin," was arrested in Leningrad in March, 1938, and by order to the Special Commission [OS] incarcerated on 2 September 1938, prisoner no. 48838, in the Corrective Labor Camp of the NKVD for a term of 5 years "for counter-revolutionary Trotskyite activity."

At the investigation I was accused of allegedly being a member of a counter-revolutionary writers' organization in Leningrad which, grouped around the well-known poet N.S. Tikhonov, published its counter-revolutionary literary works in the Leningrad press. Cited as one of these works was my long poem, "The Triumph of Agriculture," written in 1929–30 and published in 1933 in the Leningrad journal *The Star*, no. 2/3.

The investigator read me excerpts from the testimonies of the writers B.K. Livshits and E.M. Tager, who were arrested before me. I quote them from memory:

Livshits, B.K.: "In Leningrad there existed a counter-revolutionary writers' organization. It included: N.S. Tikhonov, Kornilov, Zabolotsky, Livshits and others. The organization waged a struggle against Soviet power in two ways:

1. It published its counter-revolutionary works in the Leningrad press (for example, Zabolotsky's 'Triumph of Agriculture').

2. It artificially exaggerated the authority of the members of the counter-revolutionary organization."

Tager, E.M.: "Around N.S. Tikhonov in the Leningrad Division of the Soviet Writers' Union were grouped the right-wing writers Kornilov, Zabolotsky, Kuklin, Tager and others. Tikhonov published Zabolotsky's counter-revolutionary poem 'The Triumph of Agriculture' in *The Star*. When Zabolotsky was unmasked by the critics, Tikhonov hastily organized a presentation by Zabolotsky at a discussion on formalism."

I was acquainted with the writers Livshits and Tager, albeit superficially, through the Union of Soviet Writers; nevertheless, I considered them honest and decent people. I do not know what extraordinary circumstances forced these writers to give slanderous testimony about me. Only Livshits and Tager themselves can say. But I certify, as I did at my investigation, that their testimonies are pure lies and slander, and I take full responsibility for my words. I was not allowed a personal confrontation with citizens Livshits and Tager. Likewise I could not confront N.S. Tikhonov who, according to the witnesses' words, was at the center of the counter-revolutionary organization.

I never belonged to any counter-revolutionary organization and never heard anything about its existence. With N.S. Tikhonov I was associated by our common work in the Union of Soviet Writers; I had a professional literary acquaintance with him, knew him as a Soviet man and a talented poet. I was never close to Kornilov and Kuklin, since I considered them socially unpleasant people.

As for my poem "The Triumph of Agriculture," it was written in an early period of my literary work – by the hand of a still unformed, inexperienced poet. It is a formalistic, utopian poem, which because of its defective style was in its time [deemed] a hostile, anti-Soviet work. When my mistake became clear to me, on my own initiative I spoke at a discussion on formalism at the Mayakovsky Writers' House in Leningrad. I revealed the cause of my literary mistake which, in the final analysis, became a politically significant mistake. My speech was immediately published in the newspaper *Literary Leningrad*.

At the investigation, my acquaintance with the arrested writers N.M. Oleinikov (Leningrad) and T.I. Tabidze (Tbilisi) was mentioned. With the former I was associated by virtue of our common work at the Leningrad Division of the State Children's Publishing House; with the latter – as a translator of the Georgian classics. In these literary acquaintances there was nothing counter-revolutionary, to which mutual acquaintances who know both me and the above-mentioned writers can attest.

I was sentenced in absentia by the Special Commission, with no opportunity to defend myself and refute the slanderous testimonies of Livshits and Tager.

In February, 1939 I accidentally learned from the newspaper (*Pravda* of 2/2 1939) that not only was the poet N.S. Tikhonov not arrested by the NKVD, but he was given an award for his social and literary activity. The frivolousness of accusing me of belonging to a counter-revolutionary organization became clear to me. Especially since I cannot admit the thought that I was convicted on account of my literary acquaintances.

For what reason have I, a Soviet writer, been convicted; for what reason is my art, which constitutes the meaning of my life, discredited; for what reason must my completely innocent family suffer?

I am 36 years old, I have only just entered a period of maturity as a writer. After my unsuccessful poem I produced a series of works well received by the Soviet public. My poems "Gori Symphony," "The North," "Sedov," "Farewell," "The Book of the Depths," and others printed in *Izvestiya* received widespread publicity as did *The Second Book* (published separately by Goslitizdat in 1938). Romain Rolland was interested in my poems. For my translation of "The Knight in the Panther's Skin" I was awarded a certificate by the Central Executive Committee of Georgia. My arrest prevented me from completing my verse translation of "The Lay of Igor's Campaign." I had planned another large work to occupy several years, namely the first complete translation of Firdausi's "Shah-Nama." So far only fragments of this marvellous Iranian poem have been translated into Russian. The need for a complete and precise translation has been recognized by our scientific and literary community.

Citizen Prosecutor! I have already been imprisoned for one-and-one-half years. My family (a wife and two small children) has been deported from Leningrad to the Kirov [Vyatka] region. From the time of my arrest I have not had the opportunity to read a book, write a poem. With each day I am losing my qualifications as a writer.

I request your personal intervention in my case. I ask that you convene a competent, expert commission including specialists – writers and critics – who would evaluate my literary work, its artistic and political significance.

I request that you again interrogate citizens Livshits and Tager in the presence of employees from the Prosecutor's Office and clarify the reason for their slanderous testimonies.

I request that you review my entire case again, remove from me the unmerited stamp of an enemy of the people, and return me to my art and to my family. Do not allow a poet to perish, one who is ready to devote all of his strengths and abilities to the good of Soviet culture.

N. Zabolotsky

23 July 1939

Zabolotsky's wife succeeded in garnering support for the poet's appeal from a number of prominent Leningrad and Moscow writers, including the critics Viktor Shklovsky and Yury Tynyanov, the prosaists Veniamin Kaverin, Valentin Katayev, and Mikhail Zoshchenko, and the poets Nikolai Aseyev, Kornei Chukovsky, and even Tikhonov. The politically powerful writer Aleksandr Fadeyev agreed to intercede personally with Prosecutor Pankratyev on Zabolotsky's behalf. Early in 1940, the Leningrad Prosecutor's Office sent Zabolotsky's file on to Moscow with a positive recommendation, bolstered by an affidavit from a special commission of the Leningrad Writers' Union affirming Zabolotsky as a "genuine Soviet writer." Zabolotsky's case looked so good that on March 6 a memo from the Prosecutor's Office signed by a Comrade Osipenko stated: "Today I heard some very pleasant news, but it has yet to be confirmed ..." Zabolotsky's file was turned over to the NKVD for "confirmation of a reversal of [his] sentence," and a favorable outcome was anticipated.

But unexpectedly, on July 15, 1940, Yekaterina Vasilyevna received a final, negative response: "In answer to your application, the Office of the Public Prosecutor informs you that the case of Zabolotsky, N.A., has been verified again. It has been determined that he was sentenced correctly and that there are no grounds for a review of his case." As a result of the appeal process, Yekaterina Vasilyevna learned that no small rôle in Zabolotsky's arrest and imprisonment had been played by N.V. Lesyuchevsky, a critic with whom Zabolotsky was acquainted and who caused the downfall of more than one writer. It was Lesyuchevsky who signed the file denouncing Zabolotsky, having assiduously compiled damaging statements from early reviews of "The Triumph of Agriculture." Still, Yekaterina Vasilyevna did not give up. In November,

1940, she sent a personal letter to Stalin requesting that Zabolotsky's case be reopened. A new investigation eventually did ensue, but when war broke out in June, 1941, all hopes for a change in Zabolotsky's situation were lost.

Meanwhile, Zabolotsky had gone through several upheavals in his labor camp life. For a while he continued to work as a draftsman in the project bureau. Only briefly did his luck change for the worse when he was sent out to hard labor in the quarries for spurning the advances of a free employee in his office. But the great demand for draftsmen returned Zabolotsky to his job after only one week, and by the summer of 1939 the conditions of his life had eased so much that he actually contemplated writing again. Late in the summer Zabolotsky was transferred to a separate barracks for the office workers, where he had his own plank bed and where he could listen to music on a homemade receiver – his first real contact with the outside world in over a year. Zabolotsky and his fellow workers often amused themselves before bed by playing word-association games to keep their minds limber. It is from this period that his poem "Solovei" ("The Nightingale") dates:[66]

Уже умолкала лесная капелла.
Едва открывал свое горлышко чижик.
В коронке листов соловьиное тело
Одно, не смолкая, над миром звенело.

Чем больше я гнал вас, коварные страсти,
Тем меньше я мог насмехаться над вами.
В твоей ли, пичужка ничтожная, власти
Безмолвствовать в этом сияющем храме?

Косые лучи, ударяя в поверхность
Прохладных листов, улетали в пространство.
Чем больше тебя я испытывал, верность,
Тем меньше я верил в твое постоянство.

А ты, соловей, пригвожденный к искусству,
В свою Клеопатру влюбленный Антоний,
Как мог ты довериться, бешеный, чувству,
Как мог ты увлечься любовной погоней?

Зачем, покидая вечерние рощи,
Ты сердце мое разрываешь на части?

Я болен тобою, а было бы проще
Расстаться с тобою, уйти от напасти.

Уж так, видно, мир этот создан, чтоб звери,
Родители первых пустынных симфоний,
Твои восклицанья услышав в пещере,
Мычали и выли: "Антоний! Антоний!"

The forest choir has grown still.
The siskin barely opens its throat.
In a small crown of leaves, the nightingale's body
Alone rings out, ceaselessly, over the world.

The more I chased you, perfidious passions,
The less I was able to mock you.
Insignificant bird, is it in your power
To remain silent in this radiant temple?

Slanting rays, striking the surface
Of cool leaves, have flown off into space.
The more I experienced you, truth,
The less I believed in your constancy.

But you, nightingale, nailed to art,
An Anthony attached to his Cleopatra,
How could you, mad one, trust feeling,
How could you be seduced by the pursuit of love?

Why, abandoning the groves of evening,
Do you claw my heart to shreds?
I am ill with you, and it would be simpler
To part from you, to escape danger.

This world, it seems, was made so that beasts,
Parents of the first desert symphonies,
Hearing your cries in the cave,
Would bellow and howl: "Anthony! Anthony!"

Hearing a nightingale, Zabolotsky identifies the bird's song with the poetic yearning within himself; he experiences a keen sadness that his pursuit of art has cost him so much, but realizes that it could not be otherwise. Like Anthony bound to his Cleopatra, Zabolotsky is bound to his art, and together they share the tragedy of impossible love. Both Anthony and the poet are prisoners of fate, whose downfalls are due not to any character flaw but to their helplessness before their great obsessions. Zabolotsky's poem is a rueful affirmation of himself as a poet, cursed with a nightingale inside.

Zabolotsky's energy for poetry did not last long, however. On January 30, 1940, he wrote to his wife: "Inner loneliness has already become habitual; my sensitivity is obviously numbed." And later: "My poetic instrument is growing coarse from disuse; my perception of things is dimming, but inside I feel – despite the exhaustion, the complete mental fatigue, the utter and endless burden of constant waiting – I feel like a whole person, who could still live and work ..." (3 August 1940). Zabolotsky soon had less time than ever to contemplate his elusive "instrument." In October, 1940, the project bureau was moved into the town of Komsomolsk-on-Amur and the workers relocated to a barracks three kilometers from their office. They were forced to trudge the distance to work and back four times a day, thereby losing three to four precious hours of sleep or free time. They also risked freezing in the −40° temperatures of winter: the wind was often so fierce that the whole column of prisoners had to join hands to keep from being blown over.

Paradoxically, some benefits accrued from Zabolotsky's new position. To his great joy, he was able to read books brought in by the free employees. One day he received a parcel containing five books by nineteenth-century poets, which the guards immediately confiscated, stating that regulations allowed only Soviet poets to be read. But by pointing to the publisher's imprint of "Soviet Writer" in an edition of Boratynsky, Zabolotsky managed to hoodwink his guards and keep this single volume for himself. The books helped assuage Zabolotsky's increasing sense of alienation and isolation from the world. Two years into his imprisonment, he assessed his condition:

I've begun to grow old. My bald spot stands out more and more clearly, wrinkles have appeared, my skin is no longer fresh and elastic. Time and deprivations take their toll ... From one life I've disappeared into another, I look out at you now with the eyes of a different person, one you can't understand well and one who is probably forgotten by many.

If only I could rest properly, catch up on my sleep, and mull over many, many thoughts which have long been awaiting their turn and for which there is no time. My head wants to think – it still hasn't lost that ability – and this circumstance alone brings me joy ...
If I could write now – I would begin to write about nature. The older I grow, the closer nature becomes to me. Now it stands before me as a huge theme, and everything I've written about nature so far seems like merely insignificant and timid attempts to approach it. (Letter of 19 April 1941)

When war broke out on June 22, 1941, the camp administration received orders for all prisoners to be transferred to the remote taiga for general labor. Zabolotsky immediately requested that he be sent to the Front but was drily informed that the troops would manage without him. So in torrential rains he was herded along with the other prisoners onto a barge that made its precarious way across the Amur River. From there the prisoners were transported in stages to Lysaya Gora (Bald Mountain) on the Khungara River. There, conditions were worse than Zabolotsky had previously known. He was sent out to labor with primitive tools in a quarry, breaking rocks and loading them onto carts. The guards relished their power, sometimes forcing their charges to lie prostrate in puddles of cold, dirty water. It was at Bald Mountain that Zabolotsky's health deteriorated. For the next year or so he was shuttled back and forth between Komsomolsk-on-Amur, Bald Mountain, and the settlement Start.

Despite his physical weakness, Zabolotsky rallied enough mental energy to study Armenian with Gurgen Tatosov, a close friend he had made in the Sverdlovsk transit prison. He even compiled a small dictionary of Armenian words, copied onto graph paper in calligraphy with obvious care. Zabolotsky also wrote down an Armenian song and its Russian translation, which echoes his own sentiments from the thirties:

The forest is my birthplace, the tree is my home.
I say to the wolf: "Lie down, wolf," and the wolf lies
Close by my feet. I say to the bird: "Fly, bird,"
And the bird flies up. I read the book of the earth ...

RETURN TO MOSCOW

March, 1943, finally arrived, signalling what should have been the end of Zabolotsky's term, but because of the war all prison sentences were extended. Ironically, Zabolotsky now faced the worst period of his confinement. He was transferred from the Far East to the Altai Region of Siberia, west of Barnaul, where he was compelled to work in a mine extracting soda. The labor was gruelling; fifteen years later he referred to it in a letter to a friend: "What's with your heart? I'm an old 'heart specialist,' too, since I left the health of my heart behind in the soda sludge of a Siberian lake."[67] After working for two and one-half months in the mine, Zabolotsky collapsed and was taken to the camp hospital. When he recovered, he was allowed to work in a drafting office until his release from imprisonment on August 18, 1944. Though delayed, Zabolotsky's release may have been precipitated by a second, passionate appeal he made to the NKVD in February, 1944, again requesting an immediate review of his sentence.[68] Given Zabolotsky's condition at the time, this document is remarkable for the elegance and spirited energy of its language.

Upon his release, Zabolotsky was ordered into exile in the Altai, where he worked as a technical draftsman for the railway line under construction between Kulunda and Malinovoye Ozero. His wife and two children, now seven and twelve, were reunited with him at Mikhailovskoye; and in March, 1945, the entire family moved along with the camp to Karaganda in central Kazakhstan, arriving in the midst of a fierce blizzard.[69] In Karaganda Zabolotsky worked in the project office responsible for developing the local coal basin and building the new city of Saran.

When the war ended on May 9, 1945, even remote Kazakhstan experienced a general easing of tensions, and for the first time in a long seven years Zabolotsky was able to think seriously about his own work and his fate as a poet. He turned anew to his translation of the Russian epic, "The Lay of Igor's Campaign," which had been cut short by his arrest. He had already completed the Introduction and Part One of the poem; now he attempted to recapture the spirit of the poem and resume where he had left off.[70] Given the circumstances of his life, this was no easy task. In a letter to his friend Stepanov, he explained:

Not long ago I sent you a telegram asking you to mail me the text of "The Lay of Igor's Campaign." I very much doubt that I'll manage to do any work on the conclusion of the translation, but at any rate I want to refresh the text in my mind and recall the conception I had of it in the old days ...

I doubt I'll have the strength to finish [the translation] unless the circumstances of my life change for the better. Is it really possible to carry out such a large task in snatches and at night after an exhausting day's labor? Isn't it a sin to expend only the last bits of one's energy on this translation, to which one could devote an entire lifetime and surrender all one's interests? And I don't even have a table where I can lay out my papers, or a lamp that will burn all night.

All day long you sit at work, copying blueprints and fervently awaiting the moment when you can return home and take up your pen. Then it comes, this moment. You walk three kilometers in the heat. Then, with book in hand, you eat. You take up your pen – but already you feel weak, you need rest, your head's not clear, your thoughts are fuzzy. The pen doesn't move. And you know what this kind of work is like. You can write ten versions for a single passage – and not one of them works. So sometimes you're driven to frenzy, and cursing everything, you fall asleep. The next day it's the same story. Things change only on Sundays, but my God, how many Sundays do I need?!

Now that I've entered the spirit of the text, I'm overwhelmed with reverence, amazement and gratitude to fate that out of the depths of the centuries it has brought this marvel to us ...[71]

Zabolotsky invested this project with tremendous hope, and simply put, his work on the translation saved him. The Party authorities at the Saran construction site were so impressed by his ardor and diligence that they granted him a one-month leave in July, 1945, to finish the translation at the local "House of Rest." After reading Zabolotsky's final version, the Karaganda House of Party Enlightenment sent an official letter of recommendation to the Moscow Writers' Union, requesting that Zabolotsky be brought to Moscow and reinstated in the Union. Zabolotsky was, in fact, granted permission to return to Moscow. He arrived there in January, 1946, thus ending nearly eight years of imprisonment and exile.

For the first few months Zabolotsky slept on the dining table in the Stepanovs' apartment – a rather horrifying bed, since Russia's dead traditionally were laid out on tables before burial.[72] In the spring he moved with his family to the writer V.P. Ilenkov's dacha in Peredelkino. The family later stayed with Kaverin, too, until obtaining their own small Moscow apartment in 1948.

Despite his reinstatement into the Writers' Union, Zabolotsky had to fight his way back into the literary world. A number of Moscow writers were critical of his efforts to return to public life; at a reading of Zabolotsky's translation of "The Lay of Igor's Campaign," the prominent literary historian Nikolai Gudzy, for one, sharply criticized the poet for his use of rhymed verse and his interpretations of the poem's Church Slavonicisms.[73] Like the artists of the avant-garde two decades earlier, Zabolotsky found that his greatest enemy was not the malefic Stalin himself, but a stolid public. The opposition of both critics and peers to his reemergence in the literary world caused Zabolotsky to feel shaky for years after his release. Nikolai Stepanov and Zabolotsky's Georgian friend Simon Chikovani urged him to publish some "safe" poetry in order to secure his position; but even the politically acceptable "Tvortsy dorog" ("Creators of Roads"),[74] Zabolotsky's first poem to be published since his arrest, elicited negative response.[75]

Neither were favorably disposed writers eager to help Zabolotsky directly. In 1946 Zabolotsky read his newly composed "Slepoi" ("The Blind Man") to Aleksandr Fadeyev, the powerful head of the Writers' Union. Fadeyev began to cry with emotion, then turned his sympathetic response into a weak joke, telling Zabolotsky that not only would he not publish his poem, but that it would remain "blind" and not see the light for another two hundred and fifty years.[76] Zabolotsky took Fadeyev's words as a forewarning. While he continued to

7 Zabolotsky reading the book *America* with his wife,
Yekaterina Vasilyevna, 1951

write his own poetry, he supported his family by verse translations from the Georgian.

Ever since meeting the Georgian poets Simon Chikovani
and Titsian Tabidze in 1935, Zabolotsky had been interested
in Georgian literature.[77] Before his arrest he had worked on
translations from both classical and contemporary Georgian
poetry, including the epic Rustaveli poem of which he was so
proud. Zabolotsky felt an affinity to the Georgians, and each
visit to their country enthralled him. In the spring of 1947, the
Writers' Union invited Zabolotsky to join Pavel Antokolsky,
Viktor Goltsev, Aleksandr Mezhirov and Tikhonov on a trip to
Georgia.[78] This visit was timely for him: just as the Caucasus
had succored Mandelstam and Pasternak during difficult
periods in their lives, so it now offered Zabolotsky a salvation,
both in its landscape and in the support he received from the
Georgian literary establishment. Zabolotsky wrote a number
of original poems as a result of this trip, including the lovely
"Tbilisskie nochi" ("Tbilisi Nights"), probably dedicated to
the actress Nata Vachnadze.

. . . .
Хочешь, завтра под звуки пандури,
Сквозь вина золотую струю
Я умчу тебя в громе и буре
В ледяную отчизну мою?

Вскрикнут кони, разломится время,
И по руслу реки до зари
Полетим мы, забытые всеми,
Разрывая лучей янтари . . .

Tomorrow, to the sound of the *panduri*,
Through a golden stream of wine
Shall I whisk you away in thunder and storm
To my icy homeland?

The horses will cry out, time will break apart,
And along the river channel until dawn
We shall fly, forgotten by all,
Bursting the amber rays . . .

In his early poetry, Zabolotsky used fragmentation of time
and space as a poetic device, without fully plumbing the extent
of its meanings. Here, the trope of time breaking apart carries
substantially deeper significance. Only through his traumatic
camp experience did Zabolotsky come to see the richness
toward which his unconscious mind had impelled him in
Scrolls. The result is verse at once less abstract and cerebral, the
poet's emotional function merging with his intellectual one. By
now Zabolotsky had also experienced alienation from parts of
himself and come to recognize the value of being a more
complex, conscious individual: he could see the beauty of light
not only fractured into rainbows, but also separated by harsher
prisms such as ice and hoarfrost. Where previously he had
merely intuited the darker side of life, now he knew it. Yet
paradoxically, the more fragmented Zabolotsky's personality
grew, the more integrated he became as a poet. Furthermore,
having experienced in his own life a fissure in time,[79] Zabolotsky learned how to drop through it to gain transcendence[80]
and thus escape the immediate circle of his present-tense life.
He was able to achieve a sense of time that is neither present,

nor past, nor future, but free of standard perceptions. "Tbilisi Nights" beckons with an invitation to slip through time; and in this magnificat to the North, inspired by a passion for the South, one senses the beginning of the poet's reconciliation with his homeland.

The process was not an easy one. Like other returnees from the labor camps, Zabolotsky had difficulty readjusting to civilian life. Certain holdovers from his camp experience continued to influence his behavior; for one thing, he could not shake his fear. When friends would quote from *Scrolls* to show their admiration, Zabolotsky was terrified – he did not even want to talk about the literary work that had brought about his arrest. In a tribute to Peredelkino writers, the poet Semyon Lipkin describes Zabolotsky:

> Я знаю, что собрат зверей, растений, птиц –
>   Боялся он до дней конечных
> Волков-опричников, волков-самоубийц,
>   Волчиных мастеров заплечных ...[81]

> I know that the colleague of beasts, plants and birds
>   Lived in fear to his final days
> Of the vigilante-wolves, the suicide-wolves,
>   The wolfish executioners ...

Zabolotsky's anxiety was not merely a symptom of paranoia; the threat of rearrest was never distant. In fact, Zabolotsky would have been detained in 1948 had Stepanov not managed to hide him. But even apart from the menacing political situation, Zabolotsky did not fit easily into post-war Moscow society. Because he was still officially under conviction, many people avoided him, afraid of jeopardizing their own positions. In the camps Zabolotsky had learned what was necessary for survival; now he was faced with new rules and was often unsure how to proceed. Zabolotsky's difficulties were compounded by his desire to regain a respected literary standing. Despite his previous ill treatment at the hands of the critics, he now sought their approval. Yet he had not relinquished his stringent poetic standards and was unable to compose poetry on demand. In this necessarily contradictory desire for artistry and acclaim lies Zabolotsky's personal tragedy.

Two incidents point up Zabolotsky's conflict and suggest a certain attitude that he adopted toward the outside world. The first occurred in 1949, when Zabolotsky was summoned to Moscow from Peredelkino to participate in a forum at the Writers' Union. He did not want to go: no matter what he did or did not say, he was afraid of compromising himself or others. But because his position was so tenuous, friends urged him not to ignore the summons. So Zabolotsky reluctantly left for the Peredelkino train station, where he was discovered later that evening, drunk, having passed the hours at his favorite bar. Whether Zabolotsky resorted to drunkenness out of shame or by conscious design in order to avoid potentially more unacceptable behavior cannot now be determined. Whatever the cause, he had discovered a way to exist in society: through evasive behavior he could protect his real, interior world. In other words, he could avert new disaster by adopting a safe public persona.

Over the remaining nine years of his life Zabolotsky perfected the dichotomy between his public and private selves, engaging in a doubling of sorts, as the second incident reveals. In 1958, the last year of his life, Zabolotsky was awarded the Order of Labor of the Red Banner. He willingly accepted this symbol of governmental approbation and travelled across Moscow to have an official photograph taken. But when he returned home, he methodically cut out his decorated chest from the photograph,[82] until only his solemn face remained.

Zabolotsky's benign public face protected him, but it also worked against him. For one thing, he recognized the complicity that his acceptance of the award represented. Even more troubling, perhaps, was the reaction from some of his public. Those who admired the early Zabolotsky reproached him for accepting the medal; they failed to see that for the poet it represented security, the official symbol of his freedom from harrassment. They castigated Zabolotsky also for what they considered his capitulation, as evidenced by the change in his stylistics. These critical readers had certain expectations for literature based on the way they wanted to see the world, particularly after Stalin's death. They wanted Zabolotsky to

8 Zabolotsky in Moscow, 1955

support their idea of poetry; when he failed to, they cast him down.

The fact is that even in freedom, Zabolotsky lived in limbo, and his safe public image was hard-won. The volume of verse[83] he published in 1948 – his third in as many decades – was virtually ignored by the critics. And in 1951 he was again nearly exiled from Moscow. Only the continued protestations of friends in the Writers' Union prevented his banishment and led to the official lifting of his conviction on October 6, 1951.[84] Zabolotsky was not formally rehabilitated during his lifetime.[85] However, after two favorable reviews appeared in the *Literary Gazette* in 1956,[86] one by the influential Ilya Ehrenburg, Zabolotsky was able to publish his poetry with some regularity. Sadly, however, his personal life was now falling apart. His wife had left to live with the writer Vasily Grossman, and Zabolotsky began an affair with Natalya Roskina, the daughter of the eminent Chekhov scholar.[87] This was a very difficult time for Zabolotsky, as he had come to rely on his wife's solicitude. His emotional state was so tenuous that despite his strong attraction to Roskina, he secretly worried that she was an informer because of the many provocative statements she made. Zabolotsky's affair was short-lived, lasting only three months. A year and a half later, Yekaterina Vasilyevna returned to him, without any suspicion that he had so little time left to live.

In 1957 Zabolotsky was given permission to travel to Italy with a delegation of Soviet writers, and in that same year he issued a fourth book of poems (*Stikhotvoreniia* [*Poems*]). As far as the general public was concerned, Zabolotsky's conscious ploy had succeeded: to all appearances, he was a model Soviet poet. But this period of recognition and ostensible ease lasted only a short time. On October 14, 1958, Zabolotsky suffered a heart attack and died.

CHAPTER 3

Visions of a brave new world

The earth is the cradle of reason, but you can't lie in the cradle forever."

Konstantin Tsiolkovsky

The critics who discovered a "new" Zabolotsky in the mid-1930s failed to recognize that this "second"[1] Zabolotsky had existed from the first. Alongside the urban grotesques of *Scrolls*, Zabolotsky had been composing a very different, parallel sort of verse. Such masterly poems as "The Face of the Horse" (1926), "V zhilishchakh nashikh" ("In Our Abodes," 1926), "Na lestnitsakh" ("On the Stairs," 1928) and "Nachalo oseni" ("The Beginning of Autumn," 1928) reveal his early interest in questions of the universe and man's mortality. These and similar poems express man's longing to comprehend the universe, to explore the degrees of reason granted mankind, animals and nature itself. Nature is not so much the subject of these poems as a counterpoint to man and his tenuous existence.[2] But in the furor over the publication of *Scrolls*, Zabolotsky was cast as a poet of cityscapes, and his other, more lyrical poems were overlooked.

Zabolotsky was fully conscious of the two strains coexisting in his poetry. The organization of his intended second volume of verse[3] illustrates the distinction he made between his urban poems or *stolbtsy* and his other, more philosophical lyrics. This second category of poems he placed under the heading *derev'ia* or "trees." While the *stolbtsy* reflect a modern ennui, a sense of stagnation, the *derev'ia* offer a promise of transformation. Simply put, the "new" Zabolotsky who emerged in the thirties was a poet who chose to concentrate on poems of the *derev'ia* rather than the *stolbtsy* type.

While poems about transformation suited the overall spirit of the times, Zabolotsky's highly personal vision hardly corresponded with the formulaic conventions of Soviet literature, according to which writers were expected to portray positive models for the edification of the masses. A radiant future populated by heroic socialist workers represented the ideal advanced by the new Writers' Union. As other writers were concerning themselves with the exigencies of society, Zabolotsky turned increasingly inward to contemplate the cosmos, drawing on the visionary ideas of precursors as varied as the eighteenth-century Ukrainian mystic philosopher Skovoroda and the twentieth-century biogeochemist Vernadsky. That Zabolotsky should be attracted to these thinkers is not unusual; as a provincial Russian, he had been imbued from an early age with utopian ideas. Stories about the Book of the Depths,[4] a medieval tome purportedly holding the secrets of nature and the key to the origins of social institutions, enthralled him:

> В младенчестве я слышал много раз
> Полузабытый прадедов рассказ
> О книге сокровенной . . .
>
> И слышу я знакомое сказанье,
> Как правда кривду вызвала на бой,
> Как одолела кривда, и крестьяне
> С тех пор живут, обижены судьбой.
> Лишь далеко на океане-море
> На белом камне, посредине вод,
> Сияет книга в золотом уборе,
> Лучами упираясь в небосвод.
> Та книга выпала из некой грозной тучи,
> Все буквы в ней цветами проросли,
> И в ней написана рукой судеб могучей
> Вся правда сокровенная земли.
>
> . . .
>
> "Голубиная книга" (1937)

In infancy I heard many times
My ancestors' half-forgotten tale
Of a secret book . . .

And I hear the familiar legend,
How truth called injustice to battle,

How injustice won, and the peasants
Since then have been cursed by fate.
Only far away in the ocean,
On a white stone amid the waters,
Shines a book encased in gold,
Its rays thrust against the heavens.
That book fell down from a thundercloud,
Its letters are overgrown with flowers,
And written in it by fate's powerful hand
Is the secret truth of the earth.
...

"The Book of the Depths" (1937)

In his poetry of the 1930s, Zabolotsky presents his own vision of utopia. The poetic universe he opens to his readers is so broad as to encompass other planetary systems, yet still particular enough to pinpoint the atoms swirling through it. In its plasticity, the range of Zabolotsky's perception suggests a great latency and potential.

SOCIETY TRANSFORMED

By definition, Zabolotsky's cosmography represents a description of the universe, but he did not come easily to his formulations. He was particularly influenced by three thinkers whose voices soon became part of his chorus: the poet Velimir Khlebnikov; the philosopher Nikolai Fyodorov; and the aerodynamic theorist Konstantin Tsiolkovsky. The ideas of these writers impelled Zabolotsky toward a conscious response to nature and man's rôle in it, although the *Naturphilosophie* he developed differs in all instances from the material that inspired it.

Of course, a concern with man *vis-à-vis* nature was all part of the fervor of the post-Revolutionary years, when utopian ideas were in the air, reflected in such diverse works as Yesenin's "Inonia" and Mayakovsky's "150,000,000" (where immortal man is envisioned as a beam of light living in a timeless paradise). It was hardly more surprising for a poet to propound "biological reconstruction" (Alexei Gastev)[5] than it was for a writer to predict physical immortality (Gorky).[6]

A basic premise of the current ideology was the limitless potential of man to transform the world through his labor. This idea, though hardly new, had changed in its terms since the nineteenth century. What had been merely prophecy in Chernyshevsky[7] was now reality as technology transformed life daily. Bazarov's assessment of nature as a workshop for man's use[8] was substantiated in the 1920s as man actively fulfilled the function of worker in it. And the ideas of the social utopist Timofei Bondarev on the regenerative power of labor[9] were echoed in part in Aleksandr Chayanov's *Journey of My Brother Aleksei to the Land of Peasant Utopia* (1920). Even if the Soviet emphasis on industry was not entirely original, its perspective had evolved. No longer was labor the only crucial factor for attaining an ideal society; now the laborers themselves – the people – had to "grow" in consciousness before this goal could be reached.[10] Zabolotsky took this fashionable idea one step further, maintaining that not only man, but nature itself, must grow in consciousness before a perfected world can evolve.

Over the first decade of Soviet rule, the orientation of utopian literature changed. Where early on rural utopias predominated, by the end of the NEP period urbanist views prevailed. What both varieties of utopia shared, however, was an interest in questions of immortality. In contrast to the eschatological premonitions of the preceding generation, the writers and artists of post-Revolutionary Russia were caught up in a spirit of renewed life; having effected a political revolution, it was now time for a revolution of the spirit. Thus Mayakovsky could write:

> ... встает из времен
> революция другая –
> третья революция
> духа.
>
> "Четвертый интернациональ" (1922)

> From out of time will arise
> another revolution –
> a third revolution
> of the spirit.
>
> "The Fourth International" (1922)

The heralds of the new age sought nothing less than a victory over death. Even the mundane aspects of life served to encourage this progressive idea, with movies like "In Scorn of Death" playing to eager crowds.[11] The entombment of Lenin in a special mausoleum and the coining of the slogan "Lenin is With Us" likewise may be seen as part of the widespread attempt to realize the dream of immortality.[12]

Such a feat seemed quite possible in a society where science was accorded new importance. In the Bolshevik victory, Marx's idea of science as history had seemed to prove itself. Now all sorts of experiments were conducted in institutions investigating everything from reanimation to the humanization of animals.[13] The Soviet state took great pride in these experiments, likening them to a new revolution.[14] Through technology, the state sought actively to control and organize nature in order to revolutionize society. As a kind of lay science invaded Soviet life, the theme of transformation through the labors of model workers became increasingly frequent in the literature. Even poetry was not spared. More than one leading article urged poets to forsake the "passive exaltation of the beauties of a nature which has not been subjugated by man" in favor of a "scientific approach" to their subject.[15] Plans were made to combine the disciplines of literature, science and technology in popular almanachs.[16] Despite this forced enthusiasm, however, satire of scientific methods persisted well into the 1930s. Nikolai Oleinikov, Zabolotsky's friend from the Children's Publishing House, wrote several poems about the extreme societal emphasis on science. His "Praise the Inventors" (1934) begins:

Хвала изобретателям, подумавшим о мелких и смешных
    приспособлениях:
О щипчиках для сахара, о мундштуках для папирос,
Хвала тому, кто предложил печати ставить в удостоверениях,
Кто к чайнику приделал крышечку и нос,
Кто соску первую построил из резины,
Кто макароны выдумал и манную крупу ...[17]

Praise the inventors who thought about petty and ridiculous
    contraptions:

About tongs for sugar and mouthpieces for cigarettes,
Praise him who suggested placing seals on certificates,
Who made a lid and a spout for the teapot,
Who built the first rubber pacifier,
Who thought up macaroni and cream of wheat ...

Kharms, too, had trouble with society's aims:

> Я не могу читать некоторые книги
> в них мысль заменяет слово
> но мысли жалкий фитилек
> надежда мученика злого
> мне непонятно восхищенье
> перед науки торжеством.[18]

> There are some books I can't read
> in them thought replaces the word
> but this pitiful wick of thought
> is the hope of an evil martyr
> I do not understand the delight
> in the triumph of science.

Zabolotsky differed from his colleagues in that he genuinely was excited by the advances of science. Where Oleinikov and Kharms were impious, Zabolotsky felt a certain reverence. In his fascination with science and utopian thought, Zabolotsky may be seen as very much in accord with the current Soviet ideology. But in the articulation of his ideas he encountered trouble. "The Triumph of Agriculture," for instance, did not follow any prevailing pattern for an urban utopia. Instead of presenting a purely technological society, Zabolotsky consciously portrayed a harmonious community distinguished by both urban and pastoral elements – a unique sort of administrative peasant utopia, one which oscillates *entre avenir et souvenir*, to use Apollinaire's formulation. Although Zabolotsky's intentions should not be construed as anti-Soviet, his critics were quick to take issue with his poetic renderings of the new society and man's rôle in it.

MAN AND NATURE

Zabolotsky's poetry represents an open forum in which he puts forth often contradictory ideas. Because these ideas do not always fall into neat categories, it may be hard to arrive at an unambiguous characterization of the poet's philosophy. Even so, several specific points may be made. Above all Zabolotsky believed in the interdependence of man and nature. He undoubtedly had read Engels, whose *Dialectics of Nature* generated immediate controversy when first published in Moscow in 1925. Like Engels, Zabolotsky saw man as a part of the natural world, within it and inseparable from it. As a part of nature, man must inevitably participate in its dialectical development which, according to Engels, is a process of perfection, of development into ever higher forms of life. Man himself is the highest form of nature – in Zabolotsky's words, "its best, its foremost part." Certainly the Darwinian theory of evolution lends itself better to a dialectical interpretation than to one featuring a perpetually-recurring cycle or the eternal sameness of nature. But where Darwin postulated an infinite system of perfection of species, Engels theorized a finite one in which man would achieve a perfect evolution and a perfect relationship with the natural world at the same moment as the state withered away.

Zabolotsky was intrigued by these evolutionary theories, though he had no interest in applying dialectical materialism to the natural sciences. Indeed, in his idea of man as nature's "foremost part," Zabolotsky sooner followed Schelling than Engels. Schelling had proposed the basic unity of the mind and nature, with consciousness as nature's highest power.[19] Zabolotsky accepted this postulate, but he further believed (and here he was in accordance with Soviet teachings) that man must actively participate in organizing the natural world,[20] given his privileged position in it.

Zabolotsky called himself a "monist," one who sees the world as unified matter with no distinction between the spiritual and the material.[21] Neither did he recognize a clear distinction between man and nature, adjudging their rôles to be interchangeable: teacher and student, master and man. While nature's inherent chaos must be tamed by man and brought into order, man is bound to learn a great deal from nature in the process. In his chosen subject, Zabolotsky often has been compared to the nineteenth-century metaphysical poet Fyodor Tyutchev. But where Tyutchev stressed the irrational as marking the bond between man and nature, Zabolotsky sought instead to find harmony in nature through the imposition of reason. And because man has been granted reason, he has the power to bring harmony to nature's inherent disorder. In this way he can begin to transform the world.[22]

Man is not omnipotent, however. He may be "the ruler of nature," but he is also "its child" ("i vlastelin prirody i ditia ee"). Nature, in turn, is a paradoxical (and inherently oxymoronic) figure who teaches her child about life ("uchitel'-nitsa, devstvennitsa, mat'" ["teacher, virgin, mother"]), but who elsewhere is likened to a prison that keeps man oppressed (in "Zmei" ["Snakes"] and "Progulka" ["A Stroll"]). Perhaps Zabolotsky's most telling metaphor is found in "Lodeinikov," where images of death and creation are united in the figure of "the eternal wine-press of nature" ("prirody vekovechnaia davil'nia"). Here is Zabolotsky's favorite terrain: that blurred state of being between imminent death and incipient life, the fleeting moment of transformation from one form into the next, the very instant of metamorphosis.

This focus on metamorphosis and transformation provides the key to Zabolotsky's conception of the natural cycles in both the animate and inanimate worlds. Since new life always emerges from the old, death as such does not exist. It follows then, for Zabolotsky, that all forms of life are immortal (although he did not conceive of immortality in the usual, religious sense of the word whereby the soul continues to exist apart from and outside of the body). To put it otherwise: if, as Zabolotsky affirmed, every man is a part of nature, and if all of nature is immortal (which by virtue of its metamorphoses, it is), then every man must be immortal, too. And this immortality involves not only man's body, but his thoughts as well. Zabolotsky imagined man as the "thought" (*mysl'*) of nature. By absorbing man's achievements, nature can be improved. Man, in turn, needs nature to gain immortality, which is impossible on his own. Thus the relationship between the two is reciprocal. In "Yesterday, Pondering Death" (1936)

Zabolotsky expresses the idea that man's accomplishments live on in nature:

Вчера, о смерти размышляя,
Ожесточилась вдруг душа моя.
Печальный день! Природа вековая
Из тьмы лесов смотрела на меня.

И нестерпимая тоска разъединенья
Пронзила сердце мне, и в этот миг
Все, все услышал я – и трав вечерних пенье,
И речь воды, и камня мертвый крик.

И я, живой, скитался над полями,
Входил без страха в лес,
И мысли мертвецов прозрачными столбами
Вокруг меня вставали до небес.

И голос Пушкина был над листвою слышен,
И птицы Хлебникова пели у воды.[23]
И встретил камень я. Был камень неподвижен,
И проступал в нем лик Сковороды.

И все существованья, все народы,
Нетленное хранили бытие,
И сам я был не детище природы,
Но мысль ее! Но зыбкий ум ее!

Yesterday, pondering death
My soul suddenly grew bitter.
A sad day! Ancient nature
Gazed at me from the forest gloom.

The unbearable anguish of separation
Pierced my heart, and at that moment
I could hear everything, everything – the singing of the
    evening grasses,
The water's speech, and the dead cry of the stone.

Alive, I wandered over the fields,
Entered without fear into the forest,
And the thoughts of the dead, like transparent columns,
Rose up to the heavens around me.

And Pushkin's voice was heard above the foliage,
And birds sang Khlebnikov by the water's edge.
And I met a stone. The stone was motionless,
And Skovoroda's face appeared on it.

And all existences, all nations
Preserved their daily life untainted,
And I myself was not a child of nature,
But was her thought! Her supple mind!

Nature is similarly alive and resonant in "Lodeinikov," where
flapping shirts become a metaphor for the rustling foliage of
trees: "O slushai, slushai khlopan′e rubakh!/Ved′ v kazhdom
dereve sidit moguchii Bakh/I v kazhdom kamne Gannibal
taitsia ..." ("O, listen, listen to the flapping of the shirts!/For
in every tree there sits a mighty Bach/And in every rock
Hannibal is lurking ...")[24]
Cognizant of this living inheritance from past generations of
men, Zabolotsky grappled with the task of bringing consciousness to nature. If thought was crucial to this process, then,
inversely, it was also the key to man's understanding of nature.
In 1929 Zabolotsky wrote a poem in which man first becomes
aware of nature's anguish. Significantly, he entitled it "The
Beginning of Thought" ("Nachalo mysli"):[25]

....
Речка девочкой невзрачной
Лежит тихо между трав,
То смеется, то рыдает,
Ноги в землю закопав.
Что же плачет? Что тоскует?
Отчего она больна?
Вся природа улыбнулась,
Как высокая тюрьма.
....

....
Like an unattractive girl the river
Lies quietly among the grasses,
Laughing and then sobbing,
Her legs buried in the earth.
Why does she cry? Why feel anguish?
For what reason is she ill?
All of nature smiles
Like a lofty prison.
....

Once man has recognized nature's pain, he is bound to act on his knowledge. The poet has a particular obligation to help, for in contrast to nature's inarticulateness (*kosnoiazychie*), the gift of fluent speech has been granted him. In such early poems as "The Face of the Horse" and "Iskusstvo" ("Art"), nature is unable to express its secrets; therefore the poet speaks in its place. But as Zabolotsky's poetry develops, nature gradually learns to speak for itself and tell of its hardships. Nature's own narrative voice (heard particularly strongly in "The Triumph of Agriculture") marks the first step toward its liberation. Man need only intervene to complete the process, transforming nature through his conscious acts.

"EQUALITY FOR COWS" (VELIMIR KHLEBNIKOV)

Zabolotsky once stated that much of his inspiration for "The Triumph of Agriculture" derived from one line in Khlebnikov's long poem "Ladomir" (1920): "Ia vizhu konskie svobody i ravnopravie korov" ("I see equine freedoms and equality for cows").[26] "Ladomir" is a utopian poem about the future; indeed, the future as a concept was highly important to Khlebnikov: "... the birthplace of creativity is the future. The wind of the gods of poetry blows from there."[27] In nearly five hundred lines, "Ladomir" treats of revolution and radical change ushering in a new era. Like "The Triumph of Agriculture," the poem portrays in narrative form the overthrow of an old order and the eradication of suffering. Khlebnikov's "Lyudostan" (roughly, "People Land") is an imaginary country where animals, people, and gods are united in harmony. Although Zabolotsky's long poem progresses in much the same way as "Ladomir," ending with the advent of a more harmonious existence, his holistic vision of the future differs significantly from Khlebnikov's.

Zabolotsky's utopia is based on an understanding between man and nature, both in the sense of "comprehension" and "an agreement." Because man and nature are inseparable, they must strive together for their mutual benefit; once they know how to do so, harmony will ensue. Khlebnikov's utopia results from a different process: not mutual understanding, but a fine balance of opposites forms a state of equilibrium, which Khlebnikov equated with harmony. While the opposites are interdependent, they cancel each other out[28] (like algebraic equations) once they are juxtaposed, until no tension remains. In contrast, Zabolotsky utilized the tension of opposites (conflicts, paradoxes) to create excitement and interest in his poetry.

Both poets presupposed an inner logic to the universe, and this logical basis accounts for the scientific terms of their utopias. Khlebnikov's attraction to the radical geometric constructions of the nineteenth-century mathematician Nikolai Lobachevsky anticipates Zabolotsky's discovery of the geometric "realm of pure conceptions" in "The Trees," while Lyudostan's glass cities prefigure the engineered glass structures of "The Mad Wolf." "The Triumph of Agriculture" also proclaims scientific thought as a prerequisite for an improved society. But while mathematical science is crucial to Khlebnikov's land of the future, serving as the great unifying force in the poet's search for a world order, technology is not the main feature of Lyudostan. Instead, Khlebnikov's utopia is ultimately pastoral, a place of eternal harmony and love, where the once-wretched serf "celebrates the sweet shepherdess by the stream and the dragonflies" ("I slavish' miluiu pastushku/ U rucheika i u strekoz"). In this peaceful setting, opposites are equated and equilibrium achieved: labor is balanced by leisure, lassitude by inspiration; reason is tempered with emotion, and science with imagination. "Ladomir" represents a poetic challenge to recreate the time when man was akin to both animals and gods, when the artificial boundaries of the modern world had not yet been established and man felt himself a mystical part of the universe rather than an alienated creature of society. In contrast, the utopian society of "The Triumph of Agriculture" is more of a technocracy, even though Zabolotsky's title suggests a pastoral.

Both Zabolotsky and Khlebnikov expressed a belief in the perfectability of the universe, in a progression to ever higher stages of development. (One early example from Zabolotsky, originally entitled "Immortality", has the poet claiming to be the descendant of an alley cat: "Ia prodolzhaiu zhizn' tvoiu,/ Moi pravednik otvazhnyi" ["I continue your life,/My courageous, righteous one"].)[29] But while Zabolotsky saw this evolution in terms of perfected plants, animals and humans, for Khlebnikov the stage following human perfection was governed by numbers, which held a mystical significance including the secrets of the universe. Therefore, even after harmony has been achieved in his pastoral utopia, Khlebnikov's poet remains a prisoner, an "eternal prisoner of harmony" ("vechnyi uznik sozvuch'ia"),[30] since he cannot be released into the higher realm of numbers. Zabolotsky's poet, on the other hand, is able to free himself. At first nature appears as a prison to him, as it does to Khlebnikov's poet, but the longer he searches, the more he comes to understand, and in time nature is transformed from a prison into an harmonious orchestra. Even more significantly, along with his freedom the poet gains immortality. At last he is free not only to contemplate, but to explore the vast reaches of the universe. And through this exploration of the cosmos – this transcending of boundaries – utopia will come to pass.

In their desire to eliminate the gap between man and nature and to grasp the infinite, Zabolotsky and Khlebnikov share an interest in universalism, marked by a fascination with, and a belief in, the powers of the cosmos. For both poets, the earth is not merely a self-contained entity, but part of a larger universe with which it interacts and upon which it depends for its own existence. In "Ladomir" as well as "The Triumph of Agriculture," constellations symbolize the advent of the new order, implying that a recognition of the cosmos is integral to bringing about utopia. Once harmony is established, it will reign universally, not just on earth. But whereas for Zabolotsky harmony signifies the complex interrelationship between man and nature in both its specific and cosmic senses, for Khlebnikov this working relationship is of less interest than the accord which ensues. Thus in Lyudostan universal well-being and a universal dance replace the individual dances of various nations, bringing an end to discord. Most importantly, a universal language of love will be spoken:

Лети, созвездье человечье,
Все дальше, далее в простор
И перелей земли наречья
В единый смертных разговор.

Fly, human constellation,
Ever further into space
And smelt the dialects of earth
Into a single human discourse.

Not only people, but all of nature will be united by a common tongue as the rivers of the world proclaim: "liu ... bliu ... ves' ... mir ... ia!" ("I love the whole world!")[31] This love extends even beyond the earth: "Iazyk liubvi nad mirom nositsia/I Pesnia pesnei v nebo prositsia" ("The language of love hovers over the world/And the Song of songs appeals to heaven"). Khlebnikov's repeated use of such words as *sozvezd'e* ("constellation") and *prostor* ("space") further emphasizes his cosmic orientation. At the same time his imagery reflects the prevalent idea that the Russian Revolution would spawn similar rebellions throughout the world, thereby engendering universal freedom. In "Ladomir" capitalism is destroyed as "a song" replaces "profits." But liberation is not always automatic: before man can live in harmony with the elements, the "bolt" (*zasov*) must be removed from his eyes. Only once this obstruction falls will "equine freedoms and equality for cows" come to pass.

The harmony of Ladomir is achieved by transcending gravitational bounds and embracing infinity. Khlebnikov expresses this dream of overcoming gravity in a variety of ways. His trope "textbooks flying through the air," for instance, describes radio waves; and his free use of syntax and associative connections among sounds and meanings surmounts conventional linguistic bounds. In other works, too, Khlebnikov examines the concept of gravity in its relation to modern life, proposing new architectural constructions to create a city of the future that will rise up into the cosmos and "liberate the earth for the plant and animal kingdoms"[32] even as man himself is liberated from his planet.

Other writers and artists of the avant-garde shared Khlebnikov's interest in defying gravity and sought to create in each work "a kind of 'small universe,' with its own particular organization of time and space. A work [could] become such a universal world by conquering gravity in its structural orientation."[33] Malevich's *planity*, Miturich's *volnoviki*, and Tatlin's *Letatlin* are all familar examples of this cosmic construction. What has not been noted before, however, is Zabolotsky's fascination with the relationship between architecture and the cosmos.

At Lipavsky's gatherings, Zabolotsky named both architecture and astrology among the things that interested him. Even so, it is difficult to find concrete expressions of their conjunction in his poetry (the best example is in "Osen'" ["Autumn," 1932]). But from Kharms' archive we learn that in 1933 Zabolotsky composed a poem he called "Oblaka" ("Clouds"),[34] in which builders, ancestors and animals all figure as characters, presumably appearing among the clouds in the sky as they do in "The Triumph of Agriculture." That "Clouds" deals with architecture we learn from a letter Kharms wrote shortly after hearing Zabolotsky recite his poem: "Zabolotsky came over today. He's been interested in architecture for a long time, he's written a poem where he expressed a lot of wonderful thoughts about architecture and human lives. I know that many people will be excited about "[this poem]."[35] Intriguingly, Kharms mentions a "*vtorogo zreniia* okno" ("a window of *second sight*"), which recalls Filonov's "knowing eye." And if we consider that "in the Book of the [Depths] clouds are said to derive from thoughts,"[36] then Zabolotsky's poem must have been utopian in conception.

Unfortunately, "Clouds" has been lost, so it is impossible to know to what degree Zabolotsky's ideas correspond with other artists', particularly Khlebnikov's. But since Zabolotsky allows the ancestors in "The Triumph of Agriculture" to transcend gravitational limits (and thereby death), we can postulate for both "Clouds" and "The Triumph of Agriculture" the influence not only of Khlebnikov, but also of Nikolai Fyodorov. Fyodorov believed that "art and architecture should celebrate the vertical" and that "space exploration would be a logical extension of man's vertical orientation."[37]

In his attention to Fyodorov's ideas, Zabolotsky followed Khlebnikov,[38] although he likely learned of this philosopher from other sources.

"THE COMMON CAUSE" (NIKOLAI FYODOROV)

If for Khlebnikov the future was inextricably bound with the past, so it was too for Nikolai Fyodorov (1828–1903), the father of "philosophical cosmism."[39] In the posthumously compiled *Filosofiia obshchego dela* (*Philosophy of the Common Cause*), Fyodorov propounded a world view based on a reverence for ancestors. He promised a new era of immortality and universal peace which, despite its future vision, had a retrospective orientation, founded as it was on a cult of ancestry. Immortality could be accomplished through the resurrection of one's ancestors, an act that would serve to reawaken a feeling of kinship among men and recreate a fraternity of mankind with universal consciousness. Such dreams of unity and harmony attracted Zabolotsky, finding reflection in his poetry.

While it has not proved possible to substantiate that Zabolotsky actually read Fyodorov, it is reasonable to assume that he knew the philosopher's work.[40] For one thing, Fyodorov's ideas were a common topic of discussion among the intelligentsia in the 1920s,[41] and one contemporary of Zabolotsky recalls that it was possible to find Kant, Leibnitz, and Fyodorov's *Philosophy of the Common Cause* in Leningrad's second-hand bookstores.[42] The Futurist poets, whom Zabolotsky avidly read, had rediscovered the philosopher for themselves and were well acquainted with his teachings. Given their interest in the expressive abilities of handwriting, these poets were taken with Fyodorov's study of the aesthetic significance of the *ustavnye* or uncial letters in medieval manuscripts.[43] Mayakovsky in particular reflected Fyodorovian ideas in his poetry, such as the "workshop of human resurrections" in "Pro eto" ("About That").[44] And Khlebnikov's dream of mastering time to save mankind from death has much in common with Fyodorov's plan. As noted earlier, thoughts of conquering death were in the air in post-Revolutionary Russia, with the call for unity out not only to the living proletariat: "Dead of All Lands, Unite!"[45] Even if Fyodorov's direct influence on Zabolotsky is difficult to establish, the context is certainly there.

By all accounts Fyodorov was an eccentric. He lived an ascetic life in a dingy corner of a partitioned room furnished with only the barest necessities. For many years he worked as the manuscript curator of the Moscow Public Library and Rumyantsev Museum, where he earned a reputation for erudition and saintliness. Most of his modest salary he gave away to needy students and scholars, including the young Tsiolkovsky, whom he encouraged in his self-education. Like Filonov to follow, Fyodorov did not believe in selling his work,[46] so he distributed his books for free. Both Dostoyevsky and Tolstoy acknowledged debts to this original thinker who chose not to compile his thoughts, leaving the task instead to a few loyal followers. For his part, Fyodorov reproached Tolstoy for his hypocrisy in leading a life of comfort while preaching simplicity, and for what Fyodorov perceived as a lack of genuine faith.[47]

Fyodorov believed that the greatest happiness possible for mankind lay in man's exceeding the earth's mortal boundaries and creating an immortal universe. He worked out the means for attaining this utopian state through scientific calculations culminating in the actual resurrection of the past in the form of mankind's ancestors. This physical resurrection – the crux of Fyodorov's belief – also presented the greatest problem, for resurrection necessarily entailed the eradication of death. Puzzling out this task led Fyodorov to develop his theories on the regulation of death. Khlebnikov echoes his ideas in "Ladomir," where "smert' smerti budet vedat' sroki" ("the death of death shall govern over time"). Even resurrection seemed eventually possible to Khlebnikov:

> Если погибнем – воскреснем!
> Каждый потом оживет.
>
> "Воля всем" (1922)

> If we die – we'll resurrect!
> Each will again come alive.
>
> "Freedom for All" (1922)

But if the Fyodorovian-Khlebnikovian vision of universal resurrection entailed actual physical rebirth, Zabolotsky departed from their interpretation in his belief that extratemporal existence does not necessarily demand physical reproduction. For Zabolotsky, regeneration was one more form of transformation, in which man's essential being comes to life anew in the creations of nature. Here Zabolotsky's fascination with the Eastern religions, particularly Buddhism,[48] is relevant. Zabolotsky's concept of metamorphosis is very similar to the Eastern belief in reincarnation; his idea of transformation as opposed to resubstantiation sets him apart from Fyodorov.

"The Triumph of Agriculture" is admittedly Fyodorovian in spirit, yet Fyodorov's ideas serve merely as a springboard for Zabolotsky, whose poem offers a number of lively rejoinders to the philosopher's beliefs. For instance, where Fyodorov considered a literal rejuvenation of past generations to be the only means of eliminating oblivion, Zabolotsky brings his dead back only to *apparent* life (i.e., to recognition on the part of living generations), not to a literal one. In "The Triumph of Agriculture" he demonstrates how man can be recreated through the workings of nature, as Khlebnikov is:

Так человек, отпав от века
Зарытый в новгородский ил,
Прекрасный образ человека
В душе природы заронил.

Thus this man, separated from his age,
Buried in the Novgorod silt,
Let fall into the heart of nature
The splendid image of a man.

Here only an "image," Khlebnikov is animated several years later in "Yesterday, Pondering Death" as the birds "sing" him by the water's edge. Through Zabolotsky's resurrectional procedure, the poet has become an indivisible part of nature, living on within it.

Khlebnikov's path to immortality would be less swift by Fyodorov's method. Indeed, he would not yet be resurrected, for "until the time comes when man literally can recreate himself out of the most primal substances (atoms and molecules), he will be unable to live in all environments and take on all forms" demanded by those environments.[49] Only through re-creation will the cosmos become accessible to man. Conversely, Zabolotsky showed that man could attain immortality through his actions and achievements, which themselves live on after his bodily death.

Although the idea of a poet's work living on in posterity is not new, Zabolotsky added a different dimension to it. Where, for example, Pushkin and Boratynsky granted themselves immortality through their work, invoking future generations of readers,[50] Zabolotsky challenged his readers not only to discern his eternal presence through his verse, but also to *participate* in the unfinished act of creation:

Когда на склоне лет иссякнет жизнь моя
И, погасив свечу, опять отправлюсь я
В необозримый мир туманных превращений,
Когда мильоны новых поколений
Наполнят этот мир сверканием чудес
И довершат строение природы, –
Пускай мой бедный прах покроют эти воды,
Пусть приютит меня зеленый этот лес.

Я не умру, мой друг. Дыханием цветов
Себя я в этом мире обнаружу.
Многовековый дуб мою живую душу
Корнями обовьет, печален и суров.
В его больших листах я дам приют уму,
Я с помощью ветвей свои взлелею мысли,
Чтоб над тобой они из тьмы лесов повисли
И ты причастен был к сознанью моему.
. . .
О, я недаром в этом мире жил!
И сладко мне стремиться из потемок,
Чтоб, взяв меня в ладонь, ты, дальний мой потомок,
Доделал то, что я не довершил.

"Завещание" (1947)

When in my declining years my life dries up,
And my candle extinguished, I again depart for
The boundless world of foggy transformations,
When millions of new generations

Will fill this world with the shimmer of miracles
And finish the composition of nature –
May these waters cover my poor dust,
May this green forest shelter me.

I shall not die, my friend. In the breathing of flowers
I shall detect myself in this world.
The ancient oak, sad and stern,
Will wind its roots around my living soul.
In its large leaves I shall shelter my mind,
With the help of its branches I'll foster my thoughts,
That they might hang above you beyond the forest's gloom,
That you might be privy to my consciousness.
. . .
O, I did not live in vain in this world!
It's sweet for me to course out of the darkness,
So that you, my distant scion, taking me into your hand,
Might finish that which I could not complete.

"Testament" (1947)

Just as Fyodorov would have future generations helping to
restore their ancestors to life, so Zabolotsky felt that the living
must serve as accomplices in the work undertaken by those in
the past.

This is not to imply that Fyodorov denied the importance of
earthly achievement; he revered books as the incarnation of the
ancestors' activity. But books alone were not enough for him.
He wanted to go one step further and rekindle the spirits of the
ancestors hidden in the books, using their achievements as the
basis for reconstructing the actual men. By organizing libraries
and museums, "cathedrals of living sons with scholars at their
head, gathering the works of dead people, fathers,"[51] the living
could participate in the past and transgress the boundaries of
time. The idea of collapsing temporal and spatial boundaries
excited Zabolotsky, who in an early variant of "The Triumph
of Agriculture" toyed with making this notion a feature of
the new scientific utopia described in his poem:

> Здесь вол, зачитываясь Попом,
> Назад во времени плывет.

> Here an ox, engrossed in Pope,
> Sails backwards in time.

These lines reflect Zabolotsky's earnest interest in abolishing the constraints of time. They also convey his irrepressible sense of play. Here a castrated bull abandons himself to Pope, whose name sounds hilarious in its suggestion of *popa* or "fanny." And perhaps Zabolotsky had in mind that his ox was reading Pope's *Essay on Man* with its claim of being.

The point is that unlike Fyodorov or Tsiolkovsky, whose seriousness is often deadening, Zabolotsky treats his themes with humor and irony without, however, trivializing the philosophy underlying them. Thus in "The Triumph of Agriculture" he takes up the idea of oblivion, characterized by Fyodorov as man's greatest fear. Zabolotsky introduces a young girl in a grave, worm-eaten and forgotten by the living,[52] only to mock her. He deals similarly with a girl in "Temptation," except that she ends up transformed into a tree:

> Холмик во поле стоит,
> Дева в холмике шумит:
> "Тяжело лежать во гробе,
> Почернели ручки обе,
> Стали волосы как пыль
> Из грудей растет ковыль.
> Тяжело лежать в могиле,
> Губки тоненькие сгнили,
> Вместо глазок – два кружка,
> Нету милого дружка!"
>
> Смерть над холмиком летает
> И хохочет и грустит,
> Из ружья в него стреляет
> И склоняясь говорит:
> "Ну, малютка, полно врать,
> Полно глотку в гробе драть!
> Мир над миром существует,
> Вылезай из гроба прочь!"
> . . .
> Дева ручками взмахнула,
> Не поверила ушам,
> Доску вышибла, вспрыгнула,
> Хлоп! И лопнула по швам.
>
> И течет, течет бедняжка
> В виде маленьких кишок.

Где была ее рубашка,
Там остался порошок.
Изо всех отверстий тела
Червяки глядят несмело,
Вроде маленьких малют
Жидкость розовую пьют.

Была дева – стали щи.
Смех, не смейся, подожди!
Солнце встанет, глина треснет,
Мигом девица воскреснет.
Из берцовой из кости
Будет деревце расти,
Будет деревце шуметь,
Про девицу песни петь,
Про девицу песни петь ...

In the field there is a mound,
In the mound a young girl clamors:
"It is hard to lie in my coffin,
My small arms have turned black,
My hair is like dust,
Feather-grass grows from my breasts.
It is hard to lie in the grave,
My fine lips have rotted,
I have two small circles instead of eyes,
My sweetheart is not here!"

Death flies over the mound
Laughing and mourning,
Death shoots his rifle at the mound
And bending over says:
"Stop your nonsense, little one,
Stop bawling in your coffin!
A world exists above this world,
Climb out of your coffin!"
...
The girl began to flail her arms,
She could not believe her ears,
She knocked out a board, leapt up,
And bang! split apart at the seams.

And the poor thing oozes and oozes
What look like small intestines.
Where once was her blouse

Only powder remains.
From all the orifices of her body
Worms timidly peer out,
Like little babies
They drink the pink liquid.

There was a girl – and now there's soup.
Laughter, wait now, don't you dare!
The sun will rise, the clay will crack,
The girl will resurrect in a flash,
From her shinbone
A sapling will grow,
The sapling will rustle
And sing songs of the girl,
And sing songs of the girl ...

Wittily posed, "Temptation" illustrates Zabolotsky's understanding of death as oblivion: a "soup" or lack of coherence
among disparate particles. But once a tree sprouts, new life will
commence, characterized by a cohesive, integral form. Thus
transformation, or metamorphosis, is Zabolotsky's way of
overcoming death.[53]

Zabolotsky's focus on the particles of creation suggests a
familiarity with Fyodorov.[54] But however much his poetry
fosters a belief in immortality, it still acknowledges the fear of
death and oblivion. In fact, death is one of the major themes in
Zabolotsky's early verse,[55] despite the poet's protestations that
"death never did, does not and never will exist."[56] Predictably,
however, Zabolotsky's treatment of death is more often than
not ironic as he frequently uses animals to express man's
primal terror. The bull in Part Two of "The Triumph of
Agriculture" is full of angst:

Как понять мое сомненье?
Как унять мою тревогу?
Кажется, без потрясенья
День прошел – и слава Богу!
Однако, тут не все так просто,
На мне печаль как бы хомут.
На дно коровьего погоста,
Как видно, скоро повезут.
О стон гробовый!

Вопль унылый!
Там даже не построены могилы.

How can I understand my doubt?
How ease my fear?
It seems the day has passed
Without event – thank God!
But all is not so simple here,
Sadness weighs on me like a horse collar.
Surely I'll be taken soon
To the bottom of the cows' churchyard.
O deathly moan!
Doleful howl!
Graves are not constructed there.

Only the promise of resurrection (that "red atom of rebirth/
the fiery torch of life" ["Krasnyi atom vozrozhden'ia,/Zhizni
ognennyi fonar'" – "The Triumph of Agriculture"]) redeemed
earthly existence for Fyodorov, who adjudged it man's duty to
understand his essential components, his *prima materia*, so that
he could effect resurrection. Fyodorov believed that man could
work with this *prima materia* to reconstruct his race from sons
back to fathers. The genetic material is already there: "Vse
veshchestvo est' prakh predkov" ("All matter is the dust of
ancestors").[57] Man need only breathe new heat into the ashes,
so to speak, in order for them to flame anew. Zabolotsky, too,
considers the theme of *prima materia*, but he makes it seem
alchemistic and magical, as in "Pekarnia" ("The Bakery,"
1928), "Tsaritsa mukh" ("Queen of the Flies," 1930), "The
Mad Wolf," and "Venchanie plodami" ("A Crowning with
Fruits," 1932).

Fyodorov perceived mankind as a single large family bound
by a common ancestry and fate. Man's problems in the
modern world stem largely from the fact that he has lost touch
with this kinship and communality; this loss is the cause of
dissension. To rectify the situation, Fyodorov called for an
actual reacquaintance with one's past through the resurrection
of ancestors. Believing as he did that the foundation of each
individual life rests on the "bones of others,"[58] and that each
birth is at the expense of someone's death, Fyodorov con-

sidered sons duty bound to the task of resurrection. Fyodorov would have every living person devote his life to this communal task, this "common cause." Zabolotsky's progressive soldier in "The Triumph of Agriculture" mocks this stance. He does not believe in the benefits of resurrection; in fact, he claims that the ancestors who have appeared have no right to exist:

> Прочь! Молчать! Довольно! Или
> Расстреляю всех на месте!
> Мертвецам лежать в могиле,
> Марш в могилу, и не лезьте!
> Пусть попы над вами стонут,
> Пусть над вами воют черти,
> Я же, предками нетронут
> Буду жить до самой смерти!

> Off with you! Silence! Enough! or
> I'll shoot all of you on the spot!
> The dead should lie in their graves,
> March into your graves, don't crawl!
> Let priests moan over you,
> Let devils wail over you,
> But I, untouched by my ancestors,
> Will live until I die!

At the same time, Zabolotsky's soldier seems to personify Fyodorov's idea that progress is directly opposed to resurrection because it presumes the superiority of the current generation over the preceding one.[59] The passage is of particular interest because it reflects Zabolotsky's own irresolution. According to Fyodorov, the soldier could ensure his own immortality by helping to restore the ancestors. But even though Zabolotsky duly brings the ancestors to life, he makes them appear silly as he plays them off against the soldier. Paradoxically, though, he suggests that as an agent of reason, the soldier is unable to fathom what representatives of the dead past know, and thus he will be deprived of a deeper, secret knowledge.

Despite the insight the ancestors promise, there is no room in Zabolotsky's utopia for actual living beings with all of their emotional baggage. Instead, the poet prefers to bring past generations to life through nature, creating a union of man and environment in which the essential particles comprising man take on other forms at his death, lodging in trees and rocks, in rivers and streams. This idea of merging with nature gave Zabolotsky great peace, in contrast to the sense of continual struggle one detects in Fyodorov. For Fyodorov, the problem of immortality took on the proportions of a great battle against death, "the result of [man's] dependence on the blind force of nature, working within and outside us, uncontrolled by us."[60] To remedy this dependence (i.e., to abolish death), man must attain mastery over nature and learn to control it. Once man gains the upper hand, he will lead nature to its perfection – the ultimate aim being the regulation of the forces of life and death and the subsequent resurrection of the ancestors. And not only will these "fathers and mothers" resettle on all the planets of the universe; they will be morally and physically perfect, having been cleansed beforehand of all imperfections from their past life.

Fyodorov, and Tsiolkovsky after him, proclaimed an era of armies marching unhindered through time and space, moving in scientific detachments to master nature. Such detachments crop up in Zabolotsky's poetry, as does Fyodorov's image of nature as "blind," requiring the hand of man to perfect it. But if for Fyodorov and Tsiolkovsky the struggle with nature took the form of a serious battle *against* its forces, Zabolotsky had a gentler vision. He sought instead an interrelationship between man and his environment, their mutual understanding, and this he expressed through often whimsical imagery:

> . . .
> А там, внизу, деревья, звери, птицы,
> Большие, сильные, мохнатые, живые,
> Сошлись в кружок и на больших гитарах,
> На дудочках, на скрипках, на волынках
> Вдруг заиграли утреннюю песню,
> Встречая нас. И все кругом запело.
> И все кругом запело так, что козлик
> И тот пошел скакать вокруг амбара.
> И понял я в то золотое утро,
> Что смерти нет, и наша жизнь бессмертна.[61]
>
> "Утренняя песня" (1932)

...
And there below, trees, beasts, birds,
Large, strong, shaggy, lively,
Gathered into a circle and on large guitars,
On fifes, violins, on bagpipes,
Suddenly began to play a morning song,
Greeting us. And everything around began to sing.
And everything around began to sing so that
Even the kid went trotting around the barn.
And I understood on that golden morning
That there is no death, and our life is immortal.

"Morning Song" (1932)

"A MOST KIND AND RATIONAL ANIMAL"
(KONSTANTIN TSIOLKOVSKY)

Fyodorov's influence on others is evident from the many anecdotes that circulate about his life. One possibly apocryphal story recounts how he inspired the young Tsiolkovsky to devote his life to studying the cosmos. Fyodorov was explaining his theories of resurrection when Tsiolkovsky asked, "But how are all these people going to be squeezed onto Earth?" Fyodorov's reply that "there are plenty of stars" allegedly awakened Tsiolkovsky's interest in an expanded universe.[62]

Konstantin Tsiolkovsky (1857–1935) was the world's first great theoretician of interplanetary flight, but because the conservative Russian scientific establishment perceived him as too eccentric and his ideas as too far-fetched, he was thwarted in his experimentation by a lack of access to sophisticated equipment. Nevertheless, Tsiolkovsky managed to produce early designs for reaction vehicles and to invent primitive rockets. He continued to work in virtual obscurity until being discovered by the new Soviet government; then he was lavished with praise and awards. By that time Tsiolkovsky was already an old man, failing in health and physically unable to spend long hours in a laboratory. So he turned to promulgating the ideas that had long interested him – theories on the universe and man's rôle in it – based on his earlier, scientific investigations into the nature of creation. These tracts Tsiolkovsky published privately in Kaluga, the provincial city where he lived; they are both brilliant and eccentric. Random titles reveal his concerns: "Monizm vselennoi" ("The Monism of the Universe," 1925); "Budushchee zemli i chelovechestvo" ("The Future of the Earth and Mankind," 1928); "Rastenie budushchego. Zhivotnoe kosmosa. Samozarozhdenie" ("The Plant of the Future. The Animal of the Cosmos. Spontaneous Generation," 1929).

In addition to writing, Tsiolkovsky frequently lectured at Proletkult gatherings, and the Biocosmist poets were directly inspired by his ideas. He was friendly with such leading critics as Viktor Shklovsky[63] and was generally familiar to the Soviet intelligentsia. In particular, the painter Ivan Kudryashov knew Tsiolkovsky's work from the models his father had built for the scientist's rockets. It is likely that Kudryashov brought these designs to Malevich's attention, and that they are reflected in the cosmic utopianism of post-Revolutionary Suprematism.[64] Tatlin, too, had seen Tsiolkovsky's work. His 1920 Tower is remarkably similar to the buildings described in Tsiolkovsky's novel *Vne zemli* (*Beyond the Earth*) from the same year.[65] And in the late twenties Aleksandr Rodchenko made stage designs for a dramatization of the novel.[66]

Although Zabolotsky shared the concerns of the avant-garde, he was not in its mainstream and so did not encounter Tsiolkovsky's writings until late in 1931, after already completing "The Triumph of Agriculture." He was so struck by what he read that he immediately initiated a correspondence with the aging scientist, pleading for more books: "Your thoughts on the future of mankind struck me so greatly that now I will not rest until I read other works of yours ... It seems to me that the art of the future is so closely linked with science that the time has come for us to recognize and learn to love our best scholars – with you in the first place."[67] Zabolotsky was twenty-eight at the time.

One can only imagine the excitement Zabolotsky must have felt as he perused Tsiolkovsky's pamphlets. Here was a respected scientist (representing for Zabolotsky the discipline

of the future) whose utopian ideas coincided in many respects
with his own, and whose inclination toward Eastern religious
thought further heightened his appeal.[68] Yet despite his
obvious enthusiasm, Zabolotsky approached Tsiolkovsky's
writings critically. His own philosophy had germinated well
before he came across Tsiolkovsky's work, so although he drew
heavily on many of Tsiolkovsky's ideas, he retained his own
vision, becoming neither the dogmatist nor the mad theorist
Tsiolkovsky had. Much of Zabolotsky's poetry of the 1930s
represents a dialogue with Tsiolkovsky and his utopian
dreams.

For Tsiolkovsky, contemplation of the cosmos replaced any
organized religion. He believed the universe to be the result of
multitudinous explosions of rarefied matter aeons ago, a
conviction that found a good audience in the Soviet state with
its emphasis on science. Oddly enough, his belief in the cosmos
came about not only through his scientific calculations, but
from two eerie visions which convinced him of the existence of
otherworldly life and the possibility of interplanetary, even
intergalactic travel. Tsiolkovsky felt that man's full potential
had not yet been explored, that he must surpass the boundaries
of earthly existence in order to come into his own. Zabolotsky's
Mad Wolf echoes these aspirations as he gazes at the evening
star:

> Она мне душу вынимает,
> Сжимает судорогой уста.
> Желаю знать величину вселенной
> И есть ли волки наверху!
> А на земле я точно пленный
> Жую овечью требуху.

> [This star] tugs at my soul,
> Convulses my lips.
> I want to know the scope of the universe
> And whether there are wolves up there!
> On earth I'm like a captive,
> I chew the guts of sheep.

A Tsiolkovskian figure, the Mad Wolf knows that the path to
wisdom lies upwards. Only deep in the beyond will he find the
secrets of the universe, including his own wolfly potential.

Tsiolkovsky prided himself on his humanism and claimed to work for the benefit of mankind. Much of his appeal for Zabolotsky lay in the fact that his science was no dry, abstract discipline. For Tsiolkovsky, science was significant only in its relation to man, and his essay on "Nauchnaia etika" ("Scientific Ethics," 1930) attempts to define the proper balance between man and the modern world. Tsiolkovsky believed in the power of man to overcome the boundaries imposed by time and space and to settle freely throughout all solar systems of the universe, but he did not consider man ready to test his capabilities. Man must first adapt to the environment of the future by reaching a state of perfection. Nature, too, must be perfected before all the possibilities of the universe can be realized.

Tsiolkovsky perceived all matter as animated, likening the cosmos itself to "a most kind and rational animal."[69] Because matter is animated, it seemed to him endowed with the ability to feel, to experience happiness and sorrow. The ultimate aim of Tsiolkovsky's perfected world was to eradicate pain so that all matter – down to the tiniest atom – would feel nothing but happiness.[70] His perception of the universe may be termed anthropocosmism or even panpsychism (in their furthest extremes), but whatever the label, the idea of a living, breathing, feeling universe stirred Zabolotsky, appearing in his poetry of the 1930s. In "Lodeinikov," for instance, the grasses come alive as they engage in a terrible battle, crushing and smothering each other, losing their vital juices. Later in the poem, trampled flowers are presented from the perspective of the plants themselves, endowed with the universal ability to feel: "Tsvety ego kasalis' sapogov/I naklonialis'" ("The flowers touched his boots/And bowed down"). And in "Nachalo zimy" ("The Onset of Winter," 1935), Zabolotsky describes the real sufferings of nature as the seasons change:

Заковывая холодом природу,
Зима идет и руки тянет в воду.
Река дрожит и, чуя смертный час,
Уже открыть не может томных глаз,
И все ее беспомощное тело
Вдруг страшно вытянулось и оцепенело

И, еле двигая свинцовою волной,
Теперь лежит и бьется головой.

Fettering nature with its cold,
Winter comes and stretches its arms into the water.
The river trembles, sensing the fatal hour,
No longer can she open her languid eyes.
Suddenly, her whole helpless body
Tenses dreadfully, then freezes,
And barely moving her leaden waves,
She now lies still and beats her head.

Nature never dies completely in Zabolotsky's world. Though it
may lose consciousness ("Priroda v rechke nam izobrazila/
Skol'ziashchii mir soznan'ia svoego" ["In the river, nature
depicted to us/The slipping realm of its consciousness"]), it
will awaken again.

Tsiolkovsky's world never finally dies, either. He saw all of
nature as an uninterrupted cycle extending well beyond our
own conceptions of time and space and embracing all of
creation from the most minute particles to the grandest
expanses. While Tsiolkovsky's interest in expanding the
boundaries of the universe may be traced back to Fyodorov,
unlike his mentor he did not view the task of regulating nature
as obligatory and communal; rather, he believed that volun-
teers could be found. Furthermore, Tsiolkovsky had no use for
ancestors either on this planet or any other and recoiled at the
thought of their ancient superstitions polluting the progressive
world. Instead, he prophesied new generations of perfected
humans who would inhabit the entire universe. This new race
of people would be achieved through artificial selection (less
perfect humans would be forbidden to procreate),[71] and ultimately the universe would be populated only by happy, perfect
people who could travel about at will. Of course, even Tsiolkovsky realized his utopian dream could not come to pass
overnight. The immediate step was for man to conquer nature
on his own Earth, thus initiating the process of perfectivization
that finally would lead to a painless new life for all (for all who
were left, that is).

In his 1928 treatise "The Future of the Earth and
Mankind," Tsiolkovsky expounded his ideas on how man

must go about vanquishing nature. Marine animals would be killed to save them from suffering the predations of other beasts. On land, harmful snakes, insects and other horrors would be exterminated, and there would be no weather left to speak of. The blandness of this new world did not trouble Tsiolkovsky, for it would be maximally energy-efficient. Man would dominate an earth where both buildings and plants were structured to capture the sun's energy and use it to their greatest advantage. Once his environment was perfected, man would be ready to perfect his race.

Tsiolkovsky obviously believed in using nature to man's advantage. In spite of his conviction that all matter is living, he vouchsafed it no sentimentality, killing off thousands of plant and animal species in a single, short treatise, all in the name of eradicating evil from the universe. If evil for Fyodorov was exemplified by death, for Tsiolkovsky it represented anything that stood in the way of ultimate happiness for all atoms. Anything that hindered man's gaining dominance over the earth – which Tsiolkovsky believed would render all atoms happy – was an evil in his eyes.

Here Zabolotsky's philosophy inevitably diverged from Tsiolkovsky's. While he shared Tsiolkovsky's belief that all of nature is capable of emotion, Zabolotsky preserved a generous attitude toward it, evincing a pathos by which he as a man shared in nature's sufferings. Where Tsiolkovsky's "perfection" meant outright annihilation – the creation of a sterile atmosphere devoid of much that was truly natural – Zabolotsky's goal was to perfect nature by guiding and nurturing it. He did see man's rôle in terms of utilizing nature but made it clear that utilization did not mean exploitation: "The time will come when man, the exploiter of nature, will turn into man, the organizer of nature."[72] Zabolotsky, in fact, eschewed man's complete dominance over nature. In "Priroda chernaia, kak kuznitsa" ("Nature, Black as a Smithy"), nature becomes a pupil of man in order ultimately to become his teacher:

Природа черная, как кузница,
Кто ты – богиня или узница?
Когда бы ты была богиней,
То не дружила бы с пустыней.

Давно бы, верно, умерла.
Природа черная, как кузница,
Отныне людям будь союзница.
Тебя мы вылечим в больнице,
Посадим в школу за букварь,
Чтоб говорить умели птицы
И знали волки календарь.
Чтобы в лесу, саду и школе
Уж по своей, не нашей, воле
Природа, полная ума,
На нас работала сама.

Nature, black as a smithy,
Who are you – goddess or prisoner?
If you were a goddess
You would not have befriended the desert.
You likely would have died long ago.
Nature, black as a smithy,
Henceforth be the people's ally.
We will heal you in the hospital,
Seat you behind a primer in the school,
So that the birds might speak
And the wolves learn the calendar.
So that in the forest, garden and school
By your own will, no longer ours,
Nature, full of reason,
You yourself might work upon us.

Zabolotsky's poetic idea reflects Marx's dictum about free will, that freedom is necessity of which man has become fully conscious. The same would seem to apply to nature, which will act "by [its] own will" once it finally understands what is necessary.

Tsiolkovsky had his own ideas on the subject. In "The Will of the Universe" he wrote: "Our labor and thought will conquer nature." Nothing more exalted exists than a "strong and rational will," and "man himself is the manifestation of the will of the universe."[73] Although man believes that he acts by his will alone, he actually is fulfilling the greater will of the universe. He is the "master" ("khoziain") and the "ruler" ("gospodin") of nature, yet he is inextricably bound with the universe whose greater will is carried out through him. It is impossible to determine where man's will begins and the universe's leaves off, for they are as one.

How then is man's will to be carried out on earth? For Tsiolkovsky, the answer was simple enough: through "labor and thought," or in other words, technology. Technology — science and machines – would bring about the new order of the future. In "The Future of the Earth and Mankind," armies of men arrive to "utterly annihilate" ("unichtozhaiut do tla") the existing plant and animal life in the tropical regions. Similarly, in Zabolotsky's "Triumph of Agriculture" a tractor arrives to replace the plough and "utterly eradicate" the old world ("My staryi mir do tla snesem"). But where Tsiolkovsky's annihilation is frighteningly real, Zabolotsky's is basically metaphorical. Still, Zabolotsky was taken enough with the idea of a technological future to celebrate the machine in "The Triumph of Agriculture" and later in "Lodeinikov," where industry takes over as nature's new conductor (without, however, undermining man's essential oneness with nature):

> ... И среди полей
> Огромный город, возникая разом,
> Зажегся вдруг мильонами огней.
> Разрозненного мира элементы
> Теперь слились в один согласный хор,
> Как будто, пробуя лесные инструменты,
> Вступал в природу новый дирижер.
> Органам скал давал он вид забоев,
> Оркестрам рек – железный бег турбин
> И, хищника отвадив от разбоев,
> Торжествовал, как мудрый исполин ...
>
> Суровой осени печален поздний вид,
> Но посреди ночного небосвода
> Она горит, твоя звезда, природа,
> И вместе с ней душа моя горит.

> ... Suddenly a huge city,
> Arising all at once amid the fields,
> Lit up with millions of lights.
> The elements of the uncoordinated world
> Now merged into one harmonious chorus,
> As if a new conductor, testing the forest instruments,

Had entered into nature.

He pocked the organ-cliffs with pit-mines,
Gave the river orchestras the iron drive of turbines,
And curing the predator of pillage
He triumphed like a wise giant ...

The late face of stern autumn is sad,
But in the nighttime sky
Your star burns brightly, nature,
And together with it burns my soul.

It is important to bear in mind that while many of Zabolotsky's independently-developed ideas correspond with Tsiolkovsky's postulates, two very different genres are at issue.
Tsiolkovsky wrote tracts based in scientific theory, with an
added element of fantasy. Zabolotsky wrote poetry which plays
with both science and fantasy, but which is finally based in
metaphor. What connects the two is their common utopian
idea. Zabolotsky was struck by this coincidence of thought,
and after receiving a parcel of pamphlets from Tsiolkovsky, he
wrote to him again, this time quoting five stanzas from "The
Triumph of Agriculture" where the soldier presents his
utopian dream of "dwellings in the ether" ("zhilishcha efira").

In general, your thoughts on the future of the Earth, mankind,
animals and plants excite me greatly and are quite close to my own.
In my published long poems and verses I tried to solve them as best
I could. Now, after familiarizing myself with your work, I must
rethink a lot of it ... [There follows an 88-line quote from Chapter 5
of "The Triumph of Agriculture," beginning with "Cows, I had a
dream ..."]
    Thus, having settled people in space [*efir*], I left the earth for
animals and plants which develop into highly-organized beings.[74]

In the letter Zabolotsky also demonstrated his treatment of the
theme of transformation by quoting a fragment from "The
School of Beetles":

ШКОЛА ЖУКОВ
говорят люди будущего
Художники

... Мы нарисуем
Историю новых растений.

Дети простых садоводов –
Стали они словно бомбы.

Первое их пробужденье мы не забудем,
Час, когда в ножке листа обозначился мускул,
В теле картошки зачаток мозгов появился
И кукурузы глазок
Открылся на кончике стебля . . .

THE SCHOOL OF BEETLES
people of the future are speaking
Artists

. . . We shall draw
The history of new plants.
The children of simple gardeners –
They have become like bombs.

We shall not forget their first awakening,
The hour when in the foot of a leaf a muscle was revealed,
[When] in the body of a potato appeared the rudiment of brains
And the eye of corn
Opened on the tip of a stalk . . .

THE REALM OF ATOMS

The poetic fragments Zabolotsky quoted express the
imminence of a new and better world made possible by the
progress of technology. But while he agreed with Tsiolkovsky
on the importance of scientific advancement, he found another
of Tsiolkovsky's core ideas difficult to accept – that of man as a
"realm of atoms" ("gosudarstvo atomov"). In his correspondence with Tsiolkovsky, he voiced his skepticism. Tsiolkovsky
saw man – indeed, all of the universe – as made up of atoms.
Each atom could be broken down into its component parts,
and each of these parts was alive with an individual existence.
Furthermore, Tsiolkovsky considered "atoms and their parts
immortal, and therefore decayed matter is renewed once again
to yield life, a life that is even more perfect, according to the law
of progress."[75] Tsiolkovsky's law of progress is not unlike
Zabolotsky's principle of metamorphosis. But while both men
were concerned with the problem of death and re-creation,
their interpretations diverged.

Tsiolkovsky believed that in order for utopia to be achieved, all living matter down to the most minute part of an atom must feel happy,[76] the happiness of each individual particle yielding the greater happiness of the matter it comprises. He was preoccupied with these "worlds within worlds" ("miry v mirakh"), each of which he considered as complex as the solar system itself.[77] By seeing the universe – and man in particular – as a complex realm of immortal atoms, Tsiolkovsky was able handily to deal with death, considering it only an illusion of the weak human mind. Because the existence of the atom and of inorganic matter is not marked by memory or time, there can be no beginning or end to their existence, hence no "death" as we understand it. When a man "dies," Tsiolkovsky explained, the atoms from his particular realm disperse and form new connections in other bodies, thus creating new realms. They merge from an old life into a new, "subjective, uninterrupted, happy life." In the foreword to his "Monism of the Universe," Tsiolkovsky assured his readers that his new perception of the universe would bring them unmitigated joy, because "the cosmos contains only joy, satisfaction, perfection and truth." He explained that there is no death because the individual atoms do not die; only the particular realm they existed in ceases to function as such. The new realms may be formed in another human being, or in a plant, an animal, or even inorganic matter, since atoms are free to travel about the universe at will, combining and recombining.

But Tsiolkovsky disregarded the fact that the individual consciousness dies. This reality troubled Zabolotsky, who could not accept the idea of a "realm of atoms" breaking up at will. What then would happen to the individual, to the "I"? While Zabolotsky posited that man could come to life again through nature (compare Skovoroda as a rock or Pushkin in the foliage in "Yesterday, Pondering Death"), the man who previously existed – the man as such – would be lost forever when the atoms comprising him scattered throughout the universe. Zabolotsky wrote to Tsiolkovsky that the given association of atoms making up any individual seemed too precious to lose:

... It's not clear to me why my life will originate after death. If the atoms comprising my body wander throughout the universe and enter into other, more perfect organisms, then their given association will not be restored, and consequently I will not originate again. I assume that an atom getting into an organism from the outside will absorb the life of this organism and begin to think that it has lived in this organism from its very conception. But the same scenario will take place with each one of my atoms: they will enter into the composition of different organisms and absorb *their* life, forgetting about life in *my* body – exactly as they now have no memory of their previous existences.[78]

In this letter Zabolotsky stated that "feeling oneself to be a realm is, evidently, a new triumph for human genius"; he probably wished he could share Tsiolkovsky's peace of mind. He had already recognized the ability "to feel oneself a realm" in Khlebnikov, whose poem "Ia i Rossiia" ("Russia and Me") he subsequently quoted for Tsiolkovsky. Here the "I" appears as a realm of atoms, all of which are longing to be set free:

Россия тысячам тысяч свободу дала.
Милое дело! Долго будут помнить про это.
А я снял рубаху,
И каждый зеркальный небоскреб моего волоса,
Каждая скважина
Города тела
Вывесила ковры и кумачовые ткани.
Гражданки и граждане
Меня – государства
Тысячеоконных кудрей толпились у окон,
Ольги и Игори,
Не по заказу,
Радуясь солнцу, смотрели сквозь кожу,
Пала темница рубашки!
А я просто снял рубашку:
Дал солнце народам Меня
Голый стоял около моря –
Так я дарил народам свободу,
Толпам загара.

Russia gave freedom to thousands upon thousands.
A fine thing! Long will it be remembered.
But I took off my shirt,

And each mirrored skyscraper of my hair,
Each chink
In the city of my body
Hung out its carpets and red calico cloths.
The male and female citizens
Of me – of the realm
Of thousand-windowed curls crowded at these windows,
Olgas and Igors,
Not on command,
Rejoicing in the sun, they looked through my skin.
The dungeon of the shirt had fallen!
But I simply took off my shirt:
Gave sun to the peoples of Me
Stood naked next to the sea –
Thus to the peoples I granted freedom,
To the throngs – a suntan.

Khlebnikov in this poem, and Tsiolkovsky in general, conceived of the universe in terms of its smallest particles. Zabolotsky chose instead to regard the mass first as an entity, then proceed from this larger aggregate to its smaller components.[79] The composite of interrelated parts interested him, not the individual particles which separately could hold no meaning. He explained to Tsiolkovsky: "The more perfect the organism, the better each of its component parts feels. The more perfect the atom – the better the electron feels, the more perfect the man – the better the atom, and the more perfect human society, the better it is for the man. Personal immortality is possible only in the organization itself. Neither man, nor atom, nor electron is immortal."[80] Understanding the workings of nature – its organization – will allow man to live on within it.

As early as 1929–30, when Zabolotsky was writing "The Triumph of Agriculture," he already sensed that death need not be absolute: "Smerti blednaia podkova/Prosveshchennym ne strashna" ("The pale horseshoe of death/Does not frighten the enlightened"). And in "The Mad Wolf" he wrote:

Тому, кто видел, как сияют звезды,
Тому, кто мог с растеньем говорить,
Кто понял страшное соединенье мысли –
Смерть не страшна и не страшна земля.

He who has seen how the stars shine,
Who can talk with plants,
Who has understood the terrifying conjunction of thought –
To him death is not terrifying, nor is the earth.

Yet Zabolotsky still had to wrestle with the problem of individual death, an issue Tsiolkovsky treated all too dispassionately, focussed as he was on the atom rather than the man. Zabolotsky voiced his struggle in "Lodeinikov":

Природы вековечная давильня
Соединяла смерть и бытие
В один клубок, но мысль была бессильна
Соединить два таинства ее.

The eternal winepress of nature
United death and existence
Into a single mass, but thought was powerless
To unite its [nature's] two secrets.

"Thought" is powerless to unite life and death because it refuses to relinquish the notion of an individual I, an I that would be lost at man's decease. Transformation, however, can lead to an understanding of the universe even as it negates the finality of death:

Так, путешествуя
Из одного тела в другое,
Вырастает таинственный разум.
"Школа жуков"

Thus, travelling
From one body into another,
Mysterious reason grows.
"The School of Beetles"

And a recombination of particles (a metamorphosis, in effect) might afford a preview of the future:

Надеюсь, этой песенкой
Я порастряс частицы мирозданья
И в будущее ловко заглянул.
"Безумный волк"

I hope that with this song
I've shaken the particles of creation
And peeked cleverly into the future.
"The Mad Wolf"

By 1947, Zabolotsky could write with conviction:

> Я не умру, мой друг. Дыханием цветов
> Себя я в этом мире обнаружу.

> I shall not die, my friend. In the breathing of flowers
> I shall detect myself in this world.

The future he envisions differs markedly from Tsiolkovsky's, however. Where Tsiolkovsky's utopia is populated by a bland, perfected race of people, Zabolotsky's has a slew of eager animals and plants. His universe boasts abundant living species, unlike Tsiolkovsky's sterile cosmos. And where Tsiolkovsky destroys in order to create new life, Zabolotsky transforms without complete destruction, attempting to recreate the existing world in new terms. Zabolotsky's poetry does, however, present a pattern not unlike Tsiolkovsky's "law of progress": the infant world born in torment in "The Triumph of Agriculture" is the last to endure the suffering of birth, and each successive world in the later poetry has already been perfected to a degree. The Chairman in "The Mad Wolf" affirms this progression:

> Века идут, года уходят,
> Но все живущее – не сон:
> Оно живет и превосходит
> Вчерашней истины закон.

> Ages pass, the years go by,
> But all that's living is no dream:
> It lives and surpasses
> The law of yesterday's truth.

Furthermore, the society of wolves, born well after the infant world in "The Triumph of Agriculture," already realizes that the future of life is not limited to earth alone, but extends into the cosmos as well:

> Мы, волки, несем твое вечное дело
> Туда, на звезды, вперед!

> We wolves will carry your eternal cause
> Ever forward, to the stars!

NATURE TRANSFORMED

With such bombast, Zabolotsky's wolves may be seen as latter-day Futurists echoing Marinetti's proclamation, "Erect, on the summit of the world, we are casting once again our challenge to the stars."[81] But the future portrayed in Zabolotsky's verse is not militant like Marinetti's. Instead, Zabolotsky offers a strangely lulling vision of a diverse, yet balanced universe, bound by communality and lit by vivid constellations which incorporate all of the rich variety of life on earth. In his "Merknut znaki zodiaka" ("The Signs of the Zodiac Flicker," 1929) dogs, sparrows, flies, flounders, beetles, spiders and cows share the skies with witches, goblins, naiads, and cannibals:

> Меркнут знаки Зодиака
> Над просторами полей.
> Спит животное Собака,
> Дремлет птица Воробей.
> Толстозадые русалки
> Улетают прямо в небо, –
> Руки крепкие, как палки,
> Груди круглые, как репа.
> Ведьма, сев на треугольник,
> Превращается в дымок.
> С лешачихами покойник
> Стройно пляшет кекуок.
> А за ними бледным хором
> Ловят Муху колдуны,
> И стоит над косогором
> Неподвижный лик луны.
>
> Меркнут знаки Зодиака
> Над постройками села,
> Спит животное Собака,
> Дремлет рыба Камбала.
> Колотушка тук-тук-тук,
> Спит животное Паук,
> Спит Корова, Муха спит,
> Над землей луна висит.
> Над землей большая плошка
> Опрокинутой воды.

Леший вытащил бревешко
Из мохнатой бороды,
Из-за облака сирена
Ножку выставила вниз,
Людоед у джентельмена
Неприличное отгрыз.
Все смешалось во общем танце
И летят во все концы
Гамадриллы и британцы,
Ведьмы, блохи, мертвецы.

Кандидат былых столетий,
Полководец новых лет –
Разум мой! Уродцы эти –
Только вымысел и бред.
Только вымысел, мечтанье,
Сонной мысли колыханье,
Безутешное страданье –
То чего на свете нет.

Высока земли обитель.
Поздно, поздно. Спать пора.
Разум, бедный мой воитель,
Ты заснул бы до утра.
Что сомненья, что тревоги?
День прошел и мы с тобой –
Полузвери, полубоги –
Засыпаем на пороге
Новой жизни трудовой.

Колотушка тук-тук-тук.
Спит животное Паук,
Спит Корова, Муха спит.
Над землей луна висит.
Над землей большая плошка
Опрокинутой воды . . .
Спит растение Картошка
Засыпай скорей и ты!

The signs of the Zodiac
Flicker over open plains.
The Dog is sleeping,
Sparrow Bird is slumbering.
Water nymphs with fat behinds
Fly away straight to the sky,

Their hands are strong as wood,
Their breasts are round as turnips.
A witch seated on a tripod
Is transformed into smoke.
A corpse gracefully dances
The cakewalk with wood elves.
After them, in a pale chorus,
Wizards catch the Fly,
And above the hillside
Stands the moon's immobile face.

The signs of the Zodiac
Flicker over village buildings,
The Dog is sleeping,
Flounder Fish is slumbering.
Little Beetle tap-tap-tap,
Spider's sleeping fast,
Cow sleeps, Fly sleeps,
Over earth hangs the moon.
Over earth, a large saucer
Of overflowing water.
A Wood Gnome pulled a little log
From his shaggy beard,
From behind a cloud, a siren
Thrust out her foot,
From a gentleman, a cannibal
Gnawed off his private parts.
All merged in a common dance
And baboons, Britons,
Witches, fleas, and corpses
Fly about in all directions.

Candidate of bygone ages,
Captain of new years,
O my Psyche! These monsters
Are only ravings and inventions.
Only dreamings and inventions,
Glimmerings of sleepy thought,
Inconsolable distress –
That can't be found on earth.

Earth's abode is high.
Late, so late. It's time to sleep.
Psyche, my poor warrior,

You should sleep till morn.
Why have doubts, why worries?
Day has passed, and you and I –
Half barbaric, half divine –
Fall asleep upon the threshold
Of a new life filled with toil.

Little Beetle tap-tap-tap.
Spider's sleeping fast,
Cow sleeps, Fly sleeps,
Over earth hangs the moon.
Over earth, a large saucer
Of overflowing water . . .
Sweet Potato has dozed off,
Now it is your turn to sleep!

Zabolotsky presents his version of the universe in images
that are both comforting (tapping beetles and sleeping cows)
and troubling (cannibals, wizards and witches). Here is the
zodiac in grotesque animation. With its strong trochaic beat
and dream visions, the poem is like a lullaby; at the same time
it is hallucinatory, full of "ravings" and "inventions," veering
off from the delightful and childish into the monstrous, like an
X-rated Disney cartoon. From this poem it is evident that
Zabolotsky is not after perfection in his universe, but variety,
and he makes his world large enough to encompass many
different forms of life. Like Khlebnikov's creations, Zabolotsky's come together in a "common dance," transcending
time and space and acknowledging their deep kinship. As for
man, he straddles the threshold of a new era of labor, mindful
of both the past and the future, his ostensible child's vision
informed by an adult consciousness.

Zabolotsky offers his readers solace, introducing them to a
world where transformations negate the finality of death. His
vision is, finally, an optimistic one. In his dream of seeking a
mastery over the problem of death, and in dreaming of a
Golden Age, Zabolotsky continued the Russian tradition of
home-grown utopian thought.[82]

CHAPTER 4

Mad wisdom: the long poems

Wahnsinn, der sich klug gebärdet!
Weisheit, welche überschnappt!
Heinrich Heine, *Atta Troll*

Not long before his death, Zabolotsky described a play he
wanted to write, "a play in which the characters were people,
stones, animals, plants, thoughts, atoms. The action would
take place in the most diverse places – from interplanetary
space to a living cell."[1] Zabolotsky possessed an abiding
interest in the interrelationships of the universe, a theme he
had broached in the 1920s in his first poems on nature. In these
early works, man more often than not emerges as the loser in
his tenuous relationship with the environment – an unconventional, if not antagonistic, stance for those years when writers
were expected to depict man in control of natural forces.
Instead of working to exploit nature, Zabolotsky's man finds
himself trapped within it and its ceaseless transformations:

> Лес качается, прохладен,
> Тут же разные цветы,
> И тела блестящих гадин
> Меж камнями завиты.
> Солнце, жаркое, простое,
> Льет на них свое тепло.
> Меж камней тела устроя,
> Змеи гладки, как стекло.
> Прошумит ли сверху птица
> Или жук провоет смело
> Змеи спят, запрятав лица
> В складках жареного тела.
> И загадочны, и бедны,

153

Спят они, открывши рот,
А вверху едва заметно
Время в воздухе плывет.
Год проходит, два проходит,
Три проходит. Наконец,
Человек тела находит –
Сна тяжелый образец.
Для чего они? Откуда?
Оправдать ли их умом?
Но прекрасных тварей груда
Спит, разбросана кругом.
И уйдет мудрец, задумчив.
И живет, как нелюдим,
И природа, вмиг наскучив,
Как тюрьма, стоит над ним.

"Змеи" (1929)

The cool forest sways,
Here various flowers sprout,
And the bodies of sparkling reptiles
Are coiled among the rocks.
The sun, direct and hot,
Pours its heat upon them.
Arranging their bodies among the rocks,
The snakes are sleek as glass.
Whether a bird chatters overhead
Or a beetle boldly wails,
The snakes sleep, hiding their faces
In the folds of their roasting flesh.
Poor and enigmatic,
They sleep with open mouths,
And up above, barely perceptible,
Time floats in the air.
A year elapses, two years,
Three. Finally,
A man finds the bodies –
The heavy pattern of sleep.
What is their purpose? Where do they come from?
Can they be justified by the mind?
The heap of splendid creatures
Sleeps, scattered around.
Pensive, the wise man departs.
He lives antisocially,

And nature, bored in an instant,
Stands over him like a prison.

"Snakes" (1929)

Having glimpsed the metamorphoses of nature, the wise observer retreats into solitude to ponder these mysteries without distraction, for until he understands them he will continue to feel oppressed. The poem is spared a dark vision, however, as Zabolotsky acknowledges the magic of the universe alongside its mystery. The snakes basking in the sun appear as brilliant jewels, and they shed their skins like escape artists, leaving behind no trace of living flesh. Their essence continues to be felt in the discarded skins, which seem suspended in time, more alive than dead.

This awareness of a magical presence is keenly sensed in another poem begun in the same year as "Snakes": "The Triumph of Agriculture." Here, in his first long poem, Zabolotsky abandoned the city once and for all and turned his attention instead to the countryside and collectivization, the leading question of the day. Just as his neophyte imagination had been struck by the city with its constantly shifting faces, so now Zabolotsky turned back with fresh eyes to the land and the tumultuous changes taking place where he had been born, bringing a wealth of knowledge and a highly developed sense of play to the serious questions about nature he was debating. While such hallmarks of his early verse as innovation, verbal pranks, and a penchant for the grotesque contributed to the poem's bold style, a conscious philosophical dimension added new depth. The result is a highly intellectual, yet extraordinarily animated poem with dramatic personae ranging from an anxious bull to a dilapidated plough, each of which expresses a keen view of the new world being created by man.

"The Triumph of Agriculture" posits a universe that is animate in all of its aspects, from infinitesimal particles to infinite space; as we have seen, this view provoked strong and quick critical reaction. Censors seized the issue of the journal carrying "The Triumph of Agriculture" and excised the poem. In order to salvage their issue, the journal's editorial board substituted a new version of the poem, drastically changing its tone,[2] but Zabolotsky still found himself out of step with the changing literary orders of the day. He was stunned by the force of the critics' rancor. Had he not written a poem that took as its major theme the transformation of the countryside through labor, leading to a new, productive era for all? Surely this idea was in keeping with the new models for literature and very much in the spirit of the times. But as Zabolotsky discovered, the problem with "The Triumph of Agriculture" lay not so much in its theme as in his expression of it.

"THE TRIUMPH OF AGRICULTURE"

In a prologue and seven parts, "The Triumph of Agriculture" tells its tale of rural transformation. In Part One, "A Conversation About the Soul," peasants avidly discuss the question of mortality: does a soul remain after death or only "stinking gas"? The peasants feel oppressed by nature's unpredictability, agreeing that lately nature has seemed particularly chaotic, even sinister. Part Two, "The Sufferings of the Animals," is narrated from the animals' point of view. They are even gloomier than the peasants as they contemplate their fate. The conversation is led by a bull who describes the horrors of anonymous death in a slaughteryard. Part Three, "The Exile," shifts back to the human realm, where a self-satisfied kulak flaunts his prosperity in the midst of "blighted nature," ignoring the dying crops around him. He is ruining the harvest for his own personal gain. As he counts his money, the night grows deeper, becoming "witch-like" in a developing storm, and the raging wind howls its vision of nature transformed through electricity. As Part Four, "A Battle with the Ancestors," begins, so does the storm. By Part Five, "The Beginning of Science," a new and peaceful day has dawned. A soldier relates his fabulous dream of an "Animal Institute" where life is always healthy, happy and progressive. The arrival of a tractor signals the advent of a new era, and Part Six, "The Infant World," describes this new life.

The final section of the poem, "The Triumph of Agriculture," portrays a transformed world where machinery has replaced manual labor. Science has been incorporated into the villagers' lives: an old man explains philosophy to a dog while an engineer explicates mechanical designs to some cows. But beyond the surface contentment of village life, nature continues its relentless cycle of life and death as worms begin their work of decomposition on the plough. And as the newly-literate peasants read their newspapers, the evening above them "floats through the air, laughing."

By choosing to read "The Triumph of Agriculture" as a lampoon of Stalin's policies, the critics misunderstood the prevailing spirit of play in Zabolotsky's poem. Worse, they perceived the poem as a breach of faith on the part of Zabolotsky who, as a Soviet poet, was expected to uphold and glorify the socialist State. Such catchwords as "class enemy," "bourgeois" and "formalistic" appeared in the reviews with frightening frequency, given the fate of others who fell from official grace. Yet Zabolotsky's intentions in the poem were far from satirical; indeed, "The Triumph of Agriculture" may be interpreted as a paean to the new age of collective farming.

Words had to be chosen carefully in the Soviet Union of the early thirties, but an indictment of the times does not sufficiently explain the discrepancy between authorial intention and readers' interpretation. The problems Zabolotsky encountered lie in the tone of his poem and in the devices he used. For one thing, "The Triumph of Agriculture" expresses ambiguity both as an aesthetic stance and as a mark of the poet's own conflicts. Furthermore, the poem is rife with images of a grotesque and carnivalesque nature, which by definition contain a certain degree of derision. While this secondary satirical element was wrongfully perceived as dominant, it does place the poem within the genre of Saturnalian poetry, where utopian thought is closely linked with satire.[3] Zabolotsky necessarily made his poem political by expressing his dream of social equality; by giving voice to many different creatures, he repeatedly "challenge[d] the claims of a dominant hierarchy."[4] Critics who expected an unequivocally loyal voice felt their hackles rise, and they were further offended to find not only that different people speak in Zabolotsky's poem, but that spirits, animals, and objects are given voice, too. This aspect of whimsy led a number of critics to call Zabolotsky *"iurodivyi"* and to cite "The Triumph of Agriculture" as an instance of *iurodstvo*, by which they meant absurdity.[5] Particularly in the Middle Ages, but also continuing into more modern times, *iurodivye* or "holy fools in God" roamed the Russian countryside, placing themselves at the people's mercy and offering in return supposedly God-granted divinations. Their posture as fools was often consciously adopted in order to disguise social and political criticisms. By casting Zabolotsky as a *iurodivyi*, the critics implied that his poem represented a masked attack against governmental policies.

Although they were correct in finding elements of both satire and folly in Zabolotsky's poetry, the critics failed to understand them as part of the poet's larger system of imagery based in play and fully in keeping with the traditions of Saturnalian verse. Saturnalia presupposes a return of the Golden Age of Saturn, an age in which abundance and gaiety dominate.[6] The earliest description of this age as a utopian ideal is found in Hesiod's *Works and Days*, where a life free from anxiety and toil is recalled. Virgil, too, evokes a golden age in the *Georgics*, but in contrast to Hesiod, his new era is predicated on labor, which serves as an agent of transformation. In the motto of *labor omnia vincit*, we find the premise for Zabolotsky's "Triumph of Agriculture," where a new and better life transpires through the efforts of man.

Zabolotsky's depiction of a refashioned world is not clear-cut, however. The new world of "The Triumph of Agriculture" does not simply supersede the old; rather, it emerges through a complex process of transformation whereby the old world is "turned inside out," resulting in a certain "regeneration of archaic forms"[7] and finally in a new society where elements of a chaotic past continue to coexist with all the attributes of a modernized present.[8]

PROPHETIC DREAMS

Yevgeny Zamyatin has written that "utopias bear a + sign,"[9] by which he meant that in a utopian presentation, positive elements predominate. When the reverse is true, the depiction appears as satire.[10] Even though Zabolotsky freely incorporates negative elements into "The Triumph of Agriculture" by means of grotesque imagery, and even though the laughter that prevails is undercut by the demonic,[11] the balance in the poem is tipped toward the positive. Such dynamics between positive and negative rendered "The Triumph of Agriculture" both comic and dangerous. Playing poetically with the powers of darkness,[12] Zabolotsky unwittingly entered a game where the stakes proved excessively high.

The tension between the plus and minus signs in "The Triumph of Agriculture" is evident right from the start. The very title of the poem indicates its utopian nature: carnival, as an expression of the utopian ideal, is a festive, triumphant (*torzhestvennyi, torzhestvuiushchii*) time, the affirmation of better days ahead. When agriculture triumphs,[13] "Budet uzhin i uzhín" ("There will be supper and harvested hay," Part 7). In ancient times, people prayed to Saturn, the god of agriculture, for a good yield. Since carnival is a celebration of the return of Saturn's Golden Age, Zabolotsky's title carries a double meaning: not only will agriculture triumph, but by implication the age of Saturn will as well.

"The Triumph of Agriculture" describes a world in which the sufferings of animals cease and the plight of mankind is alleviated. But this utopia develops from a Prologue where, in sharp contrast to the poem's millennial title, the presence of sinister forces is sensed:

> Нехороший, но красивый –
> Это кто глядит на нас?
> То мужик неторопливый
> Сквозь очки уставил глаз.
> Белых житниц отделенья
> Поднимались в отдаленье,
> Сквозь окошко хлеб глядел,
> В загородке конь сидел.
> Тут природа вся валялась
> В страшно диком беспорядке:
> Кое-где дерево шаталось,
> Там – реки струилась прядка,
> Тут – стояли две-три хаты

Над безумным ручейком.
Идет медведь продолговатый
Как-то поздно вечерком.
А над ним – на небе тихом
Безобразный и большой
Журавель летает, с гиком
Потрясая головой.
Из клюва развевался свиток,
Где было сказано: "Убыток
Дают трехпольные труды."
Мужик гладил конец бороды.

Sinister, but beautiful –
Who is it that peers at us?
A peasant slowly
Fixes his gaze through his glasses.
Segments of white granaries
Arise in the distance,
Grain peeks through a window,
A horse sits in his yard.
All of nature welters
In wild and terrible disorder:
A tree staggers off somewhere,
There, a strand of river surges,
Here, two-three cabins hover
Above a raging streamlet.
Sometimes an oblong bear
Walks late into the evening.
Above him, in the silent sky,
Ugly and huge,
Flies a crane, whooping
And shaking its head.
From its beak a scroll unwinds,
Where is said: "Three-field
Labors yield loss."
The peasant strokes the tip of his beard.

A presence that is unseen but felt, the terrible chaos of nature, a stream that is "mad," not babbling – all contribute to a sense of terror as remembered from childhood. This terror, however, also involves awe, since the unknown force is "beautiful" as well as "sinister." Fascinated, we are drawn into the poem. The mention of childhood here is not arbitrary, for Zabolotsky's language recalls children's rhymes in both diction and tone. The grain peers out from a small window ("okoshko") like a mischievous Gingerbread Man or *kolobok*.[14] And the regular trochees of the first two lines recall riddle form as they pose their question. Zabolotsky's personification of both animals and inanimate objects is also a familiar device from fairy tales.

This use of the diction of fairy tales supports the utopian idea of "The Triumph of Agriculture." In general, motifs and stylistic techniques from the fairy-tale genre were widely used in the literature of post-Revolutionary Russia as a way of demonstrating a utopian future in an idealized present.[15] Not only was the fairy tale deeply rooted in the Russian consciousness, it was instructive as well. The fledgling Soviet government faced a whole nation of naive children who had suddenly to be educated in the changing ways of the world, and fairy tales provided a wealth of hortative lessons: greed is man's undoing; laziness is a vice; evil ultimately will be vanquished by good. But while fairy tales acknowledged the magic of the universe in its unexplained mysteries, the new Soviet tales, diverging from the tradition, sought to explain everything in scientific terms. The geniality of Zabolotsky's art lies largely in his concept of a scientific utopia which nevertheless admits to the magic of the universe and unexplained presences in the world.

The form of the Prologue reflects the way in which Zabolotsky mixes the different traditions: here trochees, a meter associated with folk verse, are used in the service of a *poema*, an epic form. The Prologue represents a battleground of forces, where *starina* (the old) vies with *novizna* (the new). We find the old in the countryside, where such words as *valialas'* "weltered", *besporiadok* "disorder", *shatalos'* "staggered", *struilas'* "surged", and *bezumnyi* "mad" point up its chaos. Yet this entire vocabulary is confined to a highly regular meter, so that despite the *besporiadok* of nature, the stanza manifests an overriding sense of *poriadok* or order (a function of the new) – at least until the very end. The trochaic tetrameters shift to iambs in lines 15 and 21–24, but until the final line the beat is regular, as is the consistent pattern of alternating masculine and feminine rhyme endings. Only the last word of the stanza, *borody*, breaks the meter (◡–◡–◡–◡◡–), ending the Prologue on a jarring note and creating ambiguity.

The imagery of the stanza also expresses discordancy, even though the chaos is ostensibly under control. Here Zabolotsky employs the grotesque by not strictly observing the distinctions between various categories of being. He blurs the differences among humans, animals, and plants, stressing instead their commonality as inhabitants of the same universe. In rapid succession he presents a muzhik; followed by grain animated to peek out a window; then a horse; then Nature "lolling in terrible and wild disorder." Next comes a loafing tree; then an "oblong bear"; and finally an ugly crane. The various animate and personified living forms appear as if in a wild circus procession, evoking a carnival atmosphere. In its colorful imagery affording a highly visual panorama of the village, Zabolotsky's scene may be compared to the vivid depictions of village life painted by Bruegel.[16] And like Bruegel's world, Zabolotsky's is askew; only his fancifulness offsets the grotesque.

The last creature in the procession is a crane, which appears bearing a highly modern message in striking incongruity with its primordial mien. This bird threatens to impose order onto the chaotic countryside by introducing *ratio* into illogicality through a more productive method of crop rotations. Russia's time-honored three-field system was not easily abolished. In fact, Zabolotsky's father had tried to teach the local peasants about productivity as early as 1912 or 1913. Kim Vasin remembers how "the agronomist . . . said it was time to change from three-field to nine-field labors, that they had to sow clover and invest in machinery."[17] The intrusiveness of the official message is marked by the high frequency of gutterals accompanying the bird's whooping arrival: *gik, golovoi, kliuva, svitok, ubytok*. The crane also signals the metrical shift into iambs that eventually break down in the final line. But even though the bird is prophetic, a harbinger of the future, it still resonates with the past. Two thousand years earlier, Hesiod had offered this advice:

At the time when you hear the cry of the crane
going over, that annual
voice from high in the clouds, you should take notice and
make plans.[18]

Zabolotsky offers the same message, only his peasant is likely
to resist. The Prologue ends as the peasant strokes his beard in
contemplation.

The transformations augured by the crane are far-reaching
and based in scientific achievement. Significantly, the details
of the transformed world are seen in the dream of a soldier who
represents the more rational future:

> Коровы, мне приснился сон.
> Я спал, овчиною закутан,
> И вдруг открылся небосклон
> С большим животным институтом.
> Там жизнь была всегда здорова ...
> . . . .
> Я дале видел красный светоч
> В чертоге умного вола,
> Коров задумчивое вече
> Решало там свои дела.
> Осел, над ними гогоча,
> Бежал, безумное урча:
> Рассудка слабое растенье
> В его животной голове
> Сияло, как произведенье
> По виду близкое к траве.
> Осел скитался по горам,
> Глодал чугунные картошки,
> А под горой машинный храм
> Выделывал кислородные лепешки.
> Там кони – химии друзья –
> Хлебали щи из ста молекул,
> Иные, в воздухе вися,
> Смотрели, кто с планет приехал.
> Корова, в формулах и лентах,
> Пекла пирог из элементов
> И перед нею в банке рос
> Большой химический овес.
> . . . .
> Здесь учат бабочек труду,[19]
> Ужу дают урок науки –

Как делать пряжку и слюду,
Как шить перчатки или брюки.
Здесь волк с железным микроскопом
Звезду вечернюю поет,
Здесь вол, зачитываясь Попом,
Назад во времени плывет ...

Cows, I had a dream.
I was sleeping, wrapped in sheepskin,
When suddenly the horizon opened
And I beheld a great animal institute.
There, life was always wholesome ...
....
Next I saw a red torch
In the hall of a wise ox.
A pensive council of cows
Was deciding its affairs.
Chortling, an ass
Ran about, rumbling madness:
In his animal's head
The frail growth of reason
Shimmered like a product
Close to grass in appearance.
The ass wandered through the mountains
Gnawing cast-iron potatoes,
While under the mountain a mechanical temple
Isolated tablets of oxygen.
There, horses – friends of chemistry –
Ate a cabbage soup of one hundred molecules,
While others, hanging in the air,
Watched for animals from other planets.
A cow in formulas and tapes,
Baked a pie of elements
And before her in a jar grew
Great chemical oats.
....
Here they teach butterflies labor,
They give grass snakes lessons in science –
How to make yarn and mica,
How to sew gloves and pants.
Here a wolf, with an iron microscope,
Sings the evening star,
Here an ox, reading Pope,
Flies backwards in time ...

9 Zabolotsky's caricature of his son, Nikita, as a
"learned agronomist," 1950s

Here is the essence of Zabolotsky's early utopian vision. The world the soldier envisions is distinguished not so much by comfort as by enlightenment: although the animals at the Institute are still "wreathed" in "incomplete consciousness," they work hard at improving their ken. The "bloody art of living" has given way to a chemical diet that causes no one pain. The future is a scientific utopia in which the animals, free to pursue their own interests, peacefully seek answers to the mysteries of the universe.[20] Zabolotsky departs from the norm in his dream of equality not just for people, but for animals and plants as well. This mix of the rural and the technological sets Zabolotsky apart, and much of the originality of his utopian idea lies in his conception of a perfected society where the machine age coexists with the pastoral. Rarely do such disparate visions coincide.

Zabolotsky's soldier represents a typical Russian idealist in that he sees the future in his dreams – unlike his Western counterpart, who more often finds it in his travels.[21] But revelations of the future are not limited to humans in Zabolotsky's poem. The animals are also privy to a deeper insight and are, in fact, the first to witness a utopian vision. Huddled in a shed, in the midst of nocturnal gloom and despair,

> Казалось – прорван мир двойной,
> И за обломком тканей плотных
> Простор открылся голубой!
>
> "Вижу я погост унылый,"
> Сказал бык, сияя взором,
> "Там, на дне сырой могилы,
> Кто-то спит за косогором.
> Кто он – жалкий, весь в коростах,
> Полусъеденный, забытый,
> Житель бедного погоста,
> Грязным венчиком покрытый?

> The binary world, it seemed, was pierced:
> Beyond a shred of dense tissues [i.e., clouds]
> A light blue expanse spread open.
>
> "I see a melancholy country churchyard,"
> Said the bull with radiant gaze,

"There at the bottom of a damp grave,
Someone sleeps beyond the hillside.
Who is he – pitiful, scab-encrusted,
Half-eaten, forgotten,
The inhabitant of a poor churchyard,
Covered with a filthy wreath?"

This passage evokes Khlebnikov, since light blue is a recurrent color in his poetry and is associated with creative power.[22] The visionary bull relates the poet's sad fate, to lie buried and half-rotten in a forgotten churchyard, crowned with a "filthy" *venchik* (the wreath placed on the deceased by Orthodox custom). However, in defiance of the physiological process of putrefaction, the poet's artistic creation, "The Tablets of Destiny" (*Doski sud'by*), hovers above him "undecayed," "the wise witnesses to his life." Despite his decomposition, Khlebnikov emerges as a symbol of lasting art and a diviner of fate, whose "Tablets" proclaim a utopia of freedom and equality. Zabolotsky took Khlebnikov's ideas about liberation to heart, and the prophecy of the latter's vision of harmony seems realized at the end of Zabolotsky's poem,[23] where the sky is awash in Khlebnikov blue:

Крестьяне, сытно закусив,
Газеты длинные читают,
Тот – бреет бороду, красив,
А этот – буквы составляет.
Младенцы в глиняные дудки
Дудят, размазывая грязь,
И вечер цвета незабудки
Плывет по воздуху, смеясь.

The peasants, having eaten well,
Read long newspapers.
That one, handsome, shaves his beard,
While this one does his alphabet.
Smearing dirt,
Infants toot on their clay pipes,
And evening the color of a forget-me-not
Floats through the air, laughing.

Yet even as the strong, final word of the poem expresses pervasive mirth – laughter so widespread it infects the very air

– the image of the laughing sky communicates the presence of something sinister in the newly-created world. Zabolotsky's inverted universe is simultaneously funny and frightening,[24] and this conjunction caused him trouble. The critics construed his impish sense of play as blasphemous in the serious context of a poem about collectivization; one critic went so far as to complain that instead of calling forth fear (*strakh*), [he] elicits a smile (*ulybka*)."[25] In fact, Zabolotsky's laughing sky manifests a dual nature, acknowledging the presence of a never-distant demonic force even as it represents all that is life-affirming and renewing, particularly in connection with agriculture. In early societies peasants would laugh as they sowed their fields in order to ensure a fruitful harvest; they hoped to provoke the earth goddess to laughter so that the grass and grain would flourish.[26] The laughter in "The Triumph of Agriculture" may be seen as a ritual performed by an unnamed divinity as he creates the world anew,[27] with the potential for both cruelty and grace. It is left for the reader to decide which power will prevail as "The Triumph of Agriculture" closes.

LIBERATION

"The Triumph of Agriculture" chronicles the transformation of society from agrarian to mechanized. Even though a more progressive world results, Zabolotsky was criticized for focussing on biological rather than social processes in his work.[28] Critics were confounded, too, by the symbolism of the poem, which expresses the idea of renewal through images of liberation – from the Aquarian figuration in the soldier's dream, to the animals' release from labor, to the peasants' freedom from illiteracy. More problematic than the obvious thematics of liberation, however, was Zabolotsky's use of language as a liberating force. Like Khlebnikov's polymetric compositions, Zabolotsky's poem is a medley of meters, rhymes, and levels of language, and these prosodic and generic intermixings are always intentional, never arbitrary. In this poem celebrating a new age, Zabolotsky sought to demonstrate that a new age of

Soviet poetry was also at hand. Like other poets of his day, he worked to liberate poetic language from itself.

But Zabolotsky's language triggered complaint. A poem employing a vocabulary both odic and vulgar, technical and grandiloquent, was difficult to categorize. Also troublesome were the meter shifts that frequently occur when elements of Soviet life are introduced into the poem. Just as the trochees in the Prologue give way to iambs when the crane appears, so a reverse shift takes place when another herald of the new age, the tractor driver, enters the scene. His words invert the established iambic tetrameter of Part Six, resulting in a series of trochees. An even more jarring break occurs in Part One, where the soldier representing the new Soviet order interrupts the peasants as they discuss their fears. He jeers at their superstitions and provides rational explanations for natural phenomena. Although an underlying sense of the iambic tetrameter is maintained throughout his speech, the actual meters of the lines vary, and at least one defies scansion ("Togo sluchaia, kogda o tverdoe razob'etsia"). Some of these rhythmic breaks seem akin to an orchestra's breaking into discordant music whenever an operatic villain appears on stage.

Throughout "The Triumph of Agriculture" semantically choppy lines keep company with graceful stanzas of classical meter. The poem relies on strong breaks in rhythmic movements, leading to the mixing of metrical patterns from traditional iambs to free verse. The effect on the reader is pronounced. The broken patterns serve to underline the rhythmic basis of the interrupted verse, but no sooner do we grow accustomed to the even flow of a lilting passage than we are jolted into a twentieth-century reality of fitful syntax and erratic rhyme. (So, too, was the peasant jolted into the reality of collectivization.) In this way Zabolotsky periodically startles his reader, drawing him into the drama of the verse-making. Zabolotsky's rhythmic breaks are also crucial to the sense of the poem: the characters in "The Triumph of Agriculture" are identified not only by name, but by the form their speeches take. A shift in meter signals a shift in action, and the variety of forms adds interest to the poem, helping to sustain it over many lines.

Such constant changes reinforce the conclusion that "The Triumph of Agriculture" is about liberation. One form liberates its predecessor, as it were, yielding a sense of infinite creative possibility. In moving freely from the realm of the fairy tale into that of science, from slang expression to heroic declamation, Zabolotsky shows his universal intentions, his desire to embrace the world in all of its forms. His consequent reluctance to smooth over his text with a single voice no doubt contributed to the hostile reception of the poem; perhaps the multiplicity of voices suggested too strongly the chaotic nature of society's transformation. In fact, the voices manifest a certain ambivalence toward the changes taking place in the countryside: while Zabolotsky welcomed the new freedoms they entailed, he sensed in them something unsound. "The Triumph of Agriculture" seeks to allay uncertainty by transforming potential nightmare into dreamscape.

Because the poem turns on the theme of transformation, it depicts a universe which is always mutable[29] and therefore holds eternal promise. The poem's disparate voices create an impression of wide-openness, and the grotesque imagery and language play express the liberation intrinsic to Zabolotsky's utopian ideal. Beyond a release from the burden of labor (for the animals) and the burden of limited knowledge (for the peasants), liberation brings community and equality, as foretold by Khlebnikov. At the end of the poem the ass – no longer a "Buridan's ass" unable to make a free choice – "sings freedom in the barn" ("v khlevu svobodu pel osel"); a horse converses with cabbage; and an old man explains philosophy to a dog. Even the machinery shares in the general well-being. The sense of oneness that the animals felt all along ("zhivotnykh sostavnoe telo" ["the animals' composite body"]) now permeates the countryside at large ("semeistvo dereviannykh sel" ["a family of wooden villages"]), and the characters become equal – human, animal, plant, and object alike.[30] But because Zabolotsky's ideas did not always result in unambiguously positive expression, his poem did not easily convey his real intentions. The final image of the laughing sky typifies the ambiguity the critics found so nettlesome.

THE LAST LAUGH

By ending "The Triumph of Agriculture" on the word *smeias'* ("laughing"), Zabolotsky avoids resolution. As we have seen, laughter hints at the existence of "minus signs" in Zabolotsky's utopia, implying that there is another side to the magical transformations in the poem. Despite their regenerative function, these transformations, in their kinship with the grotesque, express the intrinsic ambivalence of life. This thematic equivocality is heightened by a semantic one as the voices in the poem continually shift. The various characters debate their ideas, engaging in a strange sort of Menippean satire, and their battles often leave a confusing impression. Zabolotsky does not help his reader by telling him what to think. Here, for instance, is how he presents the soldier in Part Five:

> Кто он – демон или бог?
> И звезда его крылата
> Блещет, словно носорог.

> Who is he – demon or god?
> His winged star
> Glitters like a rhinoceros.

The comparison of the red star on the soldier's uniform – a symbol of Soviet power – to a rhinoceros seems almost blasphemous; and in his profanation of the sacred we can detect Zabolotsky's mixed feelings about the changes wrought by collectivization. As for the source of the simile, it could arise from Zabolotsky's affinity for Khlebnikov and these lines from "Menagerie" ("Zverinets"): "Where the rhinoceros carries in his whitish red eyes the inextinguishable rage of an overthrown tsar and alone of all beasts does not hide his scorn for people or for slave rebellions. Ivan the Terrible is concealed in him."[31] Although the connection to Khlebnikov remains speculative, Zabolotsky does seem to be likening the soldier's disdain for the unenlightened peasants to the enduring rage of the cruel rhinoceros. Certainly, he became aware of the mixed message of these lines. In the final version of "The Triumph of Agriculture" prepared just prior to his death, he changed the lines to read:

> И звезда его, крылата,
> Устремилась на восток.
>
> And his star, winged,
> Was directed toward the east.

Bearing Zabolotsky's equivocality in mind, the interpretation of even such simple lines as "Bezobraznyi i bol'shoi/Zhuravel' letaet" ("Ugly and large/A crane flies") becomes more complex. In "The Triumph of Agriculture" the crane bearing the message of Soviet society is portrayed as ugly, but we know from Zabolotsky's later verse that he regarded the crane as a graceful and noble creature. In "Zhuravli" ("Cranes," 1948) he refers to their "wondrous majesty" ("divnogo velich'ia"), giving them "silver wings," a "proud spirit" and "high aspirations." Zabolotsky's positive portrayal of the bird has even come to be identified with him: the figure of a crane is engraved on his tombstone.

The ambiguity of "The Triumph of Agriculture" is most pronounced at the end where, with glorification of the new society in full voice, Zabolotsky transports his reader to the humble grave of the wooden plough. His decision to dramatize the plough's demise may have been motivated by the frequent reports regarding mechanization that appeared in the late 1920s. At least one article played on the peasants' emotions by referring to the plough as a nurturer, calling it a "wet-nurse" and "mother," only to campaign for the peasants to grow up and finally lay it to rest.[32] But Zabolotsky does not allow his plough to pass unremembered:

> Умерла царица пашен,
> Коробейница старух.
> И растет над нею важен
> Сын забвения – лопух.
> И растет лопух унылый,
> И листом о камень бьет,

И над ветхою могилой
Память вечнюю поет.

The empress of ploughed fields has died,
The pedlar of old women.
Over her grows burdock –
Proud son of oblivion.
The melancholy burdock grows,
Beating its leaves against the stone,
And over the decrepit grave
It sings a dirge.

When Zabolotsky reworked "The Triumph of Agriculture" late in life, he ended the poem on this peaceful, if gloomy, note, with the burdock singing a dirge for the plough. By eliminating the final stanza, he abandoned the laughing sky with its implicit ambiguity.

In the original version of his poem Zabolotsky indicates that even in a perfected world contradictions persist (he was, after all, an admirer of Engels' *Dialectics of Nature*). Over the course of the poem he reflects on these universal antinomies and seeks a harmonious solution to them. The apparent confusions of his poem mirror the chaos of the real world, but the contradictions he discovered prompted him to explore different varieties of perceptual experience. Not surprisingly, his imagination was engaged by the transformations taking place in his own society: he sensed in them a real drama in which he could participate.

"The Triumph of Agriculture" resulted from Zabolotsky's passionate consideration of the changes occurring around him, yet it would be wrong to see the poem as entirely conscious, for Zabolotsky's sense of wonder at the metamorphosis of society brims over into the poem. Like an explorer or scholar, he pursued the questions that perplexed him. Sincerely (if naively) determined to find a resolution to them, Zabolotsky was more than saddened by the critical reception of his work; he was crushed. As he had earlier remarked: "What I write is not parody; it is exactly what I see" ("eto moe zrenie").[33]

Because the world Zabolotsky celebrates is continually in a state of flux, ever evolving and ambiguous, it is difficult to ascribe a single, definitive "meaning" to "The Triumph of

Agriculture": the guises are always changing. This lack of closure reveals Zabolotsky's ability to perceive several levels of meaning simultaneously and his desire to represent the world in its multiformity. As Picasso has said, "A green parrot is also a green salad and a green parrot. He who makes it only a parrot diminishes its reality."[34]

Who does have the last laugh in "The Triumph of Agriculture"? The answer is not straightforward. The final image of the laughing sky returns us to the poem's initial, provocative question, reminding us that unseen forces are still at play in the world. Zabolotsky has not yet found the answer to his query of "Who is it that peers at us?", but he hints at what it might be. Although several more years were to pass before Zabolotsky wrote "The Trees" with its startling insight into the mysteries of creation, "The Triumph of Agriculture" brought him closer to understanding. In exploring the transition from chaos to order, the poem illustrates varieties of transformation as reason is imposed. Harmony is attained by the end of the poem, but the laughing sky suggests that disorder still hovers nearby. And in this pervasive laughter the presence of an irrational force is revealed; it is, perhaps, the unruliness of the poet's own imagination, which cannot be suppressed.

"THE MAD WOLF"

Zabolotsky's critics were unhappy with his depiction of a new and progressive world in "The Triumph of Agriculture," but little did they suspect that the poet himself, for quite different reasons, felt dissatisfied with his work. Zabolotsky did not believe he had adequately portrayed his vision of scientific achievement in harmony with nature's laws. Like the animals populating his poem, he felt his ideas more keenly than he could articulate them. In his exuberance to embrace the future, he neglected to explore fully the interim stages of development along the way. In a number of poems written after "The Triumph of Agriculture," Zabolotsky does examine the phases necessary for the advent of a harmonious world. These poems make clear the evolution of his utopian idea.

Of particular interest is "The School of Beetles" (1931).
Like "The Triumph of Agriculture," this poem involves
animals – along with the rest of nature – aided by man in the
quest for universal equality. Yet whereas in the earlier poem
only the technology offered by man could liberate the animals
from their drudgery, here they receive a greater gift, one that
enables them to help themselves. This is the gift of reason, and
it proves man's willingness to sacrifice himself to atone for past
injustices:

> . . . .
> Сто наблюдателей жизни животных
> Согласились отдать свой мозг
> И переложить его
> В черепные коробки ослов,
> Чтобы сияло
> Животных разумное царство.
> Вот добровольная
> Расплата человечества
> Со своими рабами!
> Лучшая жертва,
> Которую видели звезды!
>
> . . . .
> One hundred observers of animal life
> Have agreed to give up their brains
> And transfer them
> Into the craniums of donkeys,
> So that the rational kingdom
> Of animals might shine.
> This is mankind's
> Voluntary repayment
> To its slaves!
> The greatest sacrifice
> The stars have ever seen!

Zabolotsky goes on to show that the process of enlightenment is not one-sided. Nature has much to offer man. By
observing the world around him, man can learn how to pattern
his life; he need only be attentive. The astute carpenters in
"The School of Beetles" examine the properties of different
trees and their woods in order to apply their knowledge to the

sphere of human endeavors. In this way they are already wiser than the peasants in "The Triumph of Agriculture," who hopelessly discuss existential problems without realizing that the answers lie close at hand. And in their willingness to learn from the surrounding environment, the carpenters are the immediate forerunners of Zabolotsky's keenest observer of nature, the Mad Wolf.

Cast by virtue of species into the animal kingdom, the Wolf aspires to an upright spine and the knowledge it will bring once he can direct his gaze upward, at the sky. Not quite human, yet more than beast, the Wolf in his very first lines declares his occupation as observer of the world around him. He is certain that the mysteries of life and the future of wolves on earth will be revealed to him by the stars: "Ia, zadrav sobaki bok,/ Nabliudaiu zvezd potok" ("Having mangled a dog's flank,/I observe the course of the stars.")

Like "The Triumph of Agriculture," "The Mad Wolf" is constructed on a cosmic vision, representing an intermediate stage between the previous poem's ambiguous utopia and the vision of perfect harmony expressed in "The Trees," which followed two years later. In "The Mad Wolf" Zabolotsky portrays a utopian state congruent with the Soviet ideal, where members of society work together under the leadership of a wise chairman. The poem also conforms with Soviet dicta in its enthusiasm for the "NTR" (the scientific and technological revolution)[35] and in its lack of compassion for the old order left behind (here no dirges are sung over the past). Even the Marxist idea of the perfectability of man through socialism is discernible in the poem through the allegorical figures of the Bear, the Wolf, the Chairman and the Young Wolves. Yet despite its orthodox views, "The Mad Wolf," like "The Triumph of Agriculture," is highly unorthodox in its technique: Zabolotsky presents his picture of an orderly future society by means of broken rhythms, erratic rhymes, and conflicting views.With its old order represented by a sluggish bear and its progressive new society comprised of singing wolves instead of humans, "The Mad Wolf" challenged prevailing literary dogma. As Zabolotsky gave voice to his intellectual struggles, his imagination led him to write in a way that did not entirely correspond with the carefully prescribed canons for Soviet literature. Through humor, literary echoes, and grotesque perceptions, his characters come to represent opposing philosophical stances,[36] and once again, many different voices resound.

"The Mad Wolf" relates the story of a lone visionary determined to discover for himself and reveal to posterity the mysteries of the universe. At its simplest level of interpretation, the poem may be seen as a Marxist fairytale; and in keeping with the fabulous subtext, its visionary hero is a wolf, the eponymous mad one (*bezumnyi*). Over the course of the poem, this wolf progresses from a feral state to a higher, more perfect one, in the process sacrificing himself as much as any proletarian hero would. Zabolotsky dramatizes the wolf's single-mindedness of purpose as he experiences both failures and successes in his quest for knowledge, and the wolf's active efforts reflect the Marxist belief that the philosopher's task is not simply to interpret the world, but to change it. Yet despite its patently socialist vision, Zabolotsky was unable to publish "The Mad Wolf" during his lifetime; it first appeared seven years after his death.[37] The narrative begins as the wolf engages in conversation with a bear, who in his resistance to change represents the settled ways of the forest. The two animals quarrel and part, ending Part One of the poem. Part Two takes place ten years later in a stone hut which has sheltered the Mad Wolf since he abandoned his den. The wolf not only wears clothing but has long since mastered the art of writing. Over the years he has gained much knowledge, and now he describes the experiments he has pursued ever since achieving upright posture. He has attempted to overcome the prevailing laws of nature by effecting transformations between the realms of animals and plants. Although now old, he is not yet ready to abandon his pursuits. One final task remains: he wants to fly. The wolf is confident that he will succed in this, his greatest challenge.

Part Three introduces new characters who make up a society of wolves, heir to the Mad Wolf's dreams. Led by a wise chairman, these young wolves assemble in the forest to honor the Mad Wolf on the anniversary of his death. In chorus, they relate the fateful events of the night he attempted to fly. But they are unenthusiastic about this ceremony; students, engineers, doctors, and musicians, they are eager to get on with the transformation of the forest and see no point in dwelling on the past. Their chairman, however, solemnly reminds them of the importance of the Mad Wolf's revolutionary vision. Without his heroism, they would all be languishing still in the primeval forest instead of building new bridges and social structures. Here the poem ends with a panegyric to the Mad Wolf and his dreams.

While the utopian ideals expressed in "The Mad Wolf" are stirring, the poem succeeds not merely because of its fairytale Marxism. Zabolotsky polemicized his own conflicts in "The Mad Wolf," creating universality and giving the poem unexpected breadth. As he worked to master the *poema* form, Zabolotsky saw himself participating in literary history: "In Russia, poetry lived one century – from Lomonosov to Pushkin. Perhaps now, after a great interval, a new poetic era has come. If so, then it's just beginning. That's why it's so hard to find rules for composing large pieces."[38] Having finally found a form large enough to support the creative interplay of all the varied elements comprising his poetic world, Zabolotsky set about creating his own rules; and unlike other, less bold poets of his era, he made use of unconventional – at times heretical – sources to convey his ideas.

In "The Mad Wolf" Zabolotsky goes beyond a standard depiction of a revolutionized populace to embrace a truly visionary belief in the importance of innovation not only for art but for society. This belief involved an awareness of those intangible components of creativity which cannot be rationally explained, and which Zabolotsky understood as a kind of magic. Where in "The Triumph of Agriculture" he recognized the existence of unexplained powers in the universe, in "The Mad Wolf" he makes their presence concrete. Underlying the poem are legends that explain the world in terms of its transformations.[39] The same sorts of kinships between man and nature that Ovid explores in his *Metamorphoses* are explored by the Mad Wolf; but where Ovid seeks "to tell of bodies changed to different forms,"[40] the wolf attempts to create these forms. Ovid's metamorphoses are ordained by the gods; the Mad Wolf's result from science. Even so, their magical undercurrent is felt. For Zabolotsky, science involved minute observation, which embraced the spiritual as well as the analytical. Thus when the wolf listens closely to the rustlings of the birch, he not only learns about its inner processes but also experiences the healing mysticism of the forest.

> Имею частые с природой разговоры . . .
> Бывало, ухом прислонюсь к березе –
> И различаю тихий разговор.
> Береза сообщает мне свои переживанья,
> Учит управлению веток,
> Как шевелить корнями после бури
> И как расти из самого себя.

> I have frequent conversations with nature . . .
> I press my ear to a birch –
> And I discern a quiet conversation.
> The birch informs me of its feelings,
> Teaches me the management of branches,
> How to move roots after a storm
> And how to grow out of oneself.

The wolf wants to prove, in an orderly, scientific fashion, the correspondences among living realms which previously he could only intuit. Despite his progressive views, he consults a sorceror (*vorozheia*) to find out whether his neck can be straightened. His reliance on the sorceror and the alchemistic nature of his subsequent experiments leave the impression that finally magic, not science, serves as the catalyst for the Mad Wolf's endeavors, no matter how analytical they may seem. What strikes one about this wolf is not so much his feeling for natural rhythms or his intellectual aspirations, but rather his attempt to use them in tandem.

In his experiments, the Mad Wolf seeks to create new forms of life:

> Я открыл множество законов.
> Если растенье посадить в банку
> И в трубочку железную подуть –

Животным воздухом наполнится растенье,
Появится на нем головка, ручки, ножки,
А листики отсохнут навсегда.
Благодаря моей душевной силе
Я из растенья воспитал собачку –
Она теперь, как матушка, поет.
Из одной березы
Задумал сделать я верблюда,
Да воздуху в груди, как видно, не хватило:
Головка выросла, а туловища нет ...

I've discovered a multitude of laws.
If you sow a plant in a jar
And blow on it through an iron tube –
The plant will fill with animal air,
A small head, arms and legs will appear on it,
And its leaves will wither forever.
Thanks to my spiritual strength[41]
I cultivated a dog from a plant –
Now it sings like a mother.
Out of a certain birch tree
I planned to make a camel,
But evidently I hadn't enough air in my chest:
A head grew, but no body ...

Here Zabolotsky gives expression to a truly grotesque, teratological vision. The wolf's breath (the "animal air"), by which he infuses his animal spirit into the spiritless plant, causes the plant to take on beastlike characteristics. The plant becomes a dog, though hardly an ordinary one. This dog neither howls nor barks, whimpers nor bays. Instead it "sings like a mother,"[42] an attribute embracing not only human physical characteristics, but psychological ones as well: the act of mothering; the singing of lullabies. Thus in the wolf's experiment the entire spectrum from plant life through animal to human life is traversed. The hylozoistic conviction that in all things there resides a spirit – often with human characteristics – is essential to Zabolotsky's thought. Like other Russian modernists, he was attracted to primitive belief systems and doubtless was familiar with the popular Mari legend that tells of a rock harboring human life.[43] This "living rock" is the icon of the Mari utopia,[44] a cliff where a warrior-hero lies buried yet ready to spring to action should his people need him. The rock is "living" not only because the warrior resides in it, but also because it is an enduring reminder of him. The hallowed site of "The Mad Wolf" is similarly a rocky cliff, a powerful symbol of the wolf's dreams and an image of hope for a better life.[45] Both legend and poem implicate the human element into the natural world; the Mad Wolf is indeed a wolf, but he is human in his aspirations.

This human aspect of the Mad Wolf's character represents a new development in Zabolotsky's thought. In his early poetry Zabolotsky demonstrated his idea of human empathy for nature's sufferings: trees groan; rivers moan; animals suffer helplessly. But in "The Mad Wolf" Zabolotsky moves for the first time beyond empathy to an actual identification with the natural world. The wolf is the first of Zabolotsky's characters not only to articulate his desires, but to act on them. Furthermore, his actions serve a social agenda: through individual sacrifice he brings about a better society. Although in this respect Zabolotsky follows Soviet prescription, inevitably he departs from the rule: "The Mad Wolf" expresses the highly primitive belief that the forest has secrets to share if one is receptive enough to listen. Unlike the bear who simply, blindly worships the sun, the wolf has a keen ear for the unspoken wisdom around him, and through sensitivity to his surroundings, he is able to effect change. Here the intricacy of Zabolotsky's vision becomes apparent. The wolf practices science, but he believes in magic; and without one or the other element his experiments are bound to fail.

Strange as the wolf's pursuits seem, they mirror the fantastic state of Soviet science in the 1920s, when scientists regularly – and with State approval – sought to fuse animals and new forms of life. Even the respected architect Konstantin Melnikov cherished plans for an "Institute for Changing the Form of Man."[46] Significantly for Zabolotsky, the critical element in the wolf's experiments turns out to be neither the equipment nor the procedure, but the spirit – an ineffable factor at best. The wolf's experiments succeed only to the extent of his "spiritual strength." Precisely this strength is lacking in his second attempt as he fails to turn a birch into a camel, creating a monster instead: the great salivating mouth, yellow teeth and bulbous eyes of a camel's head dangle misbegotten from the trunk of a slender birch. Here Zabolotsky's implication is clear: without a guiding spirit behind it, science will not succeed, for finally the creative spirit is the crucial determinant.[47]

SPIRITED BORROWINGS

Thanks to his father's eclectic bookshelf,[48] Zabolotsky early on developed an interest in literature, which later fed his poetry. In "The Mad Wolf" Zabolotsky reinvigorates the Russian literary tradition by borrowing from his predecessors, echoing or distorting their words, but always infusing them with new meaning. A few examples will demonstrate how various passages from the poem reflect several centuries of Russian letters.[49]

The wolf's attempts to explain his deep desire to learn more about all creation cast him as a Lomonosovian figure. Mikhail Lomonosov, the eighteenth-century poet and scientist who experimented as much with the elements as with metrics, pondered the expanse of the universe while dreaming of learning its secrets, and the wolf's words echo his in such poems as "Vechernee razmyshlenie o bozhiem velichestve pri sluchae velikogo severnogo siianiia" ("Evening Meditation on God's Greatness on the Occasion of the Great Northern Lights," 1743). The association with Lomonosov lends the wolf's experiments a credibility they might otherwise not have: visionary scientists historically have seemed daft to their contemporaries.

Lomonosov is not the only Russian poet whose lines resonate in the Mad Wolf's speech, however. Echoes from Pushkin are also audible in the wolf's musings. The blank verse in Part Two of the poem reinforces an identification with Pimen, the monk from *Boris Godunov*. By echoing lines of Pushkin familiar to his readers,[50] Zabolotsky associates the wolf with idealism and the high romantic aspirations of youth. Like the allusions to Lomonosov, these echoes place the wolf squarely on the side of the angels, who represent in this case not only the forces of goodness, but also some of the most beautiful poetry in the world. The poetic company the wolf keeps works to elevate him in the reader's estimation.

By modelling the Mad Wolf on Pimen and presenting him as a sort of religious figure, Zabolotsky creates a new martyr in the venerable Russian tradition. Yet the wolf's saintliness often appears as silliness as Zabolotsky explores the boundaries between *sapientia* and *stultitia*. In one of the Mad Wolf's most hopeful, but least successful experiments, he digs a hole in the ground, sticks his leg in it up to the knee, and stands there for twelve days and nights, hoping to take root and become a plant.[51] The wolf suffers greatly in this sacrifice to the cause of science: "Ves' otoshchal, ne pivshi i ne evshi" ("I wasted away, not drinking or eating"). The colloquial tone of the wolf's words belies the exalted aspirations behind his experiment, and the implicit comparison to a saint makes his activity seem all the more absurd. In his posture, the wolf is like the *stolpnik* or stylite Saint Simon, an ascetic who lived for thirty-five years on top of a pillar to mortify his flesh and gain redemption. But unlike Saint Simeon (as he is known in Russian hagiography), the redemption that the Mad Wolf seeks is less for himself than for the other beasts of the forest. He is, after all, "the reformer of wolves' lives."[52]

In his search for truth and his self-maceration, the Mad Wolf may be seen as a kind of furry Christ figure, determined to devote his whole life to the betterment of his kind: "A ia ot moego dushevnogo perezhivan'ia/Ne otkazhus' ne v koei mere!" ("But I will not in any measure/Renounce my life of the spirit!"). He believes that the animals can regain universal happiness by anchoring themselves to the earth from which they were once torn. Typically, he interprets their uprooting literally:

Приятно жить счастливому растенью –
Оно на воздухе играет, как дитя,
А мы ногой безумной оторвались,
Бежим туда-сюда,
А счастья нет как нет.

> The happy plant enjoys its life –
> It plays like a child in the air,
> But we've wrested loose our legs,
> We run here and there,
> And there's no happiness in sight.

The text gradually returns to a classical context from a religious one as features of eighteenth-century prosody begin to appear. Beginning with the anaphoric lines "Tomu, kto videl . . . /Tomu, kto mog . . ." ("He who has seen . . . /He who can . . ."), Zabolotsky's resonant diction, hyperbole and odic intonation mirror eighteenth-century style. But, as ever, the poet engages in play. Following such ecstatic lines as "Idi ko mne, moia bol'shaia sila!/Derzhi menia!" ("Come to me, my great strength!/Hold me!") or "Moia glava siiaet" ("My head is radiant"), come the jarring "Vse sukhozhil'ia rvutsia iz menia" ("All of my tendons are straining") and "Vse briukho vozdukhom naduetsia, kak shar" ("My belly will swell with air, like a balloon"). The use of such down-to-earth words as *sukhozhil'ia* and *briukho* tempers the Lomonosovian rapture of the preceding lines (an effect Gavriil Derzhavin also sought to achieve with his *bytovizm*, the use of everyday detail).[53]

The various classical and hagiographic references that echo throughout "The Mad Wolf" converge in Part Three as Zabolotsky manipulates them to express his idea of an idealized Soviet future in which the Russian past still reverberates. As Part Three opens, wolves have gathered in the forest to commemorate the Mad Wolf's death. The sense of the Mad Wolf as a martyr increases as the Chairman describes the night of his death: the storm that turned the sky dark and caused the earth to tremble is an obvious allusion to the crucifixion of Christ. The Mad Wolf's resemblance to Christ in his self-sacrifice is further strengthened by the Chairman's description of the cliff from which the Wolf took flight. This skull-like cliff (*kak cherep*) carries an inevitable association with the place of Christ's crucifixion, Calvary or Golgotha, names that mean "skull" in Latin and Hebrew. Such an association makes the wolf seem worthy of canonization in his attempt to fly; yet even as this hagiographic theme reaches its poetic culmination, Zabolotsky is already on to other allusions.

When the Chairman finishes his story, individual groups of wolves begin to speak. Engineers, doctors, and musicians, they represent an inversion of the theme of transformation from old Russian literature, where Vseslav in *The Lay of Igor's Campaign* turns into a wolf: here the wolves have turned into professionals with human occupations. In a song particularly resonant with literary associations, the wolf-engineers describe how they will "build a bridge to the far shore of earthly happiness." A "coachman in a glass hat" will lead them across this bridge, singing.

The idea of a bridge as a symbol of earthly well-being carries both religious and literary overtones. In the Bible, God's sign of the covenant with Noah is a rainbow – a bridge between heaven and earth (Genesis 9:13–17). In Russian literature, a bridge is the focus of Manilov's dreams of happiness in Gogol's *Dead Souls*. The coachman's song ("Gai-da, troika,/Energiiu utroi-ka!" ["Giddap, troika,/Increase energy threefold!"]) implicitly equates the new Soviet industrial state with Gogol's famous characterization of Russia as a speeding troika. And the glass hat of this modern-day coachman who inexorably leads the wolves to happiness recalls the numerous glass utopias in Russian literature, popular ever since Vera Pavlovna's dream in Chernyshevsky's *What is to be Done?*: Dostoyevsky's Crystal Palace; Zamyatin's glass dome; Khlebnikov's city of glass in "Ladomir."

Glass constructions figure, too, in Mandelstam's "Kontsert na vokzale" ("Concert at the Station," 1921) where he describes the Pavlovsk Railway Station, juxtaposing "the station's sphere of glass," "the glass forest of the station," and the "glass vestibule" ("vokzala shar stekliannyi," "stekliannyi les vokzala," "stekliannye seni") with the steam engine as symbols of progress through industry. Echoing Mandelstam's image of a "glass forest," the Chairman in Zabolotsky's poem pictures a glass building in the woods: "Ia zakryvaiu glaza i vizhu stekliannoe zdanie lesa." ("I close my eyes and see a glass building in the forest."). Because *les* in Russian also means "scaffolding," the Chairman's vision of an industrial utopia involves an intricate synecdoche. His picture of a happy future reverberates with all of its accumulated utopian associations from Russian literature. Notably, this utopia is neither ambiguous nor merely symbolic: in the palpable image of a constructed building in the forest it becomes concrete, moving beyond the realm of the abstract to the possible and the real.

THE MOVEMENT OF NEW FORMS

Impelled by pagan legends, Faustian aspirations, and native poetic traditions, the visionary ideal behind "The Mad Wolf" shows considerable development from the utopia depicted in "The Triumph of Agriculture." The Mad Wolf and his schemes have brought about the well-ordered world based in scientific knowledge which was still only a dream in the previous poem. Having grasped the mysteries of the universe ("Ia ponimaiu atmosferu! ["I understand the atmosphere!"] and hence of life, the wolf has overcome the fear of death. In Zabolotsky's poetic world, this represents real progress. Furthermore, the Mad Wolf's legacy demonstrates genuine socialist optimism: a progressive community of industrious workers is guided by a farsighted chairman. In this second long poem by Zabolotsky, the current slogan "We Are Building Socialism" is imaginatively articulated. The song of the student-wolves:

> Мы новый лес сегодня созидаем.
> Еще совсем убогие вчера,
> Перед тобой мы ныне заседаем
> Как инженеры, судьи, доктора.

> Today we are building a new forest.
> Utterly wretched only yesterday,
> Before you now we gather
> As engineers, judges, doctors.

even echoes the Russian version of "The International," the proletarian hymn:

> Весь мир насилья мы разрушим
> До основанья, а затем
> Мы наш, мы новый мир построим
> Кто был ничем тот станет всем.

We will destroy the whole world
Of oppression, and then
We will build a new world that is ours.
He who was nothing will become everything.

Yet even as Zabolotsky presents his utopian-cum-socialist vision, he invests "The Mad Wolf" with another layer of meaning. Of primary importance is the fact that he calls his hero "mad," for in this epithet lies a key to his larger idea. What "The Mad Wolf" ultimately explores is the visionary component of species development – the relationship between madness and creativity.[54] A dreamer, the Mad Wolf is a vessel of creativity and a symbol of creative power. In his conscious renunciation of society and dreams of salvation for wolfdom, the wolf may be perceived as a latter-day *iurodivyi* or "holy fool."[55]

With the figure of the Mad Wolf, Zabolotsky advocates the importance of the iconoclast in any society, implying that the visionary is often the one who best can see the world for what it really is. Unlike Icarus, whose example teaches that man's place remains on earth and that one should not attempt to exceed his given limitations, Zabolotsky's Mad Wolf – who would also fly – represents the poet's belief in the importance of taking risks and attempting what is commonly held to be impossible. Whether the wolf is wisely mad or madly foolish, his behavior is clearly heroic and essential to the progress of society. Considering the growing precariousness of Zabolotsky's situation, "The Mad Wolf" may well be interpreted as a defense of his own individualistic verse.

With this thought in mind it is interesting to compare another poem from the same year, "Bitva slonov" ("The Battle of the Elephants"). Here elephants unexpectedly enter into "a battle of words! A clash of meanings!" ("Bitva slov! Znachenii boi!"), throwing Syntax into disarray. These elephants represent the subconscious, which irrepressibly asserts itself and causes old rules to be broken. The result is that

Синтаксис домики строят не те,
Мир в неуклюжей стоит красоте.

Деревьев отброшены старые правила,
На новую землю их битва направила . . .
Волк вместо разбитой морды
Приделал себе человечье лицо,
Вытащил флейту, играет без слов
Первую песню военных слонов.

Syntax builds the wrong kind of houses,
The world stands in clumsy beauty.
The old rules of the trees are cast off,
The battle has dispatched them to a new land . . .
Instead of his smashed snout, the wolf
Has put on a human face,
He's dug out his flute, and wordlessly he plays
The militant elephants' first song.

The apparent loser in this battle of words is Poetry, the high
priestess of language:

На самом деле, как могло случиться,
Что пала древняя столица?
Весь мир к поэзии привык,
Все было так понятно.
В порядке конница стояла,
На пушках цифры малевала,
И на знаменах слово Ум
Кивало всем, как добрый кум.
И вдруг какие-то слоны,
И все перевернулось!

Indeed, how could
The ancient capital [Poetry] have fallen?
The whole world had grown accustomed to poetry,
Everything was so comprehensible.
The cavalry stood in order,
With painted numbers on its guns,
And on its banners the word Intellect
Nodded to everyone, like a benevolent god-parent.
Then suddenly some sort of elephants,
And everything is overturned!

Disorder, disruption ensue. "Full of laughter," the elephants
invade the rational domains of the mind, challenging Reason.
Zabolotsky clearly is alluding here to the linguistic assaults of
the modernists on traditional poetics. Like the modernist

affront, the intrusion of the elephants does not bring utter chaos; instead,

> Поэзия начинает приглядываться,
> Изучать движение новых фигур,
> Она начинает понимать красоту неуклюжести,
> Красоту слона, выброшенного преисподней.

Poetry begins to get used to it,
To study the movement of new forms,
It begins to understand the beauty of clumsiness,
The beauty of the elephant, cast out of the nether regions.

Zabolotsky could be referring to his own poetry in these lines. Aware of the frequently cited "clumsiness" of his verse, he defends this characteristic of his work, seeing in it an uncommon beauty or at the least a renewal of language. Precisely this willingness to believe in – not just pay lip service to – the less rational parts of the mind distinguishes Zabolotsky even as he espouses socialist ideals. For him, the success of any new society has more to do with the visionary element than with the canonical or organizational virtues; hence his enthralment with Tsiolkovsky. And hence the Mad Wolf, in his struggle against the prevailing laws of the universe (akin to the elephants' battle), epitomizes Zabolotsky's transcendent idea. Because the wolf refuses to surrender his dreams, a new and better society comes to exist. As the Chairman warns the young wolves, even their progressive society must continue to revere the wolf's vision – must in itself be visionary – in order to progress.

Zabolotsky recognizes the need for balance, however, and he never suggests that the illogical should prevail. Even though the elephants are essential, they must be tamed:

> Сраженье кончено. В пыли
> Цветут растения земли.
> И слон, рассудком приручаем,
> Ест пироги и запивает чаем.

The battle is over. In the dust
Bloom the plants of the earth.
And the elephant, tamed by reason,
Eats pies and sips tea.

Thus an agreement is reached between Reason and Art, one which works both ways: the unruly elephants of the subconscious are subdued with reason, and the rational wolves learn the value of inspiration.

"The Mad Wolf" teaches that inspiration can be gleaned from nature, from a close observation of its forms. Through creativity buttressed by rational thought, man can discern patterns for his own life in these forms. Thus "The Mad Wolf" identifies the components necessary to a harmonious society, civilization, even universe. They need only be set in an equation of perfect balance for Zabolotsky's vision to be complete.

"THE TREES"

As the decade advanced, Zabolotsky became increasingly occupied with problems of form. While form is obviously integral to the poet's art, it represented for Zabolotsky more than just a vessel into which he could pour his words. What interested him beyond the inherent modes of poetry was created form: a meaningful pattern he could discern through his art, both for itself and as a metaphor for finding order in the universe. Ever since encountering Filonov's work Zabolotsky had been exploring the idea of organic development in nature, and now he conceived of all creation as an evolving organism whose inner processes determine its external configuration. This biological paradigm underlies the transcendent vision of the universe in "The Trees," a poem that seeks to reveal nature's mysteries by providing them embodiment.[56]

Several of Zabolotsky's poems from 1932 address his search for significative form. In "Predosterezhenie" ("A Warning"), he uses the metaphor of a house – a substantial, lasting structure – to convey the idea of inspired and rational thought united through form to yield meaning:

Соединив безумие с умом,
Среди пустынных смыслов мы построим дом . . .

Having united madness with intellect,
Among empty thoughts we shall construct a house . . .

The word "house" implies a dwelling full of life, a meaning the more neutral word "building" could never communicate. Furthermore, the actual conformation of the house is important, since that is where meaning resides. In "Osen'" ("Autumn") Zabolotsky develops his architectural metaphor further as he observes the way nature orders surrounding space. Here the focus is not so much on the external appearance of things as on nature's basic morphology:

> Архитектура Осени. Расположение в ней
> Воздушного пространства, рощи, речки,
> Расположение животных и людей . . .

> The architecture of Autumn. The arrangement in it
> Of atmospheric space, of groves and rivers,
> The arrangement of animals and people . . .

Zabolotsky posits the existence of an underlying design in nature, one which he is just beginning to discern; gradually he comes to see the universe as a series of geometric patterns. This perspective leads, in turn, to his perception of all of nature as constructed form, full of meaning:[57]

> . . . .
> И посреди сверкающих небес
> Стоит, как башня, дремлющее древо.
> Оно – центр сфер, и чудо из чудес,
> И тайна тайн. Направо и налево
> Огромные суки поддерживают свод
> Густых листов. И сумрачно и строго
> Сквозь яблоко вещает голос бога,
> Что плод познанья – запрещенный плод.
> . . . .

> "Венчание плодами" (1932)

> . . . .
> And among the shimmering skies
> Stands a slumbering tree, like a tower.
> It is the center of the spheres, the wonder of wonders,
> The mystery of mysteries. To the right and the left
> Its huge branches support a vault
> Of dense leaves. Darkly and sternly
> The voice of God prophesies through the apple
> That the fruit of knowledge is forbidden fruit.
> . . .

> "A Crowning with Fruits" (1932)

In this paean to the discoveries of Luther Burbank and Ivan Michurin, Zabolotsky likens the modern tree of contrived genetic makeup to a constructed tower standing at the center of the universe and containing the secrets of life. He presents the tree in terms of its basic structure, its vaults and supports, a miraculous edifice that nourishes man both literally and figuratively. In seeking to understand its construction, man precipitates his quest for knowledge. Zabolotsky's own quest is satisfied in "The Trees," where man himself is likened to a tower, a structure fashioned of all living things.[58] Here the trees reveal to him at last the appropriate forms for his envisionings – their natural housings.

"The Trees" investigates the familiar Zabolotskian theme of the mysteries of the universe and man's place within it. This time the seeker of knowledge is Bombeev, who opens the Prologue with queries about the origins of life. In Part One, "An Invitation to a Feast," Bombeev bids the woodland trees join him for a celebration at his home beyond the forest. By Part Two, "The Feast at Bombeev's," the revelry is already underway, but despite the celebration, Bombeev is discontent. He launches into a long speech to the trees in which he compares nature to a stove, the athanor of life.[59] In the stove he finds an apt metaphor for nature in the evolutionary process: whatever is put into it unformed comes out improved. But whereas the stove has mastered the mechanics of perfection, nature is still striving to do so, and Bombeev is troubled by what he sees. The natural chain of predation, which he not only witnesses but participates in, saddens him, and he deplores the fact that nature's stove, fired by elemental fires,[60] is inscrutable to man.

In the middle of Bombeev's impassioned speech the forest warden suddenly arrives, causing the trees to cry out in fear and anguish. The warden chastises Bombeev for disrupting the order of his forest and luring away the trees. Bombeev defends himself as master of his own home and proclaims himself the initiator of a new order in the world. The warden presents his own vision of a "glorious century of great trees, long rivers, cool mountains, powerful steppes," expressing only disdain for Bombeev's "Golden Age." Like the soldier in "The Triumph of Agriculture," the warden represents the man of progress, and he urges the trees to follow him back to the forest to take root again under the "vaults of wisdom."

As Part Three, "Night in the Forest," begins, the trees have returned to their orderly lives. The emperor-trees have taken off their crowns; the soldier-trees are hard at work. All take part in the new life of the forest, which grows ever more complex. Suddenly the cello-trees step forward, and the entire forest breaks into song. This fabulous woodland orchestra awakens various slumbering beasts, who climb to the tops of the trees, poised for revelation. Amid the melodies they hear, a new order begins to take shape, characterized mathematically by new planes and forms. As the axe-trees cleave the air into parallelograms, the trees "lose their outlines" and become geometrically defined. The forest is transformed into an aggregation of triangles and semicircles over which the Tree of the Sphere reigns. With this enigmatic image of a Sphere Tree presiding over all, the poem ends.

"The Trees" is a highly conceptual poem that explores the origins of being. Through complex architectural and geometric metaphors, Zabolotsky examines the connections among all living things. The image of a tower represents the basic construct of evolution as it is set forth by the Forest Warden:

> Да, человек есть башня птиц,
> Зверей вместилище лохматых,
> В его лице – миллионы лиц
> Четвероногих и крылатых.
> И много в нем живет зверей,
> И много рыб со дна морей,
> Но все они в лучах сознанья
> Большого мозга строят зданье.
> Сквозь рты, желудки, пищеводы,
> Через кишечную тюрьму,
> Лежит центральный путь природы
> К благословенному уму.
> Итак, да здравствуют сраженья,
> И рев зверей, и ружей гром,
> И всех живых преображенье
> В одном сознанье мировом!

Yes, man is a tower of birds,
A receptacle of shaggy beasts,
In his face are millions of faces
Of four-legged and winged animals.
And many beasts reside in him,
And many fish from the depths of the seas,
But all of them in the rays of consciousness
Of his great brain construct a building.
Through mouths, stomachs, gullets,
Across the intestinal prison,
Lies nature's central path
To the blessed mind.
So long live battles,
And the roar of beasts, and the thunder of weapons,
And the transformation of every living thing
Into a single universal consciousness!

This tower is like a zoological Tower of Babel, where many different beasts work hard at comprehension, but unlike the builders of the Biblical tower, the denizens of Zabolotsky's come to mutual understanding and enlightenment: they attain a single consciousness. Furthermore, their path to enlightenment involves physical, as well as mental, development – knowledge must literally be digested before it can reach the mind. The mind of man represents here the highest achievement of species development, but Zabolotsky does not portray this stage in the evolutionary process as an end-product or culmination. Rather, he implies that even though man and his intelligence manifest the knowledge and instinctual information that has been passed on from earlier, less perfect species, much progress must be made before universal perfection is achieved.

Zabolotsky's theme reflects his interest in the biological debates on heredity and environment that were current in the thirties, particularly those focussing on the hereditary transferal of learned experience.[61] All along he had believed that the transferal of knowledge from nature to man was possible, and in "The Trees" he brings his idea to poetic fruition. The final lines of the poem present a vision of the innate and harmonious forms of nature whence man himself evolved:

Звери вздымают на лестницы тонкие лапы,
Вверх поднимаются к плоским верхушкам деревьев
И замирают вверху, чистые звезды увидев.
Так над землей образуется новая плоскость:
Снизу – животные, взявшие в лапы деревья,
Сверху – одни вертикальные звезды.
Но не смолкает земля. Уже деревянные девочки
Пляшут, роняя грибы в муравейник,
Прямо над ними взлетают деревья-фонтаны,
Падая в воздух гигантскими чашками струек.
Дале стоят деревья-битвы и деревья-гробницы,
Листья их выпуклы и барельефам подобны.
Можно здесь видеть возникшего снова Орфея,
В дудку поющего. Чистою лиственной грудью
Здесь окружают певца деревянные звери.
Так возникает история в гуще зеленых
Старых лесов, в кустарниках, ямах, оврагах,
Так образуется летопись древних событий,
Ныне закованных в листья и длинные сучья.
Дале деревья теряют свои очертанья, и глазу
Кажутся то треугольником, то полукругом –
Это уже выражение чистых понятий,
Дерево Сфера царствует здесь над другими.
Дерево Сфера – это значок беспредельного дерева,
Это итог числовых операций.
Ум, не ищи ты его посредине деревьев:
Он посредине, и сбоку, и здесь, и повсюду.

The beasts raise slender paws onto the stairway,
Climb up to the flat tops of the trees
And freeze there, having glimpsed the pure stars.
Thus above the earth a new plane is formed:
Below – the animals, having grasped the trees with their paws,
Above – only vertical stars.
But the earth does not fall silent. The wooden girls
Are already dancing, dropping mushrooms into an anthill.
Directly above them the fountain-trees fly up,
Their giant cups of spray falling in the air.
Further on stand the battle-trees and tomb-trees,
Their leaves swollen like bas-reliefs.
Here one can see Orpheus arising again,
Singing on his pipe. With pure, leafy breast
The wooden beasts surround the singer.

Thus history arises in the thick of the old
Green forests, in the bushes, pits, ravines;
Thus the chronicle of ancient events assumes a form,
Now shackled in the leaves and long boughs.
Further on, the trees lose their outlines, and to the eye
Appear now as triangles, now semicircles –
This is already the expression of pure conceptions,
The Tree of the Sphere reigns here over all others.
The Tree of the Sphere is the sign of the infinite tree,
The sum of numerical operations.
Mind, do not seek it among the trees:
It is among them, and to the side, and here, and everywhere.

In graceful dactyls whose tone recalls Lucretius' classic work on the nature of things, Zabolotsky offers his own vision of the universe in terms of its spatial dimensions. Initially the forest appears in Dionysian, chaotic splendor, filled with music and dancing, but as form is gradually imposed on the primeval world, the forest constricts. Suddenly, though, the universe opens up, disclosing its limitless scope, and the forest no longer seems self-contained, but part of an infinite cosmos. Such expansiveness gives the forest added meaning as *space*, emphasized by Zabolotsky's vocabulary (*"snizu, sverkhu, vertikal'nye,*[62] *priamo, posredine, sboku, zdes', povsiudu"* ["below, above, vertical, straight, among, to the side, here, everywhere"]). Its dimensions seem nearly palpable.

This insight into the true nature of the forest is achieved through the imposition of form, which acts as the agent bridging the gap between disorder and order. The ancient forest is now revealed as a mass of semicircles, triangles, and parallelograms. For the poet, recognizing these shapes is an act of inspiration, but the process of ordering them (the very fact of their geometric description) is an act of reason or intellectuality. Thus, in this ultimate vision of pure forms, Zabolotsky unites *bezumie* and *um*, making the two modes of thought compatible and divining a solution to his quest.

SYMMETRY (VLADIMIR VERNADSKY)

Zabolotsky's final vision in "The Trees" represents his thought at its most recondite, but his "Notes to the long poem

'The Trees,'"[63] discovered among his papers, aid interpretation. These notes consist of two citations:

"An amount of matter equal to the weight of the earth's crust may, by force of multiplication, be created in insignificant, not geological time, as long as the external environment does not impede this process. *Cholera vibrio* and *bakterium coli* could yield this mass of matter in 1.6–1.75 days ... One of the most slowly multiplying organisms – the e1lephant – could yield the same amount of matter in 1300 years ... Of course, in reality no single organism ever yields such amounts."   (Vladimir Vernadsky[64])

"Thine enemies are thine own ideas, which rule in thy heart and torment it constantly; they are the whisperers, the slanderers, the opponents of God, who continually disparage the prevailing order of the world and try to restore the most ancient laws. In darkness they eternally torment themselves as well as those who agree with them, seeing that nature's governance over everything is not in accordance with their demonic desires or their murky conceptions, but rather according to the highest counsel of our Father, which has endured sacrosanct through yesterday and today and which will continue throughout all the ages. Those who do not understand malign the configuration of the heavenly orbs; they criticize the quality of the earth and fault the sculpting by God's most sage right hand of the animals, trees, mountains, rivers, and grasses. They are not satisfied with anything; according to their unhappy and ridiculous ideas, the world needs neither night nor winter, old age nor labor, hunger nor thirst, sickness nor most of all death: what good are they? Oh, our meager knowledge and understanding!"   (Grigory Skovoroda[65])

At first glance these extracts would seem to have little in common, their authors – a twentieth-century Russian biochemist and an eighteenth-century Ukrainian mystical philosopher – separated by more than the centuries in which they lived. Vernadsky created the discipline of biogeochemistry, the study of the living nature of the earth in its atomic aspect, and for him all theories had to be expressed in scientific terms. Skovoroda, on the other hand, proceeded from the premise of divine ordination in his conception of the three interrelated worlds comprising Creation.[66] Yet a common concern with order links the two thinkers: both sought to formulate the grand design of the universe, to clarify its symmetry.[67]

Furthermore, neither was conformist in his views. Vernadsky used data more often extrapolative than purely scientific to expound his theories,[68] while Skovoroda's religious teachings frequently defied Church doctrine. In their writings Zabolotsky found kindred ideas, and his perception of them as mavericks heightened their appeal, just as the heterodoxies of Tsiolkovsky and Fyodorov had attracted him.

Vernadsky wrote his *Biosphere* in 1926, years after hearing Élie Metchnikoff's famous Parisian lectures on immortality and the possibility of the prolongation of life.[69] Like Tsiolkovsky, Vernadsky focussed on the small particles of creation – the atoms and isotopes – in order to uncover the larger mysteries of life. But while both scientists professed a belief in hylozoism,[70] Vernadsky did not acknowledge any spiritual basis to life, seeing the cosmos as manifest solely in matter and energy.[71] He posited an overriding, symmetrical scheme to the universe to which the individual components of living matter could be conformed. Through his work on the evolution of the biosphere, he developed the idea of the noosphere, an era of reason brought about by labor and scientific thought. In this eager extension of Marxism, Vernadsky explained that man could participate in the natural historical process by exerting control over nature, by "humanising" it (*ochelovechenie*), in his terms. Man's activity would eventually manifest not just physical strength, but geologic strength as well: immortal and autotrophic, he would no longer be limited by the constraints of time.

Vernadsky's description of a biosphere that includes all living forms, mutually dependent in their actions, is based in scientific thought; after all, matter and energy are interconvertible. But his work contains a visionary component as well. In order for life as we know it to exist, specific arrangements of certain molecules must occur, and these biomolecules must obey the laws of physics and chemistry. Vernadsky's criteria for judging life do not always correspond with a strict biological definition of life, however. His sometimes wacky ideas appealed to Zabolotsky, who responded earnestly to the concept of universal interdependence and the belief that man is capable of transforming nature through reason.[72]

Like Tsiolkovsky, Vernadsky was a philosophizing scientist, but our interest in both men lies not so much in their ideas as in what Zabolotsky did with them. Zabolotsky brought his playful, unsentimental vision to bear on their often soft-headed theories, inflating them, breathing new life into them. In his poet's hands, their grandiose schemes took on new meaning. Thus "The Trees" offers a vision of universal symmetry similar to Vernadsky's, but Zabolotsky's method is inductive and intuitive: he does not reveal his overarching scheme until the end of the poem. At first only disconnected forms appear as Bombeev ponders the origins of life. Each of Bombeev's questions is answered in chorus by the existing and incipient forms of life around him: the parts of a flower; the elements of a stormy sky; and the essence of life itself.[73] "Ciphers" (*nuli*) represent the tremendous energy that is latent in all matter, and here Zabolotsky is highly conscious of evolving states of being. In his perception of nothingness as potentially fecund, Zabolotsky had much in common with other artists of the avant-garde.[74] However, he sought to express his abstract ideas in terms of concrete forms – the ever-important *predmet*. For this reason Zabolotsky was attracted to Vernadsky, who conceived of time and space not merely as theoretical concepts, but as actual entities composed of matter and energy.[75] Vernadsky studied the universe on the basis of the symmetry and geometry of space. Zabolotsky similarly sought to show the underlying patterns of the universe in "The Trees."

At the end of the poem the forest changes in appearance. Its disconnected, incomplete forms have evolved into an organic unity, which is visually manifest even though it remains conceptually abstract. The symbol of the harmony achieved is The Tree of the Sphere,[76] an entity that is far more than just the "sum of numerical operations." Because spheres have no points of beginning or end, the tree is "infinite," representing nothing less than boundless possibility: the idea that man can go beyond the limits of time and space. The Tree of the Sphere also reflects a "perceptual experience" ("chuvstvennyi opyt")[77] on the poet's part – a moment of insight into nature that Vernadsky believed could come about only through man's close involvement in its processes. Zabolotsky's choice of a sphere to represent this moment is meaningful. By choosing a geometric shape to signify his insight, Zabolotsky continues the modernist tradition of using non-representational forms to illuminate spiritual concepts. (Kandinsky had this sort of representation in mind when he stated that "the circle of all the primary forms points most clearly to the fourth dimension."[78]) The sphere serves to make the immaterial material and gives form to the rhythmic, cyclical force of matter in constant flux that Zabolotsky detected in nature. By expressing nature's unseen essence, the sphere takes on an almost religious significance. In bold, geometric terms, Zabolotsky represents the living force behind existence, and his sphere is pregnant with meaning, an embryo of all possibilities."[79]

The Tree of the Sphere was a new discovery for Zabolotsky, but he may have anticipated it as early as 1928, when he first rendered a moment of insight in geometric terms:

> . . .
> Как сон житейских геометрий,
> В необычайно крепком ветре
> Над ним домов бряцали оси,
> И в центре О мерцала осень.
> И к ней касаясь хордой, что ли,
> Качался клен, крича от боли,
> Качался клен, и выстрелом ума
> Казалась нам вселенная сама.
>
> "Начало осени"

> . . .
> Like a dream of everyday geometries,
> In an unusually strong wind
> The axes of houses clanged above him,
> And in the center of O flickered autumn.
> And touching it like a chord[80]
> The maple staggered, screaming with pain,
> The maple staggered, and the universe itself seemed
> To us like a shot of intellect.
>
> "The Beginning of Autumn"

Precisely this "shot of intellect" or understanding makes possible Zabolotsky's awareness of the forest in "The Trees" as composed of geometric forms. Beyond its mathematical aspect,

Zabolotsky could now recognize in the Tree of the Sphere the solution to nature's great secrets, the incarnation of the essential mystery of life. Thus the Tree of the Sphere becomes a scientific correlative to pantheism, the poet's counterpart to God. And it is here, in the intersection of the scientific realm with the spiritual – in the conceptual continuum of the Sphere – that Zabolotsky found the correspondence between Vernadsky and Skovoroda.

INSIGHT (GRIGORY SKOVORODA)

Several centuries before Vernadsky, Skovoroda had emphasized the moment of insight, believing it would lead to an understanding of one's place in the universe, and thence to happiness. But for Skovoroda, at least initially, the intuitive act was directed within, rather than beyond, the self. He summed up his Socratic idea in two simple words: "Znai sebe" ("Know thyself").[81] From a knowledge of himself man would progress to a knowledge of the world; and in perfecting himself, he would be perfecting the world. Skovoroda's belief is similar to the teachings of the Vedantic school, which hold that the cosmos will become accessible through meditation on the self, and Zabolotsky's interest in Eastern religions may have heightened the philosopher's appeal for him. He studied the final lines of Skovoroda's dialogic "Conversation," which warn against being laggard in the pursuit of knowledge:

We have entered into the interior of our flesh, as if into the bowels of the earth. We have found that which we had not seen. We found in people new arms, and legs, everything new. But this is not yet the end. Continue on the path to our perfect world ...[82]

Skovoroda argued that the perfected world must not remain within man alone; man is obliged to transmit whatever he learns. Zabolotsky fitted this idea into the twentieth-century, post-Darwinian context of man bringing his knowledge to bear on nature and helping it to evolve.

Zabolotsky read Skovoroda avidly; according to his widow he rarely parted with a volume of the philosopher's works.[83]

Although direct references to Skovoroda are rare, the philosopher's influence on Zabolotsky's poetry can be detected at virtually all stages of his career.[84] For one thing, the expressiveness of Skovoroda's non-literary Russian, mixing not only various levels of language but also dialects, engaged Zabolotsky, who combined different styles in his own work. Perhaps most appealing to him was Skovoroda's conviction that even inanimate things possess a soul. Skovoroda considered the soul to be the crucial component of all living things, the determinant of life:

> Без души трава – сено,
> Деревья – дрова,
> Человек – труп.[85]

> Without a soul grass is hay,
> Trees are firewood,
> Man is a corpse.

Zabolotsky concurred with Skovoroda that form alone is not sufficient to yield life; there must be something beyond it. But in postulating what that provenance might be, Zabolotsky approached the problem of form from a different angle, and in doing so he gave substance to Skovoroda's ideas. We have seen that a number of Zabolotsky's poems demonstrate the importance of form for uniting thoughts to yield meaning; without meaning, the object is inherently empty and lifeless. For Zabolotsky, the element that gives life – the equivalent to Skovoroda's soul – is, quite simply, art. In "Iskusstvo" ("Art," 1930), Zabolotsky equates this necessary component with inspiration. Here, a house is likened to "a cemetery of trees," "a cabin of corpses," "a gazebo of the dead" ("kladbishche derev'ev," "shalash iz trupov," "besedka iz mertvetsov"). The house contains only dead things "if we forget the man/who built and erected it" ("esli zabudem cheloveka,/kto stroil ego i rubil"). What finally distinguishes life, then, is the creative impulse, even as form molds it to provide meaning. Man has been granted the ability to transform intrinsically lackluster objects into vibrant ones, affording them a level of existence previously unknown:

10 Zabolotsky with his daughter, Natasha, in Peredelkino, 1956

Но я, однообразный человек,
Взял в рот длинную сияющую дудку,
Дул, и, подчиненные дыханию,
Слова вылетали в мир, становясь предметами.
Корова мне кашу варила,
Дерево сказку читало,
А мертвые домики мира
Прыгали, словно живые.

But I, a monotonous man,
Took into my mouth a long, shining fife,
I blew, and submitting to my breath,
Words flew out into the world, becoming objects.
The cow cooked me porridge,
The tree read a fairytale,
And the dead houses of the world
Jumped, as if they were alive.

Just as the Mad Wolf blows his spirit into plants, so the poet
breathes life into his words, which are objectified once they are
cast out into the world. This image both recalls and reinforces
Zabolotsky's assertions from the OBERIU Declaration. Nevertheless, Zabolotsky's ideas have evolved, for in "Art" the poet

stresses that it is not enough for words to become concrete: they must also inspire and inform the universe. Thus the words in "Art" affect whatever they touch, and newly inspired, the wooden shapes of the houses transform the world. A similar conception lies at the heart of the transformed forest in Zabolotsky's fecund vision at the end of "The Trees."

Zabolotsky recognized the importance of man's rôle in transforming nature, a rôle likewise acknowledged by Skovoroda. By imposing form man can bring meaning to bear on the universe, whether he serves as the agent of a divine spirit or of an artistic one. Zabolotsky's man as a "receptacle" of millions of creatures is akin to Skovoroda's man as a "small world" ("chelovek est' malen'kii mirok"):[86] both metaphors express a belief in the seen and unseen worlds of man, and hence of nature. Skovoroda urged man to recognize the unseen worlds, considering the readily visible ones such as appearance or material wealth less worthy. Through observation of himself and of the surrounding world, man must learn to discern the patterns of the universe. This Zabolotsky understood, and in his long poems he attempted to define the unseen forces of life. By the end of "The Trees" he is able to answer the initial questions posed in two of his poems: "Eto kto?" ("Who is this?") and "Kto vy?" ("Who are you?").

Even in the thirties, years after his association with Filonov's school had ended, Zabolotsky continued to be compelled by the idea of the seen and the unseen. He undoubtedly was familiar with Skovoroda's theory characterizing the unseen as the "head" of the universe, the seen as the "tail."[87] Carrying this classification one step further, Skovoroda placed "thought" (*mysl'*) within the category of the unseen: that which cannot be seen but which rules.[88] Skovoroda then proceeded to equate thought with man, since in ruling the body, thought ultimately comprises it.[89] Zabolotsky, in his turn, expanded on this idea, judging man to be the ruler not only of himself, but of all of nature:

> И сам я был не детище природы,
> Но мысль ее! Но зыбкий ум ее!
> > "Вчера, о смерти размышляя"

And I myself was not a child of nature,
But its thought! Its vacillating mind!
"Yesterday, Pondering Death"

By affirming man as nature's mentor, Zabolotsky poetically collapses the age-old division between *Natur* and *Kultur*, effectively creating in "The Trees" a union of nature and history on a utopian plane. Here is a vision of conciliation between man and the natural world:

Так возникает история в гуще зеленых
Старых лесов, в кустарниках, ямах, оврагах,
Так образуется летопись древних событий,
Ныне закованных в листья и длинные сучья.

Thus history arises in the thick of the old
Green forests, in the bushes, pits, ravines;
Thus the chronicle of ancient events assumes a form,
Now shackled in the leaves and long boughs.

In accordance with Tsiolkovsky's "law of progress" this new world is the finest of all Zabolotsky has created: it is not merely a world, but a "new plane of existence," a higher reality than has ever before been known.[90]

This new reality is characterized by the integration of science and art, the poles of the rational and the inspired. "The Trees" reveals the intuitivist basis of Zabolotsky's aesthetics as he subtly affirms that in spite of its many benefits, science can never fully replace art. The forest warden who triumphs in bringing the trees back to the forest for classification can do so only after he has been exposed to Bombeev's chaotic world; he can execute only what others have discerned before him. In this respect Zabolotsky's visionary wolf was the necessary precursor who lay the inspired foundations for the warden's orderly world.

Even if the precise nature of Zabolotsky's revelation remains elusive, we cannot doubt that he experienced one and that he believed he had come to understand the order of the universe through his discovery of the inherent harmony in trees and their forms. Most importantly, in the process of discovery he perceived the spirit that lies beyond all the associations he

previously was able to make. If "The Trees" seems enigmatic
at the end, it is because what Zabolotsky saw cannot finally
ever be demonstrated, only intuited. In an earlier poem he had
attempted to define this presence by giving it a name:

> Природа в стройном сарафане,
> Главою в солнце упершись,
> Весь день играет на органе.
> Мы называем это: жизнь.
> Мы называем это: дождь. . . . .
> Или, когда угрюм орган,
> На небе слышен барабан.
> И войско туч пудов на двести
> Лежит вверху на каждом месте,
> Когда могучих вод поток
> Сшибает с ног лесного зверя, –
> Самим себе еще не веря,
> Мы называем это: бог.

"Поэма дождя" (1931)

> Nature in a well-cut dress,
> Resting her head against the sun,
> Plays an organ all day long.
> We call this: life.
> We call this: rain. . . . .
> Or, when the organ is morose,
> A drum is heard up in the sky.
> And hosts of two-hundred-*pood* clouds
> Lie up above in every spot;
> When a flood of mighty waters
> Knocks the forest beast from his feet,–
> Not yet believing ourselves,
> We call this: God.

"Poem of the Rain" (1931)

Once Zabolotsky has actually *seen* this presence, however, he
finds any appellation – even "God" – insufficient, and so he
refuses to name it.

Zabolotsky set no smaller task for himself than to describe
the indescribable. Just as the ancient Hebrews used the
Tetragrammaton to avoid desecrating the Lord's name as they
praised it, so in "The Trees" Zabolotsky encoded a system of
abstract geometric symbols instead of using metaphorical or

dramatic characterization to represent the great and ineffable spirit he had discerned. His refusal to identify precisely this spirit implies a reverence for it, for naming would be a travesty, a reduction at the least. Zabolotsky realized that any attempt at specificity would automatically impose limits on that which he perceived as limitless; denomination would only serve to contain the infinite.

In acknowledging a pervasive spirit behind life, Zabolotsky's vision offers an original expression of the intangible; his recognition of the essential and true brings the longed-for utopia. Just as Skovoroda believed that contentment could be attained by discerning the presence of God in everything, so Zabolotsky found his "kingdom of God" in the Tree of the Sphere: "It is among [the trees], and to the side, and here, and everywhere." By allowing his intuitive nature to guide his intellect, by balancing reason with inspiration, Zabolotsky opened himself to this ecstatic vision.

CHAPTER 5

Autumnal observations

> Yea, my heart had great experience of wisdom and
> knowledge.
>
> *Ecclesiastes*

In "The Trees" Zabolotsky penetrated beyond the finished
forms of nature to conceive a single image of creation, the
Sphere. This vision reduced his complex cosmography to its
most essential form and revealed art as the medium through
which the universal can be discerned. Zabolotsky expressed
awe before his discovery, and the magisterial voice at the end of
the poem denotes the culmination of his poetic quest. Here a
tone of reverence prevails over the poet's customary irrever-
ence. The sublime intonation of "The Trees" shows how far
Zabolotsky has evolved from "The Triumph of Agriculture":
the voice of childlike wonder in his first long poem has now
become hoary; its eloquence suggests accumulated wisdom.

If, in order to remain vital, poetry must continually accumu-
late new layers without discarding the old,[1] then Zabolotsky's
long poems exist as the proving ground for his poetry. By the
end of "The Trees" Zabolotsky had gained much wisdom,
which allowed him to recognize not only the underlying
symmetries of nature, but also its contradictions and discord-
ancies. This recognition enabled Zabolotsky to find beauty in
the very changeability of nature, and his understanding of the
"world of contradictions" ("Metamorphoses") offered him the
possibility of unexpected insight, of epiphany. It was precisely
this insight into nature that helped sustain him through his
period of adversity. Largely thanks to his "spiritual experience," Zabolotsky was able to retain a sense of delight in

nature, even as he continued to discover its ever-changing forms, some of which no doubt stretched both his conception of the grotesque and his ability to survive. Even after his return from the camps, Zabolotsky remained receptive to intuitive perception, just as he had been in "The Trees" fifteen years earlier:

> В этот миг перед ним открывалось
> То, что было незримо доселе,
> И душа его в мир поднималась,
> Как дитя из своей колыбели.
>
> "Приближался апрель к середине" (1948)

> At that instant there opened up before him
> What hitherto had been unseen,
> And his soul began to climb into the world,
> Like a child from its cradle.
>
> "April Neared its Midpoint" (1948)

Although it is possible to trace the consistent evolution of Zabolotsky's poetic voice from his early poetry to his late, it would be mistaken to presume that his arrest and imprisonment had no influence on his subsequent work. Partly because no other poet of Zabolotsky's stature shared his specific experience (as a "modernist" making a comeback as a "classicist" following a lengthy imprisonment), it is difficult to assess the effects of his ordeal. The poet John Berryman once said that for a writer, any hardship that doesn't kill him is terrific. Such an assertion presupposes that suffering enables; that adverse experience serves to temper the writer as an artist, providing not only the material but also the discipline necessary to turn incident to good advantage. Berryman's attitude seems cavalier, however, when one confronts the labor camps. By a combination of luck and wits Nikolai Zabolotsky managed to survive the camps, yet the crucial question remains: did his long incarceration kill Zabolotsky as a poet?

Following his return from six years in the gulag and two in exile, Zabolotsky resumed writing, but in a different style. This marked difference caused critics to speak of "the two Zabolotskys." Soviet critics praised the late Zabolotsky for overcoming his earlier "formalistic" tendencies, the most extreme holding that "the years of silence and humiliation" actually helped him.[2] Western critics, in contrast, upbraided Zabolotsky for his ostensible capitulation to political demands, claiming that he was "first reprimanded into silence, and then tamed into that parrotry which seems to be the supreme law of Soviet art."[3]

From the beginning Zabolotsky's art has been approached along partisan lines, resulting in the reduction of his poetry to simplistic terms. Victimized by political machinations during his lifetime, Zabolotsky continues to fall prey to them after his death. Ironically, although never a political poet, he has been caught repeatedly in the ideological crossfire. Thus, even those critics sympathetic to his case, who intend to praise his tenacity, end up damning him with the left hand:

Zabolotsky's career presents the not unusual phenomenon of a poet who began as a "progressive" and ended as a "conservative." With the difference that Conservatism was not a natural development in the experience of aging as it often is; it was a condition of creative survival.[4]

Such an assessment raises a numbers of questions, not least the validity of the word "conservatism" as applied to poetry. But semantics aside, why couldn't "conservatism" be a natural development in Zabolotsky's career, as it was in so many others'? Why must the *a priori* assumption be that Zabolotsky could not simply have entered into a less clamorous old age? After all, even Ezra Pound, vociferous author of the modernist dictum "Make it new!", has been allowed to subside into "the experience of aging." The issue, finally, is not whether the poet changed over the course of his career, since change is inevitable, even imperative, for an artist to remain viable. Rather it is the nature of the shift in Zabolotsky's verse that provokes our interest. Was it abrupt or gradual, radical or intrinsic? That is, does there exist one Zabolotsky or two?

The argument that Zabolotsky's imprisonment and subsequent uncertain status were the primary cause of the change in his poetry is simply too pat. Certainly, beginning in the thirties Zabolotsky lived under a pall. And certainly he authored two distinct kinds of verse, circumscribed roughly by the years preceding and postdating his incarceration. But the striking difference in style between Zabolotsky's post-camp verse and that of the early *Scrolls* has misled readers and critics into supposing that an entirely new poet emerged in the 1940s; meanwhile, the deeper resonances of thematic unity among the poems are either overlooked or ignored. Despite the overt differences between his early and late poems, Zabolotsky's work develops a continuous philosophy: from beginning to end he expresses the essential pursuit of a rational harmony in nature. As early as the 1920s Zabolotsky was engaged by the circumstances of man's mortality and his relation to nature. Furthermore, many of his late poems rest on the inspired vision of a universe in balance as depicted in "The Trees." Therefore it is hardly surprising that his later verse should continue to treat the same philosophical problems, particularly given his personal history during the intervening years.

Zabolotsky never chose to enlighten his public by explaining his intentions. By nature reserved, he became on his return to society even more withdrawn. Yet although the external circumstances of his life shook him deeply, they could not destroy his core poetic vision, which remained consistent throughout his life. Quite early Zabolotsky had recognized in himself something he instinctively knew he had to protect. At eighteen, he wrote to his friend Misha Kasyanov: "You know, life is such a strange thing – if you see something in yourself, don't show it to anyone. Be anyone at all in the eyes of others, but don't let them touch your heart."[5] In Zabolotsky this statement represents no adolescent posturing, but a calculated decision made in favor of remoteness, providing him a necessary defense, but leaving his poetry dangerously open to misinterpretation.

THE FACES OF NATURE

In his early verse Zabolotsky frequently employed the metaphor of nature as a prison. This idea is presented most succinctly in "Autumn":

Нелегкая задача –
Разбить синонимы: природа и тюрьма.

It's not an easy task
To separate the synonyms: nature and prison.

Ironically, within six years nature had become Zabolotsky's captor as the expanses of Siberia imprisoned him in their remoteness. Beyond the fences of the labor camp, nature itself presented a barrier to normal life, and what had been merely the poet's metaphor became his reality. Yet in Zabolotsky's post-camp poetry nature reappears not as a warder, but as a liberator of sorts, affording the poet moments of great insight. Given nature's rôle in Zabolotsky's early verse as well as in his life, how was he able to "separate the synonyms" of nature and prison? How did he come to terms with his adversary?

The evolution of nature in Zabolotsky's poetry follows a clear pattern over the three decades of his literary activity. In his earliest poems, nature suffers uniformly, helpless to free itself from conflicts and ambiguities. "A Stroll" is emblematic of nature's confusion, where a river yields to both laughter and tears in its inability to act. Nature feels the anguish of uniform suffering in "The Triumph of Agriculture," too. But as Zabolotsky's poetry matures, so does nature's capacity for self-expression: the inarticulate steed of "The Face of the Horse" gives way to the eloquent Mad Wolf. In a parallel progression, nature leaves behind chaos for order, thanks largely to the intervention of man.

Man's relationship with nature also undergoes change in Zabolotsky's verse. Initially an exploiter of nature, by the mid-thirties man is nature's mentor and guide, enjoying a mutually supportive alliance with it. This depiction followed from Zabolotsky's poetic epiphany in "The Trees," which showed that through artistic insight man can gain access to nature's essential truths. Subsequent poems explore the ways in which man can put his knowledge to beneficial use.

The idea of nature as a receptacle of truth underlies the lovely "Lesnoe ozero" ("Woodland Lake") of 1938. Zabolotsky's picture of animals thirsting in a glade appears as a vivid, verbal portrayal of Pirosmani's painting "Three Deer by a Stream," and the clear vision of the poem seems especially striking when one considers that it was composed in a closed freight car during Zabolotsky's transport to Siberia.[6]

Опять мне блеснула, окована сном,
Хрустальная чаша во мраке лесном.

Сквозь битвы деревьев и волчьи сраженья,
Где пьют насекомые сок из растенья,
Где буйствуют стебли и стонут цветы,
Где хищная тварями правит природа,
Пробрался к тебе я и замер у входа,
Раздвинув руками сухие кусты.

В венце из кувшинок, в уборе осок,
В сухом ожерелье растительных дудок
Лежал целомудренной влаги кусок,
Убежище рыб и пристанище уток.
Но странно, как тихо и важно кругом!
Откуда в трущобах такое величье?
Зачем не беснуется полчище птичье,
Но спит, убаюкано сладостным сном?
Один лишь кулик на судьбу негодует
И в дудку растенья бессмысленно дует.

И озеро в тихом вечернем огне
Лежит в глубине, неподвижно сияя,
И сосны, как свечи, стоят в вышине,
Смыкаясь рядами от края до края.
Бездонная чаша прозрачной воды
Сияла и мыслила мыслью отдельной.
Так око больного в тоске беспредельной
При первом сиянье вечерней звезды
Уже не сочувствуя телу больному,
Горит, устремленное к небу ночному,
И толпы животных и диких зверей,
Просунув сквозь елки рогатые лица,
К источнику правды, к купели своей
Склонялись воды животворной напиться.

Across my mind, fettered with sleep, again
Flashed a crystal bowl in the forest gloom.

Through the battles of trees and the wolves' encounters,
Where insects drink the juice from plants,

Where stalks rampage and flowers moan,
Where grasping nature governs creation,
I broke through to you and froze on the threshhold,
Moving aside the dry brush with my hands.

In a wreath of water-lilies, in a headdress of sedge,
In a dry necklace of vegetal fifes
Lay a piece of chaste moisture,
A refuge for fish and a haven for ducks.
But strange, how silent and peaceful it is here!
From where does such grandeur in the wild derive?
Why isn't a horde of birds raging here
Instead of sleeping, lulled by sweet dreams?
Only one sandpiper, indignant with his lot,
Blows senselessly on the fife of a plant.

And in the fire of the silent evening, the lake
Lies in the depths, motionless, shining,
And the pine trees, like candles, stand aloft,
Closing their ranks from one edge to the other.
The bottomless bowl of transparent water
Shines and thinks its own separate thoughts.
Thus at the glow of the first evening star,
The eye of a sick man in infinite anguish
No longer feels for his invalid body,
But blazes, fixed on the nighttime sky.
And crowds of animals and wild beasts,
Poking their horned faces through the firs,
Bend down to the source of truth, their font,
In order to drink of the life-giving water.

Like the Sphere, this round lake represents the source of
nature's truth, a symbol of perfection. Not only is the lake
untainted ("transparent" and "chaste"), it exists independently of man's reason (it can "think its own separate thoughts").
Trapped in a freight car, Zabolotsky substantialized the idea of
the lake's existence (the existence of truth) to such a degree as
to make it seem real: this lake is not formless water but a
"crystal bowl," an actual "piece" of moisture one can very
nearly "feel with the fingers" ("oshchupyvat' pal'tsami").

Of particular relevance is the coda of the poem, an extended
metaphor about a dying man.[7] This man, imagined as withered, contrasts sharply with the lake, which Zabolotsky

presents in the image of a young and beautiful virgin, full of life. The actual connections of this poem to Zabolotsky's situation are clear enough; what is notable is the reversal of man's and nature's rôles from his early poetry. Now man suffers in "infinite anguish"; now man is aided by nature as he fixes his gaze on the evening star – the same star that inspired the Mad Wolf – and thereby transcends his bodily pain.

Bluntly stated, this fixation on nature as a source of beauty and truth enabled Zabolotsky to survive as a poet. Once he had learned to see nature as less of a prison, it could become an escape. Zabolotsky's letters from the camps reveal that the theme of nature grew increasingly important to him.[8] By concentrating on the dramatic Far Eastern landscape, he was able to renew his sense of wonder at the universe and therefore more easily bear the hardships of his life.[9] The image of the woodland lake likely helped; we know that Zabolotsky kept it in mind throughout his imprisonment, transcribing the poem from memory only after his release.

Of the eight poems Zabolotsky wrote in 1946 following his return from exile, six are set in nature. In "V etoi roshche berezovoi" ("In this Birch Grove") he comes to terms with his past experience and announces a new start. As in "The Nightingale," Zabolotsky uses avian imagery to express the idea of poetic creation.[10] And like the previous poem, "In this Birch Grove" is about stoicism: though the body has been battered, the voice still can sing. But where the nightingale caused the poet great pain, the oriole now allows him to triumph:

> Но ведь в жизни солдаты мы,
> И уже на пределах ума
> Содрогаются атомы
> Белым вихрем взметая дома.
> Как безумные мельницы,
> Машут войны крылами вокруг.
> Где же ты, иволга, леса отшельница?
> Что ты смолкла, мой друг?
> . . . .
> За великими реками
> Встанет солнце, и в утренней мгле

С опаленными веками
Припаду я, убытый, к земле.
Крикнув бешеным вороном,
Весь дрожа, замолчит пулемет.
И тогда в моем сердце разорванном
Голос твой запоет.

After all we are soldiers in life,
And on the borders of the mind
Atoms are already shuddering,
Like a white whirlwind hurling houses.
Like mad windmills
Wars flap their wings around us.
Where are you, oriole, sylvan recluse?
Why have you grown silent, my friend?
. . . .
Beyond the great rivers
The sun will rise, and in the morning mist
With scorched lids
I shall fall, dead, to the ground.
Screaming like a rabid crow,
Trembling all over, the machine gun will fall still.
And then in my lacerated heart
Your voice will start to sing.

Zabolotsky similarly reaffirms himself as a poet in "Ustupi mne, skvorets, ugolok" ("Give up your perch to me, starling"). Here, however, the affirmation is tempered by the poet's realization of his precarious position: though his voice has survived, he must use it sparingly. His situation is made clear by a butterfly, which like earlier Zabolotskian animals is able to see the truth:[11]

Я и сам бы стараться горазд,
Да шепнула мне бабочка-странница:
"Кто бывает весною горласт,
Тот без голоса к лету останется."[12]

I myself would be good at trying,
But a butterfly whispered to me:
"Whoever is loud-mouthed in springtime
Will end up with no voice by the summer."

The original variant of this stanza is even more direct in regard to Zabolotsky's condition:

Я и сам бы стараться горазд,
Да облезли от холода перышки.
Если смолоду будешь горласт,
Перехватит дыхание в горлышке.[13]

I myself would be good at trying,
But my feathers have grown bare from the cold.
If you are loud-mouthed in youth
Your breath will get caught in your throat.

Despite the admonishments of those around him, Zabolotsky was determined to resume his literary career. And
because he sought an audience for his verse as a necessary
condition for survival, he made the pragmatic and possibly
cynical decision to save the essential core of his poetry while
ceding its more visible parts. In other words, Zabolotsky chose
poetic vision over artistic style, and his subsequent poetry
reflects this choice. The issue is one of prosody. Even in the
highly modernist *Scrolls* Zabolotsky had demonstrated his
mastery of standard metrical forms[14] (though he always overlaid them with uncommon imagery). Now, in his late poetry,
he relied almost exclusively on traditional patterns of versi-
fication. Furthermore, his imagery became more accessible.
Yet Zabolotsky's tropes do not relinquish their power; his
images remain vivid and stark, as in this first stanza from
"Mozhzhevelovyi kust" ("The Juniper Bush," 1957):

Я увидел во сне можжевеловый куст,
Я услышал вдали металлический хруст,
Аметистовых ягод услышал я звон
И во сне, в тишине, мне понравился он.

I saw in my dream a juniper bush,
I heard in the distance its metallic crunch,
I heard its amethyst berries ring,
And in my dream, in the silence, it pleased me.

These lines exemplify the clarity and simplicity of Zabolotsky's late style, still rich in tactile language. The description
of the juniper bush, its "metallic crunch," evokes a wintry
terrain with crackling snow in a shrouded landscape. Not only
do we see the bush and imagine this landscape, we also hear

11 Zabolotsky gesturing in Moscow, *c.* 1957

and feel them. The rhyming couplets of the traditional ana-
pestic tetrameter follow a regular pattern throughout the
poem, yet their insistent, assertive masculine rhyme endings
give the poem unexpected strength. And even though the
experience is once removed, in a dream, it seems very close
because of the numerous verbs that express immediate sensation.

With such vigorous lines, what then did Zabolotsky forfeit in
his poetry? Simply put, he gave up the playfulness and
audacity of modernism. In his OBERIU period Zabolotsky had
striven for complexity, but his goal now was to be understood.
Instead of "making it difficult" he wanted to "make it transparent," rejecting an *ustanovka na zatrudnenie* in favor of an
ustanovka na prozrachnost'. Even if Zabolotsky had wanted to
continue writing in his old style, it would have made no sense
to do so. As Akhmatova and Pasternak had already discovered,
modernism had long ago become obsolete in Stalin's Russia.
Not only was there no audience for experimental verse, but to

write as though nothing had happened would have been both inappropriate and foolhardy.

Yet despite the shift in his style, Zabolotsky in no way betrayed his core vision; on the contrary, his late poems affirm the consistency of his ideas from beginning to end. With his first post-imprisonment poems, Zabolotsky picked up his poetic philosophy where he had left off nine years earlier. In "Chitaite, derev'ia, stikhi Gesioda" ("Trees, Read Hesiod's Verse"), he portrays nature as man's "younger brother" who must be schooled, exhorting the trees to read the works of Hesiod, singer of the Golden Age. In order that nature might learn, man becomes its thought, as he had earlier in "Yesterday, Pondering Death." This pedagogic process is dependent upon the poet:

> Но зайцы и птицы садятся за парты
> И к зверю девятая сходит Камена.
> Березы, вы школьницы! . . .

> But the rabbits and birds sit down at their desks
> And the ninth Muse comes down to the beast.
> Birches, you schoolgirls! . . .

Other lines reveal that Zabolotsky's poetics still involve the concretization of the object. Just as he materialized the woodland lake, describing an actual "piece of moisture" as if to substantiate the lake's existence outside his imagination, so in "Trees, Read Hesiod's Verse" Zabolotsky treats the soul as a material entity in order to emphasize its vitality. In this handling of the object, the post-camp Zabolotsky differs very little from the Oberiut who "substantialized the object to the extreme":

> . . . Покуда
> Не вытряхнут душу из этого тела,
> Едва ли иного достоин я чуда,
> Чем то, от которого сердце запело.

> . . . Until
> My soul is shaken from this body,
> I'm hardly worthy of a miracle other
> Than the one that made my heart begin to sing.

This soul, substantial enough to be shaken from the body, does not dissipate at death, and its representation seems a partial response to the peasants' questions in "The Triumph of Agriculture": "Where is the soul?/Does only powder/Remain after death?/Or only stinking gas?" The frequent references to a tangible soul in Zabolotsky's late verse imply that more than powder does remain after death. Certainly the idea of a material postmortem existence appealed to the poet, but it soon becomes clear that for Zabolotsky, materiality does not necessarily entail ubiety or presence in a particular place. While the soul may continue to exist in tangible form after death, it is defined differently than in life. Thus in "Son" ("A Dream," 1953), the poet describes his entry into another world:

> Жилец земли, пятидесяти лет,
> Подобно всем счастливый и несчастный,
> Однажды я покинул этот свет
> И очутился в местности безгласной.
> Там человек едва существовал
> Последними остатками привычек,
> Но ничего уж больше не желал
> И не носил ни прозвищ он, ни кличек.
> Участник удивительной игры,
> Не вглядываясь в скученные лица,
> Я там ложился в дымные костры
> И поднимался, чтобы вновь ложиться.
> Я уплывал, я странствовал вдали,
> Безвольный, равнодушный, молчаливый,
> И тонкий свет исчезнувшей земли
> Отталкивал рукой неторопливой.
> Какой-то отголосок бытия
> Еще имел я для существованья,
> Но уж стремилась вся душа моя
> Стать не душой, но частью мирозданья.
> Там по пространству двигались ко мне
> Сплетения каких-то матерьялов,
> Мосты в необозримой вышине
> Висели над ущельями провалов.
> Я хорошо запомнил внешний вид
> Всех этих тел, плывущих из пространства:
> Сплетенье ферм, и выпуклости плит,

И дикость первобытного убранства.
Там тонкостей не видно и следа,
Искусство форм там явно не в почете,
И не заметно тягостей труда,
Хотя весь мир в движенье и работе.
И в поведенье тамошних властей
Не видел я малейшего насилья,
И сам, лишенный воли и страстей,
Все то, что нужно, делал без усилья.
Мне не было причины не хотеть,
Как не было желания стремиться,
И был готов я странствовать и впредь,
Коль то могло на что-то пригодиться.
Со мной бродил какой-то мальчуган,
Болтал со мной о массе пустяковин.
И даже он, похожий на туман,
Был больше материален, чем духовен.
Мы с мальчиком иа озеро пошли,
Он удочку куда-то вниз закинул
И нечто, долетевшее с земли,
Не торопясь, рукою отодвинул.

An inhabitant of earth, fifty years old,
Like everyone happy and unhappy,
One day I abandoned this world
And found myself in a silent terrain.
There man barely subsisted
On the last remnants of his habits,
But he no longer desired anything
And bore no nicknames, no pet names.
Participant in an amazing game,
Not staring at the teeming faces,
I lay down in smoky bonfires
And rose up, to lie down again.
I floated away, I wandered afar,
Lacking will, indifferent, silent,
And I pushed away with a leisurely hand
The frail light of the disappearing earth.
For existence I still had
Some sort of echo of reality,
But my entire soul was already striving
To become not a soul, but a part of the universe.
There the entwinements of some vague materials

Moved towards me through space,
Bridges of endless height
Were suspended over the gorges of chasms.
I remember well the external appearance
Of all these bodies floating from space:
The entwinement of girders, the protuberance of slabs,
And the savagery of primitive decoration.
There was no trace of subtlety there,
The art of forms was clearly held in low regard,
And the burdens of labor were not noticeable,
Although the entire world was in motion and work.
And in the conduct of the local authorities
I did not see the slightest violence,
And I myself, devoid of will and passions,
Did everything necessary without effort.
I had no reason not to want,
As I had no wish to aspire,
And I was ready to wander on in the future
If it would come in handy.
A little boy wandered with me,
He chattered a lot of nonsense.
And even he, resembling fog,
Was more material than spiritual.
The boy and I went to a lake,
He cast a rod down into it,
And something that had flown up from earth
He pushed away leisurely with his hand.

For Zabolotsky, life takes its meaning from art, and because this dream world lacks any aesthetic impulse, it is dead. In the absence of beauty, "the art of forms," existence is necessarily bleak and passionless. This vision of pervasive indifference is frightening, conveyed in such phrases as "nichego uzh bol'she ne zhelal," "bezvol'nyi, ravnodushnyi, molchalivyi," "lishen-nyi voli i strastei," "ne bylo prichiny ne khotet'," "ne bylo zhelania stremit'sia" ("he no longer desired anything," "will-less, indifferent, silent," "devoid of will and passions," "I had no reason not to want," "no wish to aspire"). And the twice-repeated image of a careless hand pushing away any vestiges of another reality evinces the deep resignation of the dreamer. Even the prosody contributes to a sense of surrender. The iambic pentameter is relentless in its regularity, as is the

alternating rhyme scheme with its alternate masculine and
feminine endings – as though the poet feels indifferent to the
possibility of variety in form.

The world in "Proshchanie s druz′iami" ("A Farewell to
Friends," 1952),[15] which Zabolotsky wrote in memory of his
OBERIU friends Kharms, Vvedensky and Oleinikov, is also
devoid of forms, though here their absence reflects less a lack of
beauty than of order. The chaos of disunited elements represents the state we understand as death:

В широких шляпах, длинных пиджаках,
С тетрадями своих стихотворений,
Давным-давно рассыпались вы в прах,
Как ветки облетевшие сирени.

Вы в той стране, где нет готовых форм,
Где все разъято, смешано, разбито,
Где вместо неба – лишь могильный холм
И неподвижна лунная орбита.

Там на ином, невнятном языке
Поет синклит беззвучных насекомых,
Там с маленьким фонариком в руке
Жук-человек приветствует знакомых.

Спокойно ль вам, товарищи мои?
Легко ли вам? И все ли вы забыли?
Теперь вам братья – корни, муравьи,
Травинки, вздохи, столбики из пыли.

Теперь вам сестры – цветики гвоздик
Соски сирени, щепочки, цыплята . . .
И уж не в силах вспомнить ваш язык
Там наверху оставленного брата.

Ему еще не место во тех краях,
Где вы исчезли, легкие, как тени,
В широких шляпах, длинных пиджаках,
С тетрадями своих стихотворений.

In wide hats, long jackets,
With notebooks of your poems,
Long ago you scattered into dust,
Like lilac branches that have lost their blossoms.

You are in that country with no ready forms,
Where all is disintegrated, mixed, fractured,

Where instead of sky there's only a grave mound,
Where the lunar orbit is motionless.

There, in another, indistinct language
A synod of soundless insects sings,
There, with a small lantern in hand,
A beetle-man greets his acquaintances.

Are you comfortable, my friends?
Are you easy? Have you forgotten all?
Now your brothers are roots and ants,
Blades of grass, sighs, pillars of dust.

Now your sisters are wild carnations,
Nipples of lilac, splinters and chickens ...
And the brother you left up above
No longer has the strength to recall your language.

He has no place yet in those parts
Where you disappeared, light as shadows,
In wide hats, long jackets,
With notebooks of your poems.

Like the world in "A Dream," this world is material – a
strana or "country" – but the lack of order among its elements
characterizes death. We find the same sort of equation in, for
example, the early "Temptation" or the later "Kogda by ia
nedvizhnym trupom" ("When I as a Motionless Corpse,"
1957), where the poet describes his dead self as an "accidental
combination of particles." Zabolotsky saw the random dispersal of particles as a feature of the world of the non-living. Until
these disparate particles can reform themselves into an integral
whole, life as such will not exist.

Typical of Zabolotsky's best poetry, "A Farewell to
Friends" offsets an elegiac tone with humor, simultaneously
dolorous for its depiction of death and appealing for its
animation of an otherworldly insect population. By personify-
ing the elements of this world, Zabolotsky brings his friends
back to apparent life. And by relating his fellow poets to their
new and various "sisters" and "brothers," he can take comfort
in the idea of the material unity of all creation, living and
dead.[16]

SOCIAL AND HISTORICAL CONCERNS

As a whole, Zabolotsky's late poetry continues to elaborate his *Naturphilosophie*, but not every poem treats man's relation to nature. A number of later poems were occasioned by a different sort of relationship – that of man to society.[17] "V Kino" ("At the Movies," 1954), "Nekrasivaia devochka" ("The Ugly Girl," 1955) and "Staraia aktrisa" ("The Old Actress," 1956) all address moral and psychological problems. Where Zabolotsky's late nature poems echo Tyutchev, his civic verse recalls that of Nikolai Nekrasov.

In these latter poems humans, not animals, serve as the allegorical figures. Too often, however, their characterizations lack the playfulness of Zabolotsky's best animal fables, tending the poems toward the maudlin. Here Zabolotsky's abandonment of his early dialogue form is particularly telling. Where once he challenged his reader to participate in the poetic process, he now lapses into a certain preachiness, and at times his poems seem doctrinaire. Some of his most frequently anthologized lines exhort:

> Не позволяй душе лениться!
> Чтоб в ступе воду не толочь,
> Душа обязана трудиться
> И день и ночь, и день и ночь!
>> "Не позволяй душе лениться" (1958)

> Do not allow your soul to idle!
> In order not to mill the wind,
> The soul is bound to labor
> Day and night, day and night!
>> "Do not allow your soul to idle" (1958)

Such didactic poems, while clearly accessible to a wide readership, are Zabolotsky's least successful. In them his most characteristic attribute – seriousness of thought overlaid with whimsicality – is out of balance as the ponderous prevails. Zabolotsky's poems treating man in nature convey a tension provoked by his doubts; his civic poems, although uniformly well-executed, lack this excitement.

A number of poems in this category do combine a

heightened civic sense with other themes of enduring interest to Zabolotsky. Thus in "O krasote chelovecheskikh lits" ("On the Beauty of Human Faces," 1955) architecture becomes a metaphor for facial structures.[18] In this tribute to the variety of human physical forms, Zabolotsky likens different faces to portals, shacks, dungeons, towers, and huts. The hard sciences also attracted him for the inspired leaps by which their disciplines grew. To the end of his life he followed new advances in science, reading for pleasure such works as Erwin Schrödinger's lectures on humanism and physics and Yosif Khalifman's *Book on the Biology of the Bee*.[19] Zabolotsky's poem "Skvoz' volshebnyi pribor Levenguka" ("Through Leeuwenhoek's Magic Instrument," 1948) takes as its point of departure the experiments of the seventeenth-century Dutch microscopist Anton van Leeuwenhoek, who perfected a lens that could magnify an object three-hundred-fold. This lens reveals a "world of wonderful creations," a "realm of deaths and births," which increase the poet's understanding of universal transformations.

Alongside Zabolotsky's interest in science grew his enthusiasm for history. The past fascinated him, and he frequented used book shops in the hope of collecting the entire run of *Russkaia starina* (*Russian Antiquity*), a pre-Revolutionary journal for intellectual history lovers.[20] In childhood Zabolotsky had wandered the environs of Urzhum with his father, who gathered local artifacts and impressed on his son the importance of preserving them.[21] Later, when Zabolotsky entered the Pedagogical Institute, one of his favorite courses was a seminar in Old Russian Literature.[22] Not surprisingly, then, he undertook an historical epic, "Osada Kozel'ska" ("The Siege of Kozelsk"),[23] based on the Mongol rout of that town in 1239, and was working on this poem at the time of his arrest. During the same period he began translating "The Lay of Igor's Campaign," a project that proved to be his artistic salvation. In 1951 Zabolotsky conceived of a plan to rework the entire body of *byliny* or heroic epics into modern Russian[24] but had completed only "Istselenie Il'i Muromtsa" ("The Healing of Ilya Muromets") when he died.

As noted earlier, Zabolotsky felt a lively curiosity about the East, and his historical interests extended beyond the borders of Russia. His admiration for Khlebnikov, who frequently visualized the East in his poetry, stimulated Zabolotsky's own thoughts about the cultural differences between East and West. He read Giovanni de Piano Carpini's *Liber Tartarorum*, a history of the Mongols, as well as the sketches of Friar William of Rubruquis (Rubruck), who travelled to Mongolia in 1253 as an envoy from Louis IX.[25] Zabolotsky's investigation of Tartary culminated in the magnificent long poem[26] "Rubruk v Mongolii" ("Rubruck in Mongolia," 1958), which is infused with the immediacy of his own experience of the vast Asian steppe.[27]

By the time Zabolotsky began writing "Rubruck" his political situation had eased, and he was feeling fewer artistic constraints. Thus the poem reflects what might be termed a fresh old Zabolotsky. For instance, the description of screeching Mongol caravans relies on Zabolotsky's frequent theme of an orchestra in nature, yet he makes the screeching not only aural, but visual, as well:

> Когда бы дьяволы играли
> На скрипках лиственниц и лип,
> Они подобной вакханальи
> Сыграть, наверно, не смогли б.

> If devils played
> On violins of larch and lime trees,
> They likely could not play
> A similar bacchanal.

And when Rubruck contemplates the evening sky, the constellations he sees are strikingly similar to those in "The Signs of the Zodiac Flicker" from 1929:

> Идут небесные Бараны,
> Плывут астральные Ковши,
> Пылают реки, гори, страны,
> Дворцы, кибитки, шалаши,

> Ревет медведь в своей берлоге,
> Кричит стервятница лиса,

12 Zabolotsky relaxing in Tarusa, 1958

Проходят боги, гибнут боги,
Но вечно светят небеса!

Heavenly Rams pass,
Astral Dippers float,
Rivers, mountains, countries blaze,
Palaces, wagons, cabins,

A bear roars in his den,
A carrion fox shrieks,
Gods come, gods go,
But the heavens shine forever!

With "Rubruck" Zabolotsky was moving in a new direction, one that often echoed his earliest poetry. Significantly, at his death he was about to embark on a trilogy of long poems that would have united his early and later verse. On his desk, next to a poetic fragment from 1932 subsequently published as "Pastukhi" ("Shepherds"),[28] lay the last lines he ever wrote: "Pastukhi, angely, zhivotnye ..." ("Shepherds, angels, animals ..."). These three words testify to Zabolotsky's unwavering desire to connect the various phenomena of the universe and to his continuing investigation of life in all of its manifold forms. Furthermore, the projected titles of the trilogy – "Mudrost' Sokrata" ("The Wisdom of Socrates"), "Poklonenie volkhvov" ("The Adoration of the Magi") and "Stalin"[29] – suggest that Zabolotsky planned to explore not only the metamorphoses occurring in nature, but also those taking place in history: the transformation of fact into legend. Had Zabolotsky lived to complete this project, his poems on civic and historical themes ultimately would have been linked with his nature poems.

Zabolotsky already had effected this link in a number of his best late poems, where he considered societal griefs in relation to the cycles of nature. "Begstvo v Egipet" ("Flight into Egypt," 1955), for instance, is an allegory for Zabolotsky's own exile. "Protivostoianie Marsa" ("The Opposition of Mars," 1956) metaphorically places Stalin's excesses against a cosmic scale, and like "The Mad Wolf" makes the case for an "essential spirit" that must coexist with reason. One of Zabolotsky's most beautiful poems, "Gde-to v pole vozle Magadana" ("Somewhere in a Field near Magadan," 1956), portrays the deaths of two labor camp inmates among the vast Siberian snows. Here, as in Zabolotsky's earliest nature poems, stars appear as symbols of universal freedom.

Zabolotsky also wrote about the anguish of love in the cycle "Posledniaia liubov'" ("Last Love"). "Chertopolokh" ("Thistle," 1956) is particularly vivid:[30]

> Принесли букет чертополоха
> И на стол поставили, и вот
> Предо мной пожар и суматоха
> И огней багровый хоровод.
> Эти звезды с острыми концами,
> Эти брызги северной зари
> И гремят и стонут бубенцами,
> Фонарями вспыхнув изнутри.
> Это тоже образ мирозданья,
> Организм, сплетенный из лучей,
> Битвы неоконченной пыланье
> Полыханье поднятых мечей.

Это башня ярости и славы,
Где к копью приставлено копье,
Где пушки цветов, кровавоглавы,
Прямо в сердце врезаны мое.
Снилась мне высокая темница
И решетка, черная, как ночь,
За решеткой – сказочная птица,
Та, которой некому помочь.
Но и я живу, как видно, плохо,
Ибо я помочь не в силах ей.
И встает стена чертополоха
Между мной и радостью моей.
И простерся шип клинообразный
В грудь мою, и уж в последний раз
Светит мне печальный и прекрасный
Взор ее неугасимых глаз.

A bouquet of thistle was carried in
And set upon the table.
Before me arose fire and chaos
And a crimson dance of flames.
These stars with sharp points,
These shards of the northern dawn
Peal and moan like small bells,
Blazing up from within like lanterns.
This is also an image of the universe,
An organism spun of rays,
The flame of an unfinished battle,
The blaze of raised swords.
This is a tower of rage and glory,
Where spear is set against spear,
Where bunches of flowers, with bloody heads,
Cut right into my heart.
I dreamed of a tall dungeon
With bars as black as night,
Behind the bars was a fabulous bird,
The one that no one could help.
But I too, it seems, live badly,
For I have no strength to help.
And the wall of thistle rises up
Between me and my joy.
A wedge-shaped thorn has pierced
My breast, and now the sad and wonderful

Gaze of her unquenchable eyes
Shines on me for the last time.

"An image of the universe," the thistle embodies the conflicts and longings the poet is unable to resolve. The caged bird serves as a metaphor for his impotence, and the sense of confinement is heightened by such words as "temnitsa," "reshetka," and "stena" ("dungeon," "bars," "wall"). The edges of this poem about love are quite sharp, as if the words themselves cut into the poet's heart. And not only is the vocabulary sharp-edged, it is martial: "bitvy," "mechei," "bashnia," "kop'ie" ("battle," "swords," "tower," "spear"). Inevitably, war causes bloodshed, and as the poem progresses the color red accumulates: "pozhar," "bagrovyi," "ognei," "zari," "krovavoglavy" ("fire," "crimson," "flames," "dawn," "bloody-headed"). Yet even as the red symbolizes pain, it radiates a brilliance that dazzles the reader and infuses the poem with light: "zvedzy," "zari," "fonariami," "luchei," "vspykhnuv," "pylan'e," "svetit" ("stars," "dawn," "lanterns," "rays," "blazed up," "blaze," "shines"). "Thistle" is remarkable for the abundance of impressions it provokes; like Blake, Zabolotsky was able to see an entire world in something minute.

In "Vecher na Oke" ("Evening on the Oka River," 1957), carmine and bellicose nature turns gentle as the poet contemplates the world at sunset. He experiences an epiphany that enables him to "distinguish a multitude of wonders" in nature's "living features." Following his revelation in "The Trees," he can now feel the "genuine joy" of the landscape and see the vital beauty in the world around him. In this poem, Zabolotsky brings the Russian landscape alive with the voices of Tyutchev and Pushkin,[31] affirming both his closeness to nature and his continuity with the past.

A UNIVERSAL CONSCIOUSNESS

During Zabolotsky's lifetime Russian society was thrice transformed. Still, he continued to produce poetry at an extraordinarily high level and without abandoning his basic beliefs.

As he pursued an elusive harmony in nature, many voices spoke through him, and his worldview came to encompass a wide variety of ideas. Mandelstam has written that the critic's obligation is to determine a poet's "literary genesis, his literary sources, his *kinship* and origins";[32] this book has sought to show just how broad Zabolotsky's kinships are. Throughout his career Zabolotsky struggled to expand his cosmography to make room for new components of human experience, and in amalgamating them, he always made them new. The various guises of his poetry thus reflect not only the extent of his philosophical interests, but also the breadth of his poetic talents. It is no exaggeration to state that Zabolotsky's work as a whole has broadened the cultural context of Russian poetry.

Paradoxically, the constancy of Zabolotsky's vision caused both his public undoing and his private salvation as a poet. Guided by his own, personal conceptions, Zabolotsky was never sufficiently ideological for the Soviet State, and like so many others he became its victim. Yet precisely his certitude enabled him to resume his career after it had been so harshly interrupted. Although Zabolotsky was a Soviet poet with a sense of civic responsibility, his first loyalty remained to the aesthetic demands of his poetry; had he been committed above all to socialism, he might have survived at less personal cost. Zabolotsky acknowledged the deleterious effect of political pressures on art: "I'm only a poet and can judge only poetry. I don't know, perhaps socialism really is beneficial to technology. To art, it brings death."[33]

This is not to imply that Zabolotsky made no compromises in his art. Stung by his ordeal in the labor camps, yet determined to prevail as a poet, he made a conscious decision to alter the presentation of his poetry in order that it might reach an audience in his own time and place. The caprices of the Soviet State had indeed damaged Zabolotsky's ingenuous and spirited nature; he no longer took the artistic risks he once had. In a better world, he would not have been faced with such unjust choices. But what survived – though more temperate and less fanciful – was a more intuitive poet, a seductively mellow Zabolotsky.

Zabolotsky was one of the last voices to survive from a great age of Russian poetry, and he felt the weight of this burden. Had he decided not to return to a full literary life – had he allowed political pressures to kill his career – the loss for Russian literature would have been tremendous. As Joseph Brodsky has remarked, "Zabolotsky has done for Russian literature of the twentieth century what Gogol did for the literature of the nineteenth. All of us at one time or another came under his spell."[34]

Zabolotsky's late poetry brings to fruition the ideas that engaged him throughout his life. Gradually, anguish at the inscrutability of nature ("The Triumph of Agriculture") gives way to active attempts to fathom it ("The Mad Wolf"), until finally the potential for harmony is revealed ("The Trees"). At the end the poet achieves what he has been seeking: a oneness, a unity with nature. In earlier poems, he assumed the rôle of nature's thought, in order to reason for it; now, however, his identification is more complete, embracing as it does a universal nervous system. The poet's connection to nature is thus not only intellectual, but also fully sensory, signalling his readiness to merge with nature in yet another of its metamorphoses. Like the Mad Wolf before him, he lies down in a forest glade:

> . . . .
> Я лег на поляне, украшенной дубом,
> Я весь растворился в пыланье огня.
> Подобно бесчисленным арфам и трубам,
> Кусты расступились и скрыли меня.
>
> Я сделался нервной системой растений,
> Я стал размышлением каменных скал
> И опыт осенних моих наблюдений
> Отдать человечеству вновь пожелал.
> . . . .

"Гомборский лес" (1957)

> . . . .
> I lay down in a glade adorned by an oak,
> I dissolved completely in a blaze of fire.
> Like innumerable harps and horns,
> The bushes parted to conceal me.

I became the nervous system of plants,
I became the thought of rocky cliffs,
And once again I desired to offer humanity
The experience of my autumnal observations.
. . . .

"The Gombor Forest" (1957)

Appendix. The OBERIU Declaration
(Parts 1 and 2)*

Oberiu (The Association for Real Art) works with the House of the Press and unites those working in all forms of art who accept its program and apply it in their work.

Oberiu is divided into four sections: literature, fine arts, theater, and cinema. The fine-arts section carries on its work in experimental ways; the other sections are presented at evening programs, in stage productions, and in print. At this time Oberiu is organizing a musical section.

THE SOCIAL ROLE OF OBERIU

The great revolutionary shift in culture and the conditions of everyday life so characteristic of our age is being impeded in the area of art by many abnormal phenomena. We have not yet completely understood the undeniable truth that the proletariat cannot be satisfied in the area of art with the artistic method of old schools, that its artistic principles go much deeper and undermine old art at the roots. It is ridiculous to think that when Repin is painting the year 1905, he is a revolutionary artist. It is still more ridiculous to think that all AKHRR's [Associations of Artists of Revolutionary Russia] bear within themselves the seeds of a new proletarian art.

We welcome the demand for a universally intelligible art comprehensible in its form even to a village schoolboy, but the demand for only such art leads into a maze of the most terrible mistakes. As a result we have heaps of literary trash over-

* Translated by George Gibian and reprinted with his permission from *The Man in the Black Coat: Russia's Literature of the Absurd* (Evanston, 1987).

flowing in book warehouses, while the reading public of the first proletarian state reads translations of Western bourgeois writers. We understand very well that it is impossible to find a single correct solution for the situation that has developed. But we do not understand at all why a number of artistic schools which work tenaciously, honestly, and persistently in this area are pushed, as it were, to the back alleys of art, at a time when they ought to be supported in every way by the entire Soviet community. We do not understand why the school of Filonov has been pushed out of the Academy, why Malevich cannot carry on his architectural work in the USSR, why Terentev's *Inspector General* was so badly received. We do not understand why so-called leftist art, which has not a few merits and achievements to its credit, is considered to be hopeless junk and, still worse, charlatanism. How much inner dishonesty, how much artistic bankruptcy is concealed in such a wild approach.

Oberiu now comes forward as a new section of leftist revolutionary art. Oberiu does not concern itself with only the subject matter and the high points of artistic work; it seeks an organically new concept of life and approach to things. Oberiu penetrates into the center of the word, of dramatic action, and of the film frame.

The new artistic method of Oberiu is universal. It finds a way to represent any subject. Oberiu is revolutionary precisely by virtue of this method.

We are not so presumptuous as to regard our work as completed. But we are firmly convinced that a strong foundation has been laid and that we have enough strength to build further. We believe and know that only the left course in art will lead us to the highway to the new proletarian artistic culture.

POETRY OF THE OBERIUTY

Who are we? And why do we exist? We, the Oberiuty, are honest workers in art. We are poets of a new world view and of a new art. We are not only creators of a poetic language, but also founders of a new feeling for life and its objects. Our will to create is universal. It spans all genres of art and penetrates life, grasping it from all sides. The world covered by the rubbish of the tongues of a multitude of fools bogged down in the mire of "experiences" and "emotions" is now being reborn in all the purity of concrete, bold forms. Some people even now call us *zaumniki* (practitioners of trans-rational verse). It is difficult to decide whether that is because of a complete misunderstanding or a hopeless failure to grasp the principles of literary art. No school is more hostile to us than *zaum*. We, people who are real and concrete to the marrow of our bones, are the first enemies of those who castrate the word and make it into a powerless and senseless mongrel. In our work we broaden the meaning of the object and of the word, but we do not destroy it in any way. The concrete object, once its literary and everyday skin is peeled away, becomes a property of art. In poetry the collisions of verbal meanings express that object with the exactness of mechanical technology. Are you beginning to complain that it is not the same object you see in life? Come closer and touch it with your fingers. Look at the object with naked eyes, and you will see it cleansed for the first time of decrepit literary gilding. Maybe you will insist that our subjects are "unreal" and "illogical"? But who said that the logic of life is compulsory in art? We marvel at the beauty of a painted woman despite the fact that, contrary to anatomical logic, the artist twisted out the shoulder blade of his heroine and moved it sideways. Art has a logic of its own, and it does not destroy the object but helps us to know it.

We broaden the meaning of the object, word, and act. This work proceeds in different directions; each of us has his own creative personality, and this often confuses people. They talk about an accidental association of various people. Evidently they assume that a literary school is something like a monastery in which the monks are all exactly alike. Our association is free and voluntary. It unites masters, not apprentices; artist-painters, not wall painters. Everybody knows himself and everybody knows what links him to the others.

A. VVEDENSKY (at the extreme left of our association) breaks the object down into parts, but the object does not thereby lose its concreteness. Vvedensky breaks action down into fragments, but the action does not lose its creative order. If one were to decode it completely, the result would give the appearance of nonsense. Why appearance? Because obvious nonsense is the *zaum* word, and it is absent from Vvedensky's works. One must be more curious, not too lazy to examine the collision of word meanings. Poetry is not porridge that one swallows without chewing and forgets right away.

K. VAGINOV, whose world phantasmagoria passes before our eyes as though clothed in fog and trembling. But through this fog you feel the closeness of the object and its warmth; you feel the influx of crowds and the rocking of trees which live and breathe after their own fashion, after Vaginov's fashion, for the artist has sculptured them with his own hands and warmed them with his own breath.

IGOR BAKHTEREV, a poet who finds himself in the lyrical coloring of his object material. The object and the action, broken down into their component parts, spring into being again, renewed by the spirit of new Oberiu lyricism. But lyricism here does not exist for its own sake, it is no more than the means of displacing the object into the field of new artistic perception.

N. ZABOLOTSKY, a poet of naked concrete figures brought close to the eyes of the spectator. One must hear and read him more with one's eyes and fingers than with one's ears. The object does not crumble; on the contrary, it becomes tighter and firmer, as though to meet the feeling hand of the spectator. The development of action and the setting play a secondary rôle to that main task.

DANIIL KHARMS, a poet and dramatist, whose attention is concentrated, not on a static figure, but on the collision of a number of objects, on their interrelationships. At the moment of action, the object assumes new concrete traits full of real meaning. The action, turned inside out, in its new appearance still keeps a classical touch and at the same time represents a broad sweep of the Oberiu world view.

BOR. LEVIN, a prose writer at present working experimentally.

Such are the broad outlines of the literary section of our association as a whole and of each of us in particular; our poems tell the rest of the story.

As people of a concrete world, object, and word – that is how we see our social significance. To cleanse the world by the movements of a hand, to cleanse the object of the rubbish of ancient putrefied cultures – are these not the real needs of our time? It is for that reason that our association bears the name Oberiu – Association for Real Art.

Notes

INTRODUCTION

1 Zabolotsky was the last modernist poet to appear in the Soviet Union for many decades. However, such contemporary poets as Viktor Sosnora and Mikhail Yeryomin perpetuate the spirit of Russian Futurism.

2 Iurii Tynianov, "O Khlebnikove" ("On Khlebnikov"), *Problema stikhotvornogo iazyka. Stat'i (The Problem of Verse Language. Articles)*. Moscow: Sovetskii pisatel', 1965, p. 299.

3 Vladimir Nabokov has said of Mandelstam: "Today, through the prism of a tragic fate, [Mandelstam's] poetry seems greater than it actually is." 1967 interview with Herbert Gold in George Plimpton, ed., *Writers at Work*, 4th series, New York: Penguin, 1974, p. 98.

4 Even Zabolotsky's most perceptive biographer, A.V. Makedonov, has written: "The Zabolotsky of *Scrolls* and the Zabolotsky of 'The Homely Girl' are two different, completely different poets; it's as if they were two different men." (In "Puti i pereput'ia N. Zabolotskogo" ("N. Zabolotsky's Roads and Crossroads"), *Ocherki sovetskoi poezii (Studies in Soviet Poetry)*, Smolensk, 1960, p. 208.)

5 See Stanislav Kuniaev, "Ogon', mertsaiushchii v sosude" ("The Flame Flickering in a Vessel") in *Svobodnaia stikhiia (Free Elements)*, Moscow: Sovremennik, 1979, pp. 95–122. Zabolotsky has fared better under the policy of *glasnost'*, however. An article in the journal *October* treats Zabolotsky's early verse both seriously and favorably. See B. Sarnov's appropriately entitled "Vosstavshii iz pepla. Poeticheskaia sud'ba N. Zabolotskogo" ("Arisen from the Ashes. The Poetic Fate of N. Zabolotsky"), *Oktiabr' (October)*, 1987, no. 2, pp. 188–202. See also Alla Marchenko's reverential essay, "V pokhvalu trudam ego i ranam; Sud'ba i stikhi Nikolaia Zabolotskogo" ("In Praise of His Labors

and Wounds; The Fate and Poems of Nikolai Zabolotsky") in *Pravda*, 16 January 1989.
6 Marina Tsvetaeva, *Izbrannaia proza v dvukh tomakh* (*Selected Prose in Two Volumes*), ed. Aleksandr Sumerkin, New York: Russica, 1979, vol. 1, p. 223.

I EMERGENCE

1 Vladislav Khodasevich describes the cityscape of Petrograd in the early twenties as Zabolotsky must first have seen it: "Petersburg had become uncommonly beautiful, more than it had been for years, ever perhaps ... It was as if all of the city's excess panoply of color had been stripped away. The houses, even the ordinary ones, took on a stateliness and severity that previously only the palaces had possessed. Petersburg became deserted ... the trams stopped running, only rarely did hooves clatter or cars honk – and this immobility proved better suited to Petersburg than movement had been. Of course, nothing was added to the city, it didn't acquire anything new – but it lost everything that wasn't becoming to it. There are people who grow more attractive in the grave: that, it is said, happened to Pushkin. Without a doubt that happened to Petersburg, too." ("Dom iskusstv" ["The House of the Arts"], in *Literaturnye stat'i i vospominaniia* [*Literary Articles and Memoirs*], New York: izd-vo imeni Chekhova, 1954, pp. 399–400.) Mikhail Slonimsky, who also lived at the House of the Arts, concurs with Khodasevich: "The desolation revealed the incomparable beauty of the city, as if transforming it into a phenomenon of nature, and the city seemed to float somewhere between water and sky, light and awash with the dawn." (In *My znali Evgeniia Shvartsa* [*We Knew Yevgeny Shvarts*], Leningrad/Moscow: Iskusstvo, 1966, p. 26.) Slonimsky's vision of Petrograd echoes in part the poet Mandelstam's 1913 description of The Admiralty as "brother to water and sky" ("Admiralteistvo" ["The Admiralty"]).
2 Such perceptions frequently have been termed "child's vision" by the critics. In Zabolotsky's case, however, it is perhaps less a question of "child's vision" than of the startling impact of the city upon his primarily bucolic imagination. On Zabolotsky's "child's vision" see George Gibian, ed. and trans., *Russia's Lost Literature of the Absurd. A Literary Discovery*, Ithaca: Cornell University Press, 1971, p. 23; Veniamin Kaverin, "Zagadka detstva" ("The Riddle of Childhood"), *Prostor* (*Open Spaces*), 1969, p. 109, and his "Schast'e talanta" ("The Happiness of Talent"), *Vospominaniia o*

Zabolotskom (*Reminiscences of Zabolotsky*), Moscow: Sovetskii pisatel', 1977, p. 117 (this book subsequently will be cited as *Vospominaniia*); A.V. Makedonov, *Nikolai Zabolotskii: Zhizn', tvorchestvo, metamorfozy* (*Nikolai Zabolotsky: Life, Works, Metamorphoses*), Leningrad: Sovetskii pisatel', 1968, p. 124; and I.I. Rostovtseva, *Nikolai Zabolotskii: Opyt khudozhestvennogo poznaniia* (*Nikolai Zabolotsky: An Attempt at Artistic Cognition*), Moscow: Sovremennik, 1984, p. 158. Even the distinguished Formalist critic Boris Eikhenbaum, in recognizing Zabolotsky's contribution to contemporary poetry, credited the freshness of his verse to a child's perception of the world, wrongly believing that Zabolotsky had turned to adult poetry from children's verse, not the other way around. See I. Sinel'nikov, "Molodoi Zabolotskii" ("The Young Zabolotsky"), *Pamir*, no. 1, January, 1982, p. 67.

3 For the most part the critics did not respond favorably to *Scrolls*, using such terms as *bred* "delirium" and *galliutsinatsiia* "hallucination" to characterize the verse. See, for example, Anat. Gorelov, "Raspad soznaniia" ("The Collapse of Consciousness") in *Stroika* (*Construction*), 1930, no. 1; or A. Selivanovskii, "Sistema koshek" ("A System of Cats") in *Na literaturnom postu* (*On Literary Guard*), 1929, no. 15, pp. 31–35.

4 See, for example, Veniamin Kaverin's memoirs of the Serapion Brothers, "V starom dome" ("In the Old House"), *Zvezda* (*The Star*), 1971, no. 9, pp. 196ff; Vladislav Khodasevich, "Dom iskusstv," pp. 397–412; Viktor Shklovskii, *Sentimental'noe puteshestvie. Vospominaniia 1917–1922* (*Sentimental Journey. Memoirs 1917–1922*), Moscow: Gelikon, 1923; and Ol'ga Forsh, *Sumasshedshii korabl'* (*The Crazy Ship*), Washington: Inter-Language Literary Associates, 1964.

5 Nikolai Zabolotskii, "Avtobiografiia" ("Autobiography") in Zabolotskii, *Stikhotvoreniia* (*Poems*), ed. Struve and Filippov, Washington: Inter-Language Literary Associates, 1965, p. 2. This book subsequently will be cited as *Stikhotvoreniia*.

6 Gleb Struve, *Russian Literature Under Lenin and Stalin*, Norman, Oklahoma: University of Oklahoma Press, 1971, p. 37.

7 Zabolotskii, "Rannie gody" ("Early Years") in *Stikhotvoreniia*, p. 19.

8 Ibid., p. 5.

9 Before publishing his first volume of verse, Zabolotsky changed the traditional spelling and pronunciation of his name, most likely to avoid immediate association with his provincial origins (the Russian *boloto* means "swamp" and *za* implies even greater remoteness: "beyond the swamp"). Despite this spelling change,

one critic entitled his unfavorable review of *Scrolls* "Bolotnoe i Zabolotskii" (A. Amsterdam, "The Swampy and Zabolotsky," *Rezets* [*The Chisel*], 1930, no. 4). The modified American Library of Congress transliteration of Zabolotsky's name used here masks the change in spelling. Originally, the *ts* sound was rendered by two separate consonants, т and с. Zabolotsky later substituted the single Russian consonant *ts* (ц) to represent the same sound. The family name as used in the Vyatka region still carries the stress on the first syllable.

10 L.V. D'iakonov, "Viatskie gody N.A. Zabolotskogo" ("The Vyatka Years of N.A. Zabolotsky"), *Kirovskaia Pravda*, 8 May 1978.

11 Zabolotskii, "Rannie gody," p. 7.

12 D'iakonov, "Viatskie gody."

13 The Russian *real'noe uchilishche* comes from the German *Realschule*. This type of institution stressed a practical education, rather than being college-preparatory like the *gimnazium*. Since the Practical High School did not teach the classical languages, Zabolotsky felt somewhat handicapped in his education.

14 Jeffrey Brooks states that "the collected works of classical Russian writers [from the *Niva* supplements had become] the most important premium by the end of the century." *When Russia Learned to Read*, Princeton: Princeton University Press, 1985, p. 113.

15 Zabolotskii, "Rannie gody," p. 8.

16 Ibid., p. 14.

17 Vera Zabolotskaia, quoted in D'iakonov, "Viatskie gody."

18 Lunacharsky, however, did not find Vyatka stimulating. At the suggestion of activist philosopher Aleksandr Bogdanov (Malinovsky), Lunacharsky applied for and was granted a transfer to Vologda, where Bogdanov was serving his term of exile. See Robert C. Williams, "Lunacharsky and Proletarian Culture," *Artists in Revolution*, Bloomington: Indiana University Press, 1977, p. 38.

19 Shchelkanov's literary pseudonym was Aleksandr Rabochii ("Alexander the Worker"). Dyakonov states that Shchelkanov helped Zabolotsky publish his very first poem in *Zarevo* (*Dawn*), the monthly Komsomol journal of Vyatka Province, but I was unable to find any poem signed by Zabolotsky or approaching his style in the journal's entire run. The closest connection to Zabolotsky I could find was a letter to the editor signed by another friend, Misha Kasyanov, "member of the Urzhum [Komsomol] organization," complaining of the editorial staff's

bad taste in literary selections (*Zarevo*, 1920, no. 5 [July 25], p. 17). Zabolotsky later lived with Kasyanov in Moscow.

20 Even these humorous verses were based on eighteenth-century literary forms. Cf. such poems as Pushkin's "Gavriliada" ("The Gavriliad") or Bogdanovich's "Dushen'ka" ("Darling").

21 M. Kas'ianov, "O iunosti poeta" ("On the Poet's Youth"), *Vospominaniia*, p. 32.

22 D'iakonov, "Viatskie gody."

23 M. Kas'ianov, quoted in ibid.

24 Zabolotsky did not include any of these early poems in the authoritative edition of his work prepared shortly before his death. Those that survive are collected in Nikolai Zabolotskii, *Sobranie sochinenii v trekh tomakh (Collected Works in Three Volumes)*, vol. 1, Moscow: Khudozhestvennaia literatura, 1983. Subsequently cited as *Sobranie sochinenii*.

25 Zabolotsky praised his mentor in "Sadovnik" ("The Gardener"), an effusive poem written in 1948 for Desnitsky's seventieth birthday: "V ego sadakh – izbytok divnykh sil,/Ikh ne ub'iut ni zasukhi, ni stuzhi . . . /Uchitel' moi! Ty ne sady rastil – /Ty stroil chelovecheskie dushi . . ." ("Marvellous forces abound in his gardens,/Neither droughts nor frosts can kill them . . . /My teacher! You did not cultivate gardens – /You built human souls.") Unfortunately, Zabolotsky's metaphor recalls Stalin's pronouncement that writers are the "engineers of human souls." The entire poem, with an accompanying letter from Zabolotsky to Desnitsky, was first published in *Literaturnoe obozrenie (Survey of Literature)*, no. 5, 1983, p. 111; it is reprinted in *Sobranie sochinenii*, vol. 3, p. 355.

26 Letter of 11 November 1921 to M.I. Kas'ianov, in Nikolai Zabolotskii, *Izbrannye proizvedeniia v dvukh tomakh (Selected Works in Two Volumes)*, Moscow: Khudozhestvennaia literatura, 1972, p. 227. Subsequently cited as *Izbrannoe*.

27 Osip Mandel'shtam, "Slovo i kul'tura" ("The Word and Culture"), *Sobranie sochinenii (Collected Works)*, vol. 2, New York: Inter-Language Literary Associates, 1971, p. 223.

28 Interview with D.E. Maksimov in Leningrad, March, 1983.

29 For the full text of Zabolotsky's article, see Konstantin Grish- chinskii and German Filippov, "Tak oni nachinali . . ." ("Thus They Began . . ."), *Zvezda*, no. 11, 1978, pp. 185–187.

30 See Robert Maguire, *Red Virgin Soil*, Princeton: Princeton University Press, 1968, p. 148.

31 Pseudonym of Daniil Ivanovich Yuvachov (1906–1942). Igor Bakhterev reports that Yuvachov chose the name Kharms

because of his boyhood infatuation with Sherlock Holmes. Not only did the name "Kharms" resemble the famous detective's, but Kharms also puffed continually on an English pipe. See Bakhterev, "Kogda my byli molodymi" ("When We Were Young"), *Vospominaniia*, p. 61.

32 Lipavsky used the pseudonym Savelyev. Like Zabolotsky, he worked at the Children's Section of the State Publishing House in the late 1920s. He authored the first children's book about the Revolution, *Pionerskii ustav* (*The Pioneer Charter*, 1926). The impromptu meetings at Lipavsky's apartment continued well into the 1930s, long after the poets had gone their separate ways.

33 Quoted in T. Lipavskaia, "Vstrechi s Nikolaem Alekseevichem i ego druz'iami" ("Meetings with Nikolai Alekseyevich and His Friends"), *Vospominaniia*, p. 51.

34 Sinel'nikov, "Molodoi Zabolotskii," p. 60.

35 The New Economic Policy, during which free enterprise was permitted on a limited scale, lasted from 1921 to 1928.

36 Lidiia Ginzburg, "O Zabolotskom kontsa dvadtsatykh godov" ("About Zabolotsky at the End of the Twenties"), *Vospominaniia*, p. 120.

37 Sinel'nikov, "Molodoi Zabolotskii," p. 63. A moving footnote to Zabolotsky's desire for a black suit is found in a letter he wrote to his wife from exile in Central Asia after his release from the labor camps: "Why are you keeping my black suit, you silly thing? What is it to me? Will I be any worse off without it? Sell it whenever you can and let the children have an extra bite." (Letter of 18 February 1944, published in *Sobesednik* (*The Interlocutor*), vyp. 4, 1983, pp. 297–298.

38 For more on these writers' works for children see I.A. Rakhtanov, *Rasskazy po pamiati* (*Tales from Memory*), Moscow: Sovetskii pisatel', 1966; and Elena Sokol, *Russian Poetry for Children*, Knoxville: University of Tennessee Press, 1984.

39 Both *Ezh* (1928–1935) and *Chizh* (1930–1941) are acronyms: *Ezh* = *Ezhemesiachnyi zhurnal* (*Monthly Journal*) and *Chizh* = *Chrezvychaino interesnyi zhurnal* (*Exceptionally Interesting Journal*).

40 *Campfire*, for which Zabolotsky served on the planning committee, was founded in 1936. Zabolotsky's only contributions to this increasingly orthodox journal were his reworking of *Till Eulenspiegel* (1936, in abridged form) and an article on the Georgian national epic, "The Knight in the Panther's Skin" ("Shota Rustaveli i ego poema" ["Shota Rustaveli and His Poem"], January, 1938).

41 According to Igor Bakhterev, Zabolotsky took this name from

Kharms, who one day had decked himself out in a white slipcover and declared himself "Baker Miller." See Bakhterev, "Kogda my byli molodymi," p. 79.

42 Lidiia Chukovskaia, *V laboratorii redaktora* (*In the Editor's Laboratory*), Moscow: Iskusstvo, 1963, p. 268.

43 D. Kal'm, "Protiv khaltury v detskoi literature," *Literaturnaia gazeta* (*The Literary Gazette*), 16 December 1929. Zabolotsky, along with other members of the Children's Section, responded publicly with a letter of protest to the *Literary Gazette*, published on 30 December 1929.

44 E. Flerina, "S rebenkom nado govorit' vser'ez," *Literaturnaia gazeta*, 30 December 1929.

45 A selection of these humorous verses was first published in *Voprosy literatury* (*Questions of Literature*), 1978, no. 9, pp. 292–297; they have since been collected in *Sobranie sochinenii*, vol. 1.

46 Zabolotsky explains his term in "Chto takoe stishki" ("What Rhymes Are"): "To, chto my zovem stishki/Est' ne bole kak meshki:/Plokho sshity, khorosho li – /V nikh kartoshka, no ne bole." ("What we call rhymes/Are naught but sacks:/Whether badly or well sewn – /They hold potatoes, nothing more.") *Sobranie sochinenii*, vol. 1, p. 454.

47 This poem, from the poet's private archive, was written in 1953, late in Zabolotsky's career, and reveals his continuing interest in themes first explored in "The Triumph of Agriculture" (1929–1930). K.A. Timiryazev (1843–1920) was a botanist much touted by the Soviet government for his mechanistic philosophy and for his findings in plant genetics which refuted established scientific views.

48 Zabolotskii, "Avtobiografiia," p. 2.

49 Yermolayeva illustrated Zabolotsky's *Good Boots* (Leningrad: Gosudarstvennoe izdatel'stvo, 1928) and *Vostok v ogne* (*The East in Flames*) (Leningrad: OGIZ, 1931).

50 Nikolai Stepanov, "Iz vospominanii o N. Zabolotskom" ("From My Memories of N. Zabolotsky"), *Vospominaniia*, pp. 86–87.

51 Ibid., p. 87.

52 Lidiia Ginzburg, *O starom i novom* (*On the Old and the New*), Leningrad: Sovetskii pisatel', 1982, p. 393.

53 Quoted in Sinel'nikov, "Molodoi Zabolotskii," p. 60.

54 In *Izbrannoe* the poem is tentatively dated 1928, the year of its publication.

55 V. Kaverin, "V starom dome," p. 144.

56 In the late 1920s Kharms also had himself photographed as he recklessly climbed out of one mansard window in the *Dom knigi*

(House of the Book) offices of *Ezh* and *Chizh* and back into the next, several stories above street level. (Information from Anatoly Aleksandrov, Leningrad, August, 1985.)

57 Alisa Poret, "Vospominaniia o Kharmse" ("Reminiscences of Kharms"), *Panorama iskusstv* 3 (*Panorama of the Arts* 3), Moscow: Sovetskii khudozhnik, 1980, p. 348.

58 Anatoly Aleksandrov states that Kharms meant for *chinari* to signify "enfants terribles" (A.A. Aleksandrov, "Materialy D.I. Kharmsa v rukopisnom otdele Pushkinskogo doma" ("D.I. Kharms' Material in the Manuscript Division of Pushkin House"), *Ezhegodnik rukopisnogo otdela Pushkinskogo doma na 1978 god* (*Yearbook of the Manuscript Division of the Pushkin House for 1978*), Leningrad: Nauka, 1980, p. 72). Jean-Philippe Jaccard refutes this suggestion but offers no other translation. See Jaccard, *Daniil Harms et la fin de l'avant-garde russe*, Bern: Peter Lang, 1991, p. 51.

59 I. Ioffe and L. Zheleznov, "O Chinariakh" ("About the Chinari"), *Smena* (*The Shift*), 3 April 1927.

60 Ibid., p. 70.

61 Until coining the name OBERIU, Kharms and Vvedensky, together with Zabolotsky and Igor Bakhterev, seem still to have referred to themselves as the "Left Flank," even though they were no longer associated with Tufanov. See Ilya Levin, "The Fifth Meaning of the Motor Car: Malevich and the Oberiuty," *Soviet Union/Union Sovietique*, 5, Pt. 2 (1978), p. 288; and Bakhterev, "Kogda my byli molodymi," p. 76.

62 According to Anatoly Aleksandrov, the final "U" of the acronym was added for fun, in parody of the "isms" of the time. See his article, "Oberiu, predvaritel'nye zametki" ("Oberiu, Preliminary Remarks"), *Československa Rusistika*, vol. 13, no. 5 (1968), p. 297. This same explanation is repeated in Robin Milner-Gulland, "Left Art in Leningrad: the OBERIU Declaration," *Oxford Slavonic Papers*, N.S. vol. III, Oxford: Clarendon Press, 1970, p. 67. Mr. Milner-Gulland's information comes from Aleksandr Razumovsky, a filmmaker associated with the OBERIU.

63 In his study of Zabolotsky, A.V. Makedonov includes Yury Vladimirov in the group. See Makedonov, *Nikolai Zabolotskii*, p. 35.

64 Reported in Bakhterev, "Kogda my byli molodymi," *Vospominaniia o Zabolotskom*, 2nd edition, Moscow: Sovetskii pisatel', 1984, p. 87.

65 In his memoirs about Zabolotsky, Igor Bakhterev states that Mayakovsky commissioned the article for his journal *LEF* ("Kogda my byli molodymi," pp. 59–60). However, since *LEF*

ceased publication in 1925, Bakhterev must have in mind *New LEF*, which started up in 1927 and continued until the end of 1928. Mayakovsky himself resigned in July, 1928.

66 See the advertisement for this performance in *Afishi doma pechati* (*Posters of the House of the Press*), no. 2., Leningrad, 1928, p. 35.

67 Interview with Igor Bakhterev, Leningrad, August, 1985.

68 Lidiia Lesnaia, "Ytuerebo," *Krasnaia gazeta* (*Red Gazette*), vechernii vypusk (evening edition), 25 January 1928.

69 L. Nil'vich, "Reaktsionnoe zhonglerstvo" ("Reactionary Juggling"), *Smena*, 9 April 1930.

70 Entry for 28 October 1928, cited in Aleksandr Vvedenskii, *Polnoe sobranie sochinenii* (*Collected Works*), Ann Arbor: Ardis, 1984, vol. 2, p. 247. According to Bakhterev, Zabolotsky and Vvedensky had differences even before the first OBERIU performance ("Kogda my byli molodymi," *Vospominaniia o Zabolotskom*, 2nd edition, p. 94). In a private interview Bakhterev disdainfully suggested that Zabolotsky "wanted to be an official poet" right from the start and didn't want the highjinks of the others in the group to jeopardize his career. (Interview in Leningrad, August, 1985.) From Zabolotsky's perspective, however, Vvedensky's approach to poetry was simply incompatible with his own. Where for Vvedensky the word could be "larger than its meaning" (*slovo shire smysla*, to use the Futurist poet Aleksei Kruchonykh's formulation), for Zabolotsky this could never be the case. Tangible evidence of Zabolotsky's early distaste for Vvedensky's poetry is found in his "open letter" of September 20, 1926, "Moi vozrazheniia A.I. Vvedenskomu, avto-ritetu bessmyslitsy" ("My Objections to A.I. Vvedensky, the Autho-rity on Nonsense"), published in Vvedenskii, *Polnoe sobranie sochinenii*, vol. 2, pp. 252–253.

71 Gennadii Gor, "Zamedlenie vremeni" ("The Deceleration of Time"), *Zvezda*, 1968, no. 4, p. 174.

72 For more on Zorved, see A. Povelikhina, "Matushin's Spatial System," *The Structurist*, no. 15–16, 1975/6, p. 65; and Jaccard, *Daniil Harms et la fin de l'avant-garde russe*, pp. 90–97.

73 Forsh, *Sumasshedshii korabl'*, p. 51

74 Struve, *Russian Literature under Lenin and Stalin*, p. 53.

75 This characterization of Zabolotsky as the last Russian modernist is confirmed by Vladimir Markov in his article "Mysli o russkom futurizme" ("Thoughts on Russian Futurism"), *Novyi zhurnal* (*New Journal*), 1958, no. 38, p. 174. Markov also considers Zabolotsky the "last real poet of post-revolutionary Russia." See also note 1 to the Introduction.

76 See Shklovsky's essay of the same name, first published in 1917 in *Sborniki II*.

77 An affinity with Constructivist aesthetics can be seen in the OBERIU's use of the cupboard. As art historian Christina Lodder writes: "Whereas [Meyerhold's production of *The Magnanimous Cuckold*] had been motivated by the idea of art (Constructivism) transforming life, in [his production of *The Earth in Turmoil*] the fusion of art and life, and the imperative to transform life itself led to the idea of the 'artistic' being a direct product of the real world of objects. In other words life was transforming art and the concept of what was 'beautiful.'" In Lodder, *Russian Constructivism*, New Haven: Yale University Press, 1983, pp. 177–178.

78 Kharms stated that "the fifth meaning of the cupboard is the cupboard." In other words, he aimed to focus on the absolute meaning of the object – that which he called its "existential" meaning, independent of the variables of context. See "Predmety i figury otkrytye Daniilom Ivanovichem Kharmsom" ("Objects and Figures Discovered by Daniil Ivanovich Kharms"), published in Levin, "The Fifth Meaning of the Motor Car."

79 For a translation of Parts 1 and 2 of the Declaration, see the Appendix. The quotes that follow are from the Declaration, in my translation. The complete Russian text has been reprinted in Robin Milner-Gulland, "Left Art in Leningrad: the OBERIU Declaration," pp. 65–75; the full English translation is given in Gibian, *Russia's Lost Literature of the Absurd*, pp. 193–202.

80 Quoted in Rakhtanov, *Rasskazy po pamiati*, p. 149.

81 With the Constructivists, the word *veshch'* "object" became a catch-all for many different entities, especially in the realm of theater: both a construction and a production were referred to as *veshch'*, while even scenery was given the lofty description of *veshchestvennoe oformlenie* or "object formulation." See Alma H. Law, "The Revolution in Russian Theater," in Stephanie Barron and Maurice Tuchman, *The Avant-Garde in Russia 1910–1930*, Los Angeles: Los Angeles County Museum of Art, (distributed by the MIT Press), 1980, p. 65.

82 The formulation is Osip Brik's. Quoted in Lodder, *Russian Constructivism*, p. 102.

83 The modality of Khlebnikov's plays has been characterized as "game, parody and challenge." The same holds true for the OBERIU productions. See Barbara Lönnqvist, "Xlebnikov's Plays and the Folk-Theater Tradition," in *Velimir Chlebnikov. A Stockholm Symposium April 24 1983*, (Stockholm Studies in Russian Literature 20), Stockholm, 1985, p. 114.

84 Prutkov is the invention of Count A.K. Tolstoy and his two cousins, the Zhemchuzhnikov brothers. His humorous writings appeared between 1853 and 1863.

85 See, for example, R. Milner-Gulland, "Grandsons of Kozma Prutkov: Reflections on Zabolotsky, Oleynikov and their Circle," *Russian and Slavic Literature*, Columbus, Ohio: Slavica, 1976, pp. 313–327.

86 Veniamin Kaverin states that the poet Pavel Antokolsky, upon first hearing Zabolotsky's poems, said that they resembled Captain Lebyadkin's (Kaverin, "Schast'e talanta," p. 110). Antokolsky remembers the episode somewhat differently. In his memoirs, he writes that it was his wife, Zoya Bazhanova, who likened Zabolotsky's poetry to Lebyadkin's (Pavel Antokol'skii, "Skol'ko zim i let" ["It's Been Ages"], *Vospominaniia o Zabolotskom*, 2nd. ed., p. 199).

Lidiya Ginzburg recalls that Akhmatova found Oleinikov's poetry similar to Captain Lebyadkin's (Ginzburg, *O starom i novom*, p. 409; repeated in Ginzburg, "Nikolai Oleinikov," in *Nikolai Oleinikov, Puchina strastei* [*A Gulf of Passions*], Leningrad: Sovetskii pisatel', 1991, p. 6). The Leningrad writer Bella Ulanovskaya has traced the connections between Dostoyevsky and the OBERIU, with much attention paid to Lebyadkin and Zabolotsky, in her interesting "'Mozhet li solntse rasserdit'sia na infuzoriiu?'" ("'Can the Sun Get Angry at an Infusorian?'" (Conference speech at the Dostoyevsky Museum, Leningrad, 1974).

Even Zabolotsky's late poetry occasionally has been interpreted as frivolous. Semyon Lipkin reports that in 1953, when Zabolotsky showed his newly-completed poem "Lebed' v zooparke" ("The Swan at the Zoo") to Aleksandr Tvardovsky, the influential editor of the journal *Novyi mir* (*New World*), Tvardovsky responded, "You're not so young any more, but you're still joking" ("Ne moloden'kii, a vse shutite."). Zabolotsky was stung by Tvardovsky's reaction. (Reported in Nikita Zabolotskii, "Moskovskoe desiatiletie" ["Moscow Decade"], *Moskovskii vestnik* [*Moscow Herald*], 1991, no. 1, pp. 253–313.) And the critic B. Sarnov, while correct in linking Zabolotsky's early and late poetry, exaggerates when he finds "Lebyadkinism" at the basis of all of Zabolotsky's work (Sarnov, "Vosstavshii iz pepla. Poeticheskaia sud'ba N. Zabolotskogo," pp. 188–202).

87 See John E. Bowlt, "The Construction of Space," in *Von der Fläche zum Raum, Russland 1916–1924* (*From Surface to Space, Russia 1916–1924*), Galerie Gmurzynska, Köln, 1974, p. 7.

88 Here it is interesting to compare the theories of spatial realism as propounded by the Zorved group, as well as Pyotr Miturich's concept of a sixth sense (a *chuvstvo mira* or "feeling for the world")

as "an essential cognitive power that [gives] man a heightened insight into natural phenomena and enable[s] him to transcend the limitations of perception through five senses, and to see the world more clearly." Miturich defined this *chuvstvo mira* as "a perfectly concrete sense of the world." (See Lodder, *Russian Constructivism*, p. 217.) The Zorved likewise believed in a kind of "clairvoyance" or "inner gaze" which would yield a "perspicacity and a penetration of extraordinary power." (Margit Rowell, *Art of the Avant-Garde in Russia*, New York: Solomon R. Guggenheim Museum, 1981, pp. 74–75.)

89 Letter of 4 February 1987 from Nikita Zabolotsky to this writer.

90 See John E. Bowlt, "Esoteric Culture and Russian Society," *The Spiritual in Art: Abstract Painting 1890–1985*, Los Angeles and New York: Los Angeles County Museum of Art and Abbeville Press, 1986, p. 174.

91 Walter Benjamin, *Moscow Diary*, entry for 13 December 1926, in *October* 35 (Winter 1985), p. 20.

92 Lidiia Ginzburg, "O Zabolotskom kontsa dvadtsatykh godov," p. 122.

93 Edward J. Brown, "Mayakovsky's Futurist Period," in *Russian Modernism*, ed. George Gibian, Ithaca: Cornell University Press, 1976, p. 108. Cf. also Aleksei Kruchonykh's remark that "almost all Cubo-Futurists were first artists." (Quoted in N. Khardzhiev, "Maiakovskii i zhivopis'" ("Mayakovsky and Painting"), in *Maiakovskii. Materialy i issledovaniia (Mayakovsky. Materials and Research)*, ed. V.O. Pertsov, Moscow: Khudozhestvennaia literatura, 1940, p. 347.) Kristina Pomorska states that "the direct transformation of Cubism into poetry was Russian Futurism." (Pomorska, *Russian Formalist Theory and its Poetic Ambiance*, The Hague: Mouton, 1968, p. 20.)

94 Two of Zabolotsky's portraits from the twenties have been reprinted in *Den' poezii (Day of Poetry)* for 1978 and 1981.

95 Sinel'nikov, "Molodoi Zabolotskii," p. 60.

96 Evgenii Kovtun, "Varvara Stepanova's Anti-Book," in *Von der Fläche zum Raum*, p. 59.

97 M.V. Iudina, *Stat'i, Vospominaniia, Materialy (Articles, Memoirs, Materials)*, Moscow: Sovetskii kompozitor, 1978, p. 271.

98 Bakhterev, "Kogda my byli molodymi," p. 93.

99 Letter to L.A. Iudin of 28 June 1928, in *Sobranie sochinenii*, vol. 3, 1984, p. 306.

100 Letter of 9 August 1928, in ibid.

101 In *Sobranie sochinenii*, vol. 3, p. 386. Yudin decorated a cover for Zabolotsky's story "Indeitsy" ("Indians"), but the story was

never published in book form. Yudin's drawings accompany the story in *Ezh*, 1929, no. 7. He also completed line drawings for Zabolotsky's children's poem "Mister Kuk Barla-Barla."

102 Sinel'nikov, "Molodoi Zabolotskii," p. 68.

103 See especially *K istorii russkogo avangarda/The Russian Avant-Garde*, Stockholm: Hylaea, 1976; and Juliette Stapanian, *Mayakovsky's Cubo-Futurist Vision*, Houston: Rice University Press, 1986.

104 See Levin, "The Fifth Meaning of the Motor-Car," pp. 286–300.

105 D. Tolmachev, "Dadaisty v Leningrade" ("Dadaists in Leningrad"), *Zhizn' iskusstva (The Life of Art)*, 1927, no. 44, p. 14.

106 *Afishi doma pechati*, 1928, no. 2. Igor Terentyev had worked with Filonov and his students on a 1927 production of Gogol's play in the House of the Press. For more on Filonov's involvement see "Dnevniki Filonova v vospominaniiakh ego sestry Glebovoi" ("Filonov's Diaries in the Memoirs of his sister Glebova"), in V. Chalidze, ed., *SSSR: Vnutrennie protivorechiia (USSR: Internal Contradictions)* 10, Benson, Vt.: Chalidze Publications, 1984, pp. 197; Nicoletta Misler, "Pavel Nikolaevich Filonov. Slovo i znak" ("Pavel Nikolayevich Filonov. Word and Sign"), *Russian Literature* XI (1982), pp. 253–254 (subsequently cited as "Slovo i znak"); and Misler, "Pavel Filonov, Painter of Metamorphoses," in Nicoletta Misler and John E. Bowlt, *Pavel Filonov: A Hero and his Fate*, Austin: Silvergirl, 1983, pp. 34–37 (this book subsequently will be cited as *Filonov*).

107 Milner-Gulland, "Left Art in Leningrad," p. 74, note 1; *Filonov*, p. 37; I. Sinel'nikov, "Molodoi Zabolotskii," *Vospominaniia*, 2nd ed., pp. 110–111.

108 Igor Bakhterev recalls that "I was merely acquainted with Filonov, Zabolotsky was closer to him. He even drew in imitation of Filonov." (Letter to this writer of 9 May 1983.) Nikolai Stepanov reports that Zabolotsky liked Filonov's paintings very much and that "he himself sometimes tried to draw in the same spirit." (Stepanov, "Iz vospominanii o N. Zabolotskom," p. 87.) Finally, Dmitri Maksimov remembers that Zabolotsky's drawings were "in the style of Filonov." (Interview in Leningrad, March, 1983.)

109 Filonov, "Avtobiografiia" ("Autobiography"), TsGALI (Central State Archive for Literature and Art), f. 2348, op. 1, ed. kh. 22. Filonov's "Autobiographies" have been translated and published in *Filonov*, pp. 117–134.

110 E.F. Kovtun, "Iz istorii russkogo avangarda (P.N. Filonov)" ("From the History of the Russian Avant-Garde [P.N. Filonov]"), in *Ezhegodnik rukopisnogo otdela Pushkinskogo doma, 1977*

(*Yearbook of the Manuscript Division of the Pushkin House, 1977*), Leningrad: Nauka, 1979, pp. 216–235. For extensive information on Filonov and translations of many of his documents see also the comprehensive volume by Misler and Bowlt.

111 A reproduction may be seen in *Filonov*, plate 35, p. 79.

112 Kovtun, "Iz istorii russkogo avangarda," pp. 222–223.

113 Compare, too, Filonov's 1928 "Drayman," reproduced as Plate XXXIV in *Filonov*, p. 338.

114 Umberto Boccioni, quoted in Caroline Tisdall and Angelo Bozzolla, *Futurism*, London: Thames & Hudson, 1977, p. 78.

115 Cf. these lines from Mandelstam's "Nashedshii podkovu" ("The Horseshoe Finder," 1923): "Kon' lezhit v pyli i khrapit v myle,/No krutoi povorot ego shei/Eshche sokhraniaet vospominanie o bege s razbrosannymi nogami–/Kogda ikh bylo ne chetyre,/A po chislu kamnei dorogi,/ Obnovliaemykh v chetyre smeny/Po chislu ottalkivanii ot zemli pyshushchego zharom inokhodtsa." A. Turkov mentions the correspondence between these lines and Zabolotsky's "Dvizhenie" in *Nikolai Zabolotskii*, Moscow: GIKhL, 1966, p. 24.

116 In one print, the Futurist artist David Burlyuk depicted a horse in motion that appears to have six legs. See his "Man and Horse" from the almanach *Sadok sudei 2* (*A Trap for Judges 2*), St. Petersburg, 1913 (reproduced as Figure 8 in Susan P. Compton, "Italian Futurism and Russia," *Art Journal*, Winter 1981, p. 347.

117 "Slovo i znak," p. 244.

118 Ibid.

119 Quoted in "Dnevniki Filonova v vospominaniiakh ego sestry Glebovoi," p. 228–229. See also W. Sherman Simmons' article on KA and Malevich, where he defines the KA as "a force or principle that is able to abolish the diacritical divisions of the time and space of both prose and reality and to weave them into a fabric that is whole, continuous, and syncretistic." (Simmons, "The Step Beyond: Malevich and the KA," *Soviet Union/Union Sovietique*, 5, Pt. 2, 1978, pp. 149–170).

120 See Nikolai Khardzhiev's commentary in Velimir Khlebnikov, *Sobranie sochinenii* (*Collected Works*), vol. 4, München: Wilhelm Fink Verlag, 1971, p. 443.

121 Interestingly, E.F. Kovtun believes that the portrait in question was of Khlebnikov himself, not of a horse; he quotes from Aleksei Kruchonykh's memoirs: "I remember that Filonov did a portrait of 'Velimir the Great,' giving him on his high forehead a very prominent, swollen vein that seemed to be straining with thought." See Kovtun, "Iz istorii russkogo avangarda," p. 221.

A pencil drawing of Khlebnikov by Filonov from 1913 has been preserved in the Khlebnikov Fund at TsGALI. See *Filonov*, p. 22, note 61.

122 On the kinship between *kon'* and *ikona*, see Robin Milner-Gulland, "Khlebnikov, Tatlin and Khlebnikov's Poem to Tatlin," *Essays in Poetics* 12 (1986):2, p. 89.

123 Translated in *Filonov*, pp. 135–138.

124 Notes found in Filonov's archive outline the strict rules he proposed for establishing an academy of arts: "Summer vacations should be completely abolished, the program of study should be for 2 years ... The studio work day should last at least 8 hours. Lectures on the ideology of art should be held so that they don't interrupt the 8-hour studio day and should be read immediately following it. If you count holidays and Sundays ... then the number of hours spent in the studio alone will be 4800 over the course of 2 years." (Filonov archive, TsGALI, f. 2348, op. 1, ed. khr. 8.)

125 Valentin Kurdov, "Stranitsy bylogo" ("Pages from the Past"), *Avrora (Aurora)*, 1979, no. 5, p. 145.

126 Alisa Poret, "Vospominaniia o Kharmse," pp. 356–357.

127 "Slovo i znak," p. 240. On a different level, Filonov's reading to his students as they worked recalls other experimental groups at the Institute of Artistic Culture, where *zaum* "verbal series" (*riady slov*) were read to artists at work to determine the correspondence between what was recited and what the artists produced. See Levin, "The Fifth Meaning of the Motor-Car," p. 290.

128 "Deklaratsiia mirovogo rastsveta" in *Zhizn' iskusstva*, 1923, no. 20, p. 13.

129 Kovtun, "Iz istorii russkogo avangarda," p. 219.

130 Zabolotsky shared Filonov's belief that the observer (reader) must participate in the artistic process. In a letter to A.K. Krutetsky he wrote: "If a man's not a savage or a fool, his face is always more or less calm. The face of a poem should be just as calm. The intelligent reader will clearly see the whole play of mind and heart underneath the cover of external calm. I count on an intelligent reader. And because I respect him, I don't want to become too familiar with him." (Letter of 6 March 1958 in *Izbrannoe*, p. 265.)

131 John E. Bowlt, "Pavel Filonov and Russian Modernism," in *Filonov*, p. 8.

132 The Czech critic Jan Kříž terms Filonov's art "cosmic." See Kříž, *Pavel Nikolajevič Filonov*, Prague: Nakladatelství česko-slovenskýkh Výtvarnykh Umělců, 1966, p. 7.

133 V.N. Al'fonsov, *Slova i kraski* (*Words and Colors*), Moscow: Sovetskii pisatel', 1966, p. 185.
134 Quoted in Kovtun, "Iz istorii russkogo avangarda," p. 220.
135 "Slovo i znak," p. 254.
136 Ibid.
137 Quoted in Kovtun, "Iz istorii russkogo avangarda," p. 234.
138 Gregory Freidin has suggested that in "Ptitsy" Zabolotsky created a pastiche of Lucretius' *De Rerum Natura*. This idea bears investigation, for we know that Zabolotsky often drew on classical poetry for his verse ("The Triumph of Agriculture," for instance, owes a debt to Virgil.) It is likely that Zabolotsky read Lucretius in the thirties and became enthusiastic about his work, because when he returned from exile, one of the first books he bought to rebuild his library was a volume of Lucretius (Interview with Nikita Zabolotsky, Moscow, January, 1988). Furthermore, Zabolotsky's meter in "Ptitsy" can be seen to reflect the rough hexameters of Lucretius, and both poems are notable for their concrete imagery. Zabolotsky carries the concept of concreteness further than his predecessor, however. While both poets ruminate on the essential, unseen nature of all things, Zabolotsky quite literally dissects this nature in order to discover just what it consists of.
139 Misler interprets the gash in the cheek of Filonov's "Mother" (1916) as a manifestation of "the painter's extreme proximity to the border between animate and inanimate matter." See *Filonov*, p. 37.
140 See *Filonov*, p. 26.
141 Zabolotskii, "Avtobiografiia," p. 2.
142 Nikita Zabolotskii, "N.A. Zabolotskii i kniga" ("N.A. Zabolotsky and the Book"), *Vstrechi s knigoi* (*Meetings with the Book*), Moscow: Kniga, 1984, vyp. 2, p. 285.
143 Cf. the OBERIU conception of the object as possessing metaphysical implications beyond its relative meanings. Kharms sought to express this idea with his formulation of the "fifth" or "existential" meaning of the object.
144 Fiona Björling, *Stolbcy by Nikolaj Zabolockij. Analyses*, Stockholm: Almqvist & Wiksell, 1973, p. 13.
145 "... naturalistic and abstract theses were already introduced, to the point that physiological processes in trees were depicted along with the smells emanating from and streaming around them. [I] began to paint the processes taking place in [the trees] and creating an encircling series of phenomena." Filonov, "Avtobiografiia."

146 Filonov, "Short Explanation of Our Exhibition of Works," in *Filonov*, p. 253.

147 Regarding Zabolotsky: "*urodlivye* fantasmagorii i *bol'nye* videniia Zabolotskogo" ("Zabolotsky's freakish phantasmagorias and sick visions") (A. Selivanovskii, "Sistema koshek," p. 32); "stikhi Zabolotskogo otlichaiutsia svoim *groteskovym* postroeniem" ("Zabolotsky's verses are notable for their grotesque construction") (P. Neznamov, "Sistema devok" ["A System of Wenches"], *Pechat' i revoliutsiia* [*Press and Revolution*], 1930, no. 3, p. 78).

Regarding Filonov: "Liudi, izobrazhaemye Filonovym ... *boleznennyi*. Liudi prevrashcheny v melkikh fizicheskikh *urodov*" ("The people Filonov depicts ... are sickly. The people are transformed into petty physical freaks") (N. Gurvich, "Tri vystavki" ["Three Exhibitions"], *Zhizn' iskusstva*, May 31, 1927, p. 9; "Obshchestvenno-politicheskii *grotesk* s uklonom v *patalogicheskuiu* anatomiu – vot naibolee opredelenie togo, chto est' vystavka v Dome Pechati – shkola Filonova." ("A social and political grotesque with a tendency toward pathological anatomy – that's the closest definition of the exhibition at the House of the Press – Filonov's School.") (E.G., "Shkola Filonova" ["Filonov's School"], *Krasnaia gazeta*, vech. vyp. May 5, 1927, p. 5.) (All italics are mine.)

In addition, the mental health of both artists was questioned. Of Zabolotsky's *Scrolls*, none other than Mikhail Zoshchenko wrote: "I tut skoree predmet dlia psikhoanaliza, chem material dlia kritki." ("Here is a subject for psychoanalysis rather than material for criticism.") ("O stikhakh N. Zabolotskogo" ["On N. Zabolotsky's Poetry"], *Rasskazy, povesti, fel'tony, teatr, kritika 1935–37* [*Stories, Tales, Feuilletons, Theater, Criticism*], Leningrad: Khudozhestvennaia literatura, 1937, p. 382.) In striking comparison, Filonov's early works were considered a "psychiatric document," more suited to medical students than random viewers. (N. Breshko-Breshkovskii, "Vystavka 'Soiuz molodezhi'" ["The 'Union of Youth' Exhibition"], *Birzhevye vedemosti* [*Stock-Exchange Gazette*], St. Petersburg, 1911, 13 April, p. 6, quoted in *Filonov*, p. 37.)

148 Wolfgang Kayser, *The Grotesque in Art and Literature*, Gloucester, Mass.: Peter Smith, 1968, p. 37.

149 Filonov's sister relates the reaction of the artist Smirnov to Filonov's 1924 painting "Golova" ("Head"): " I am stunned ... I purposely brought this magnifying glass in order to examine your brother's work. These aren't lines, they're nerves!"

(Quoted in "Dnevniki Filonova," p. 248.) More than anything, Smirnov's comment reflects the emotional impact of Filonov's work.

150 Ellen Chances has compared Mayakovsky's poetic technique to Boccioni's painterly superimposition of animate objects over images of the city. See her "Mayakovsky's 'Vse-Taki' and Boccioni: Case Study in Comparable Technique," *Russian Literature Triquarterly*, Spring 1975, pp. 345–351.

151 For a detailed discussion of this non-exhibition, including excerpts from the published attacks against the artist, see *Filonov*, pp. 263–277.

152 Two more decades passed before Filonov's works were again shown in any number within the Soviet Union. In September, 1988, a major retrospective of his work opened at the Russian Museum in Leningrad, then travelled to Moscow's New Tretyakov Gallery. For a comprehensive catalogue of the exhibition, see *Pavel Nikolaevich Filonov. Zhivopis', Grafika. Iz sobraniia Gosudarstvennogo Russkogo Muzeia* (*Pavel Nikolayevich Filonov. Paintings, Graphics. From the Collection of the State Russian Museum*). Exhibition catalogue. Leningrad: Avrora, 1988.

153 See I. Istokov, "Vospominaniia o khudozhnikakh. V gostiakh u O.K. Matiushinoi" ("Reminiscences of Artists. At Olga Matyushina's"), *Sankt-Peterburg. Literaturnyi al'manakh* (*Saint Petersburg. Literary Almanach*), vyp. 1, Chicago: St. Petersburg Publishing, 1984, p. 452.

2 THE LAST RUSSIAN MODERNIST

1 Aleksandrov, "Oberiu. Predvaritel'nye zametki," p. 300.

2 The word *stolbets* means 1) column or row; 2) column of print; 3) (plural only) parchment roll. The translation of Zabolotsky's title is problematic. I have chosen to follow the existing convention and render the title as *Scrolls*, even though this English word does not satisfactorily convey Zabolotsky's meaning. The poet's biographer A.V. Makedonov believes that Zabolotsky intended *Stolbtsy* to refer to the columns of printed text on the page (Makedonov, *Nikolai Zabolotskii*, p. 47). Such an "antipoetic" interpretation of the word is in keeping with Zabolotsky's outlook at the time. His desire to express orderliness through regular columns of text is evident from his statement that "I invest this word (*stolbtsy*) with the idea of discipline, order – with everything that opposes the elements of Philistinism" (Sinel'nikov, "Molodoi Zabolotskii," p. 61).

I believe that Zabolotsky intended *Stolbtsy* in its first meaning, simply as an orderly row or series, a highly visual progression of poems. The series of poems in the book forms a column or *stolbets*, just as a series of soldiers in formation is referred to as a column. The problem of translation remains, however. "Columns" in English is unsatisfactory, as the word conjures up an image of classical Greek pillars – not at all what Zabolotsky intended. A better translation might be "Colonnade," in its secondary meaning of "a row of trees or other objects placed at regular intervals." But again the classical architectural context obtrudes. In retaining the standard translation of *Scrolls*, I am motivated by Zabolotsky's love of antiquity and ancient literature – he doubtless was pleased by this secondary meaning of *stolbtsy*. Indeed, Sinelnikov recalls that Zabolotsky's notebooks of poems, carefully penned in fine black ink with red illumination, "reminded one of ancient manuscripts" (Ibid.). Finally, it is not inappropriate to view the volume as a modern-day scroll or artifact documenting life in NEP-period Leningrad.

3 For Zabolotsky's poetic treatment of actual delirium, see his 1928 poem "Bolezn'" ("Illness").

4 V.E. Meierkhol'd, "Balagan" ("Popular Drama"), in *Stat'i, pis'ma, rechi, besedy*, Chast' pervaia. 1891–1917 (*Articles, Letters, Speeches, Conversations*, Part One. 1891–1917), Moscow: Iskusstvo, 1968, pp. 226–227.

5 The title of the poem is equivalent to "The Smiths" in English.

6 Letter of 10 September 1986 from Nikita Zabolotsky to this writer. The quotation that follows is from this letter.

7 Mikhail Matiushin, quoted in Kovtun, "Iz istorii russkogo avangarda," p. 234.

8 See, for example, Simon Karlinsky, "Surrealism in Twentieth-Century Russian Poetry: Churilin, Zabolotskii, Poplavskii," *Slavic Review*, vol. 26, December, 1967, pp. 605–617.

9 Mandel'shtam, "Slovo i kul'tura," p. 223.

10 See Anatoly Tarasenkov's comments in his "Pokhvala Zabolotskomu" ("Praise for Zabolotskii"), *Krasnaia nov'* (*Red Virgin Soil*), 1933, no. 9, p. 179.

11 See Fiona Björling, "'Ofort' by Nikolaj Zabolockij. The Poem and the Title," *Scando-Slavica*, Tomus 23, pp. 7–16.

12 For an analysis of these sources, see Anna Ljunggren, "Oblich'ia smerti: k interpretatsii stikhotvoreniia N. Zabolotskogo 'Ofort'" ("Aspects of Death: Toward an Interpretation of N. Zabolotsky's Poem 'An Etching'"), *Scando-Slavica*, Tomus 27, 1981, pp. 173–174.

13 Mikhail Bakhtin has characterized the early manifestations of different language forms (genres as well as styles) as "masks" which were all the time being substituted, where no single language had an "authentic, incontestable face." See his essay on "Discourse in the Novel," in M.M. Bakhtin, *The Dialogic Imagination*, ed. Michael Holquist, Austin: University of Texas Press, 1981.

14 Nabokov, "Pushkin, or the Real and the Plausible," trans. Dmitri Nabokov, *The New York Review of Books*, March 31, 1988, p. 36.

15 Marietta Chudakova, *Poetika Mikhaila Zoshchenko* (*The Poetics of Mikhail Zoshchenko*), Moscow: Nauka, 1979, p. 86.

16 For a treatment of Zabolotsky's ironic allusions to Dostoyevsky in *Scrolls*, see Irene Masing-Delic, " 'The Chickens Also Want to Live': A Motif in Zabolockij's *Columns*," *Slavic and East European Journal*, vol. 31, no. 3 (1987), pp. 356–369.

17 Natalya Roskina has characterized Zabolotsky's sense of humor as "naive and refined." See her *Chetyre glavy* (*Four Chapters*), Paris: YMCA Press, 1980, p. 87.

18 In two poems from *Scrolls* Zabolotsky also presents eating as a violent, even cannibalistic act. See "Rybnaia lavka" ("The Fish Shop") and "Svad'ba" ("The Wedding").

19 Nikolai Stepanov, "Nikolai Zabolotskii. Stolbtsy," in *Zvezda*, 1929, no. 3, pp. 190–191.

20 See Selivanovskii, "Sistema koshek"; Gorelov, "Raspad soznaniia"; Neznamov, "Sistema devok"; and Amsterdam, "Bolotnoe i Zabolotskii."

21 Neznamov, "Sistema devok," p. 79.

22 I. Sinel'nikov, "Molodoi Zabolotskii," *Vospominaniia o Zabolotskom*, 2nd ed., p. 120.

23 Interview with Nikita Zabolotsky in Moscow, 19 January 1988.

24 Sinel'nikov, "Molodoi Zabolotskii," p. 65.

25 Interview with Lidiya Ginzburg in Leningrad, April, 1983. In the course of their interviews with me, all who knew Zabolotsky never failed to mention his self-discipline and the rigorous standards he imposed.

26 *Zvezda*, 1929, no. 10.

27 Roman Jakobson, "O pokolenii, rastrativshem svoikh poetov" ("On a Generation that Squandered its Poets"), in *Smert' Vladimira Maiakovskogo* (*The Death of Vladimir Mayakovsky*), The Hague: Mouton, 1975, p. 9. Jakobson says that partly because of its epic nature Khlebnikov's poetry never found a wide readership.

28 V. Ermilov, "Iurodstvuiushchaia poeziia i poeziia millionov"

("Idiotic Poetry and the Poetry of Millions"), *Pravda*, 21 June 1933.

29 Anon., "Novye vremena, starye pesni" ("New Times, Old Songs"), *Literaturnyi Leningrad* (*Literary Leningrad*), 5 September 1933.

30 S. Rozental', "Teni starogo Peterburga [*Zvezda* no. 1–7 za 1933 god]" ("Shades of Old Petersburg [*Zvezda* nos. 1–7 for 1933]," *Pravda*, 30 August 1933.

31 Anatolii Tarasenkov, "Pokhvala Zabolotskomu," pp. 177–181.

32 The book was scheduled to appear in 1933. The proofs are in Pushkinskii dom (Pushkin House), fond 630, no. 69. Zabolotsky's son has published them in *Veshnikh dnei laboratoriia* (*The Laboratory of Vernal Days*), Moscow: Molodaia gvardiia, 1987. See also M.I. Kievskii, "Neizdannaia kniga N. Zabolotskogo" ("N. Zabolotsky's Unpublished Book"), *Russkaia literatura* (*Russian Literature*), 1971, no. 2, pp. 163–164.

33 Interview with Nikita Zabolotsky, 19 January 1988.

34 Erik Egeland, the biographer of the artist Ernst Neizvestny, states that Zabolotsky was once engaged to Neizvestny's mother, Bella Dejour, and that it was she who introduced Zabolotsky to Leningrad's literary circles. Egeland, who incorrectly spells Zabolotsky's name as "Zapolotsky," goes so far as to state that Zabolotsky smuggled out poems "in tiny handwriting" to Bella Dejour from prison. I have been unable to substantiate this unlikely claim, which is repeated by a second writer in the introduction to a collection of Neizvestny's essays on art. See Erik Egeland, *Ernst Neizvestny. Life and Work*, Oakville, New York, London: Mosaic Press, 1984, p. 40; and Albert Leong, "Introduction," in Ernst Neizvestny, *Space, Time, and Synthesis in Art: Essays on Art, Literature and Philosophy*, ed. Albert Leong, Oakville, New York, London: Mosaic Press, 1990, p. xxvii.

35 Nikolai Tikhonov in *Literaturnaia gazeta*, 24 May 1934.

36 Lidiia Ginzburg, *O starom i novom*, p. 403.

37 Interview with Nikita Zabolotsky, 19 January 1988.

38 Quoted in Anna Akhmatova, *Sochineniia* (*Works*), vol. 2, Munich-Washington, D.C.: Inter-Language Literary Associates, 1968, p. 179.

39 Andrei Zhdanov, in his speech at the First Congress of Soviet Writers, quoted in Edward J. Brown, *Russian Literature Since the Revolution*, Cambridge, Mass.: Harvard University Press, 1982, p. 169.

40 For an excellent analysis of this period in Soviet literature, see Régine Robin, *Le Réalisme socialiste. Une esthétique impossible*, Paris: Payot, 1986.

41 Reported in *Literaturnyi Leningrad*, 14 June 1934.
42 Most likely Zabolotsky was not invited because he was not famous enough. Although controversial in literary circles, he was not widely known among the general populace.
43 Proceedings of the First Congress of Soviet Writers, quoted in Roy Medvedev, *Nikolai Bukharin. The Last Years*, New York: W.W. Norton, 1980, pp. 86–87. For the original Russian text see *Pervyi s"ezd pisatelei. Stenograficheskii otchet*, vol. 1, Moscow, 1934, p. 550.
44 Medvedev, *Nikolai Bukharin. The Last Years*, p. 71.
45 Ibid., p. 74.
46 "Stat'i 'Pravdy' otkryvaiut nam glaza" ("Articles from 'Pravda' Open Our Eyes"), *Literaturnyi Leningrad*, 1 April 1936.
47 In his correspondence, Zabolotsky writes that he composed the poem to fulfill a promise made to Simon Chikovani when they visited Gori together. (*Sobranie sochinenii*, vol. 1, p. 619.) I find this comment less than ingenuous, however.
48 See Lazar Fleishman, *Boris Pasternak v tridtsatye gody* (*Boris Pasternak in the Thirties*), Jerusalem: The Magnes Press of Hebrew University, 1984, p. 280. Bukharin's rôle in the publication of Pasternak's poem is also mentioned in Olga Ivinskaya, *A Captive of Time*, Garden City, N.Y.: Doubleday & Co., 1978, p. 59.
49 See Zabolotsky's comments to Simon Chikovani, in *Sobranie sochinenii*, vol. 1, p. 619. Other Soviet artists similarly chose to perform well under duress. When asked if there were any way to avoid appearing in operas distasteful to her, the diva Galina Vishnevskaya replied: "No, there was nothing we could do. Suppose you were told to sing in some cantata dedicated to Stalin. Well, once you accepted the fact that you had to sing it, you couldn't do it *badly*. Certainly *I* couldn't. I put everything I had into the part, trying to turn bad music into something acceptable to the listener. Rostropovich, too, had this problem. He had to perform a lot of rubbish for the greater glory of the Soviet system. So had Oistrakh. They hated it but did it, and did it with the artistry unique to their genius. They couldn't give less than their best." In George Urban, "Interview with Galina Vishnevskaya," *Encounter*, December, 1986, p.16–17. For an interesting discussion of public expectations regarding poets' behavior under political pressure, see Aleksei Medvedev, "Poet i meshchanin. O dissidentskoi etike" ("The Poet and the Philistine. On Dissident Ethics" [on Kharms and Vvedensky]). St. Petersburg, *Nezavisimaia gazeta* (*Independent Newspaper*), January, 1992.
50 Letter to Mikola Bazhan, apparently from December, 1936, in *Sobranie sochinenii*, vol. 3, p. 324.

51 Nadezhda Mandelstam, *Hope Against Hope*, New York: Atheneum, 1976, p. 203.

52 Ekaterina Vasil'evna Zabolotskaia, unpublished commentary to Sil'va Gitovich's memoirs, "Arest N.A. Zabolotskogo" ("N.A. Zabolotsky's Arrest"), held in the family archive.

53 Speech at a meeting of Leningrad writers, subsequently published in *Literaturnaia gazeta*, 26 March 1937, p. 2.

54 Sinel'nikov, "Molodoi Zabolotskii," *Vospominaniia*, 2nd ed., p. 116.

55 Lidiia Ginzburg, "Zabolotskii dvadtsatykh godov" ("Zabolotsky in the Twenties"), *Literatura v poiskakh real'nosti (Literature in Search of Reality)*, Leningrad: Sovetskii pisatel', 1987, pp. 137, 139.

56 See Zoia Maslenikova, "Portret poeta" ("Portrait of a Poet"), *Literaturnaia Gruziia (Literary Georgia)*, 1978, no. 10–11, p. 291.

57 The successful Soviet expedition to the Arctic engaged the public spirit in much the same way as the Sputnik launch did two decades later. Even Filonov was excited by the expedition. In a diary entry for 29 May 1937 he wrote: "Our steadfast people have arrived at the Pole! The radio told me today that on May 21 at 11:35, Vodopyanov landed his machine at the Pole ... I wish these people would look at my 'Coastal Schooners,' made in 1913 ... [which] depicts the North Pole. There trees blossom with gigantic roses and a lioness with cubs looks down from the cliffs at the coastal boats. May honest people thus rejoice in the victory of our school's analytical art, when our dream of a universal, proletarian, great bolshevik art is realized, which our school can accomplish, and how glad I am that handfuls of bolsheviks have arrived at the Pole." ("Dnevniki Filonova v vospomianiiakh ego sestry Glebovoi," pp. 195–196.)

58 Reported in *Vecherniaia Moskva (Evening Moscow)*, 2 October 1937.

59 My information is culled from several important documents. In 1956 Zabolotsky wrote "The Story of My Imprisonment," which covers the initial stages of his internment, from his arrest in March, 1938, to his arrival at Komsomolsk-on-Amur in February, 1939. This memoir was first published in an English translation by Robin Milner-Gulland in the *Times Literary Supplement* (9 October 1981, pp. 1179–1181) and later appeared in Russian in the Paris-based almanac *Minuvshee (The Past)* (no. 2, 1986; reprinted in *Novoe russkoe slovo [The New Russian Word]*, 21 November 1986).

After Zabolotsky's return from the camps, he extracted passages from the letters he had sent home to his family, intending to write an introduction and present them under the title "One

Hundred Letters. 1938–1944." Although he did not complete this project, his son has compiled the letters, with commentary. Except for a few excerpts (including one misleadingly entitled "Scenes from the Far East" in Zabolotsky's collected works), these letters remain unpublished. Since the information they contain is generally unavailable, I have quoted extensively from them here (all quotations are in my own translation).

Finally, Silva Gitovich's memoirs of Zabolotsky's arrest were published in *Pamiat'* (*Memory*) after many years of underground circulation in the Soviet Union. (Sil'va Gitovich, "Arest N.A. Zabolotskogo," *Pamiat'*, Paris, 1982, pp. 336–353). Zabolotsky's widow prepared a line-by-line commentary to Gitovich's document, which elaborates on or refutes a number of points. This commentary is held in the family archive.

60 All passages quoted from "The Story of My Imprisonment" are from Mr. Milner-Gulland's translation, which contains one small error. Zabolotsky wrote that "During the first few days they did not beat me, trying to destroy me morally and exhaust me physically." In the English publication, the words "did not" have been omitted.

61 Gitovich, "Arest N.A. Zabolotskogo," p. 349.

62 According to Robert Conquest, roughly three million prisoners died in the infamous Kolyma region (Conquest, *Kolyma*, London: Macmillan, 1978, p. 227). For literary accounts of camp life there, see Varlam Shalamov, *Kolymskie rasskazy*, Paris: YMCA-Press, 1982 (published in English as *Kolyma Tales*, trans. John Glad, New York: W.W. Norton, 1980); and Evgenia Ginzburg, *Within the Whirlwind*, New York: Harcourt Brace Jovanovich, 1982.

63 Tikhonov's rôle in this affair is still not entirely clear. In light of his implication in Zabolotsky's case, it is interesting to note that in 1930, when Tikhonov had control over housing and employment for writers in Leningrad, he prevented Mandelstam and his wife from settling there. See Clarence Brown, *Mandelstam*, Cambridge: Cambridge University Press, 1973, p. 125.

64 The editors later asked Zabolotsky to change the title to "Articles from 'Pravda' Open Our Eyes," and the speech was published in *Literary Leningrad* on 1 April 1936.

65 It has been published in Russian in Gitovich, "Arest N.A. Zabolotskogo," pp. 343–345.

66 "The Nightingale" (1939) and "Lesnoe ozero" ("Woodland Lake," 1938) are the only poems Zabolotsky wrote during his imprisonment and exile.

67 Letter of 6 March 1958 to A.K. Krutetskii. In *Izbrannoe*, vol. 2, p. 265.
68 This appeal was recently uncovered in KGB files. It is reproduced in Evgenii Lunin, "Nikolai Zabolotskii: 'Ia nashel v sebe silu ostat'sia v zhivykh'" ("Nikolai Zabolotsky: 'I found in myself the strength to stay alive'"), *Avrora (Aurora)*, 1990, no. 8, pp. 125–133.
69 Iu. Popov, "Zhil poet v shakhterskom krae" ("A Poet Lived in the Mining Region"), *Industrial'naia Karaganda (Industrial Karaganda)*, no. 261, 13 November 1982. For an expanded version of this article see "Nikolai Zabolotskii v Karagande" ("Nikolai Zabolotsky in Karaganda"), *Prostor*, 1984, no. 4, p. 202.
70 For details of Zabolotsky's work on the "Lay," see Nikita Zabolotskii, "Put' k 'Slovu'" ("The Path to the 'Lay'"), *Al'manakh bibliofila (Bibliophile's Almanach)*, vyp. 21, Moscow: Kniga, 1986, pp. 211–230.
71 Letters of 26 January and 20 June 1945. In *Izbrannoe*, vol. 2, p. 297.
72 Cf. these lines from Gavriil Derzhavin's "Na smert' kniazia Meshcherskogo ("On Prince Meshchersky's Death"): "Gde stol byl iastv, tam grob stoit" ("Where viands were, now lies a coffin").
73 *Literaturnaia gazeta*, 9 March 1946.
74 Published in *Novyi mir*, 1947, vol. 1. Some Western critics have objected to this poem on political grounds. See, for instance, Henry Gifford, "Terror and the Muse," *Times Literary Supplement*, 7 August 1981, p. 895.
75 See particularly the comments by Anatoly Tarasenkov in "Zametki o poezii" ("Notes on Poetry"), where he criticizes Zabolotsky's verse for lacking "human voices" and "the noise of work" ("shum rabot") (*Novyi mir*, 1948, no. 4, p. 201).
76 Interview with Nikita Zabolotsky, Moscow, 18 May 1987.
77 Zabolotsky met these poets at an "Evening of Georgian Poetry" at the Leningrad Writers' Club on February 16, 1935. By this time, at the suggestion of Yury Tynyanov, he had already translated Grigola Orbeliani's poem "Zazdravnyi tost, ili pir posle Erevanskoi bitvy" ("A Festive Toast, or the Feast after the Battle of Yerevan"). See T.K. Puturidze, "Nikolai Zabolotskii i gruzinskaia poeziia" ("Nikolai Zabolotsky and Georgian Poetry"), *Russkii iazyk v gruzinskoi shkole (Russian Language in the Georgian School)*, 1970, no. 2, p. 58. Zabolotsky's Georgian translations have been published in separate editions in *Gruzinskaia klassicheskaia poeziia v perevodakh N. Zabolotskogo (Georgian Classical Poetry in Translations by N. Zabolotsky)*, Tbilisi: Zaria vostoka, 1958,

and *Na dvukh Aragvakh peli solov'i* (*On the Two Aragvis Nightingales Sang*), Tbilisi: Merani, 1975.

78 For anecdotes about this trip see Antokol'skii, "Skol'ko zim i let," pp. 141–143.

79 Zabolotsky refers to the period of his incarceration as "the abyss of my non-existence" ("bezdnia moego nebytiia"). See Lunin, "Nikolai Zabolotskii," p. 132.

80 This idea of transcendence through oblivion is most beautifully expressed in Zabolotsky's 1956 poem "Gde-to v pole vozle Magadana" ("Somewhere in a Field Near Magadan"), which remained unpublished during his lifetime.

81 Semen Lipkin, "Viacheslavu. Zhizn' Peredelkinskaia" ("To Viacheslav. Peredelkino Life"), in *Kontinent* (*Continent*), no. 35, 1983, pp. 7–18. I am grateful to Simon Karlinsky for bringing this poem to my attention.

82 Interview with Nikita Zabolotskii, 18 May 1987.

83 Nikolai Zabolotskii, *Stikhotvoreniia* (*Poems*), Moscow: Sovetskii pisatel', 1948.

84 Details of this episode are related in Nikita Zabolotsky, "Moskovskoe desiatiletie," p. 273.

85 Zabolotsky's formal rehabilitation "for lack of a *corpus delicti*" came in 1963, five years after his death. See Lunin, "Nikolai Zabolotskii," p. 133.

86 See the reviews by Il'ia Erenburg of 28 July 1956 and A. Marchenko of 20 September 1956.

87 Roskina describes her relationship with Zabolotsky in *Chetyre glavy*, pp. 63–98.

3 VISIONS OF A BRAVE NEW WORLD

1 Zabolotsky's first Soviet biographer, A.V. Makedonov, dates this "new Zabolotsky" from 1934 (Makedonov, *Nikolai Zabolotskii*, p. 20). See also the review in *Literaturnaia gazeta* by A. Dymshits, "O dvukh Zabolotskikh" ("On the Two Zabolotskys"), 15 December 1937.

2 Interesting comparisons could be made between the Zabolotsky of the 1930s ("Lodeinikov," for instance) and the T.S. Eliot of "The Love Song of J. Alfred Prufrock."

3 See note 32, chapter 2.

4 The Russian name for this mystical book, *golubinnaia kniga*, encompasses the idea not only of *glubina* or "depth" (the book lies in the sea), but also of *golub* or "dove." The phonetic similarity between the words is strengthened by their semantic link: *glubina*

is an attribute of the Holy Spirit whose iconic representation is *golub*. A book with seven seals is also described in the Book of Revelations.

5 For more on Gastev, see Kurt Johansson, *Aleksej Gastev. Proletarian Bard of the Machine Age*, Stockholm: Almqvist & Wiksell (Stockholm Studies in Russian Literature 16), 1983.

6 See the transcription of Gorky's lecture "O znanii" ("On Knowledge"), presented at the Workers' and Peasants' University in 1920, in M. Gor'kii, *Khudozhestvennye proizvedeniia. Stat'i. Zametki (Artistic Works. Articles. Observations)*, Moscow: Nauka, 1969, p. 107.

7 See Vera Pavlovna's Second Dream in Nikolai Chernyshevsky's *What Is To Be Done*, where labor and motion are equated with reality.

8 In Chapter Nine of Ivan Turgenev's *Fathers and Sons* Bazarov states, "Priroda ne khram, a masterskaia, i chelovek v nei rabotnik" ("Nature is not a temple, but a workshop, and man is a worker in it").

9 "Trudoliubie i tuneiadstvo, ili torzhestvo zemledel'tsa" ("Industry and Parasitism, or the Triumph of the Farmer"). Bondarev's treatise had not been published in its entirety when G.I. Uspensky publicized it in 1884 in an article of his own (G.I. Uspenskii, "Trudami ruk svoikh" ["By the Labors of One's Own Hands"], reprinted in *Polnoe sobranie sochinenii [Collected Works]*, vol. 9, Leningrad: Izd-vo. Akademii nauk, 1949, pp. 91–118). Tolstoy was quite taken with Bondarev's ideas and initiated a correspondence with him (see *Pis'ma L.N. Tolstogo [Letters of L.N. Tolstoy]*, vol. 2, Moscow: Kniga, 1911, pp. 78–80; *L.N. Tolstoi. Lettres à Bondarev*. Avec introduction de Charles-Baudoin et documents inédits sur Bondarev, Genève: Reggiani, 1918; and also E. Vladimirov, *Timofei Mikhailovich Bondarev i Lev Nikolaevich Tolstoi*, ed. N.N. Gusev, Krasnoyarsk: Krasnoiarskoe kraevoe izd-vo, 1938.).

Given both the utopian focus of Bondarev's work and its theme, it is tempting to surmise that Zabolotsky had heard of it (his father was, after all, an agronomist), particularly since the title of Zabolotsky's own *magnum opus*, "Torzhestvo zemledeliia," so closely approximates Bondarev's. Certain similarities can be found in the two works. For instance, Bondarev imagined the universe as a multitude of inhabited worlds, an idea Zabolotsky explored in his own writing. And in Bondarev's tract, an envoy comes down from heaven to inquire about conditions on earth, while in "The Triumph of Agriculture" "stately choirs of people/

descend onto the broad squares of the world." Despite such echoes, I have been unable to find any indication that Zabolotsky knew Bondarev's work.

10 See Katerina Clark, "The City versus the Countryside in Soviet Peasant Literature of the Twenties: A Duel of Utopias," in Abbott Gleason et al., *Bolshevik Culture. Experiment and Order in the Russian Revolution*, Bloomington: Indiana University Press, 1985, p. 182.

11 See the review in the May, 1923, issue of *Zhizn' iskusstva.*

12 For a discussion of Lenin and immortality, see Nina Tumarkin, *Lenin Lives! The Lenin Cult in Soviet Russia*, Cambridge, Mass.: Harvard University Press, 1983.

13 On this topic, see Mikhail Bulgakov's brilliant satire *Sobach'e serdtse (Heart of a Dog)*. Cf., too, Isaak Babel's memoirs of the poet Eduard Bagritsky: "Bagritsky died at thirty-eight, not having accomplished a fraction of what he might have. In our State, an Institute for Experimental Medicine (VIEM) has been founded. May it succeed in making sure that these senseless crimes of nature will no longer be repeated." (I. Babel', *Izbrannoe [Selected Works]*, Moscow, 1957, p. 281; cited in Chudakova, *Poetika Mikhaila Zoshchenko*, p. 164.)

14 Ivan Michurin's (1855–1935) results in plant breeding, for instance, were heralded as "a genuine revolution in the plant world of the north!" See V. Lebedev, "Sad chudes" ("A Garden of Wonders"), *Tridtsat' dnei (Thirty Days)*, 1934, no. 10, p. 62.

15 See, for example, I. Postupal'skii, "K voprosu o nauchnoi poezii" ("On the Question of Scientific Poetry"), *Pechat' i revoliutsiia*, 1929, no. 2–3, p. 51.

16 Nikolai Tikhonov, Samuil Marshak, and Veniamin Kaverin planned to collaborate with numerous scientists on one such almanach in 1931. And in his memoirs Kaverin writes about conversations he and Yevgeny Shvarts had with the physicist A.I. Ioffe about building a bridge between literature and science. Zabolotsky likely participated in similar discussions. See *Literaturnyi Leningrad*, 3 July 1933.

17 In *Tridtsat' dnei*, 1934, no. 10, p. 10.

18 In Daniil Kharms, *Sobranie proizvedenii (Collected Works)*, vol. 3, Bremen: K-Presse, 1978, p. 89.

19 Friedrich Schelling, "Allgemeine Deduktion des dynamischen Prozesses," *Schellings Werke*, Erster Band, Leipzig: Fritz Eckardt Verlag, 1907, pp. 815–816. Cf. too Alexander Herzen's perception of man's consciousness as nature's greatest achievement: "All of nature's aspirations and efforts are perfected in man."

(A.I. Gertsen, "Nauka i priroda – fenomenologiia myshleniia" ("Science and Nature – the Phenomenology of Thought"), *Sobranie sochinenii v 30-i tomakh* (*Collected Works in Thirty Volumes*), vol. 3, Moscow: Izd-vo akademii nauk, 1954, p. 127.

20 This idea was prevalent in the post-Revolutionary years. Cf. the statement by the architect Moisei Ginzburg from his 1924 book *Stil' i epokha* (*Style and Epoch*) that "the architect will no longer think of himself as the decorator of life but as its organizer." Cited in Anatole Kopp, *Constructivist Architecture in the USSR*, New York: St. Martin's Press, 1985, p. 22.

21 Nikolai Chukovskii, "Vstrechi s Zabolotskim" ("Meetings with Zabolotsky"), *Vospominaniia*, p. 230.

22 For a reading of one of Zabolotsky's nature poems in relation to Tyutchev see Sarah Pratt, "Antithesis and Completion": Zabolockij Responds to Tiutcev," *Slavic and East European Journal*, vol. 27, no. 2 (1983), pp. 211–227.

23 It is likely that this image alludes to Khlebnikov's *ptich'e penie* or "language of the birds."

24 Cf. this line from Khlebnikov: "I kazhdoe utro shumit v lesu Nitsshe" ("And every morning Nietzsche clamors in the woods"). From "Derevo" ("The Tree"), in *Sobranie sochinenii*, vol. 4, p. 278.

25 Zabolotsky later changed the name of the poem to the less ponderous "Progulka" ("A Stroll").

26 In "Stat'i 'Pravdy' otkryvaiut nam glaza."

27 Quoted in Roman Jakobson, *Noveishaia russkaia poeziia* (*The Newest Russian Poetry*), Prague, 1921, p. 4.

28 Barbara Lönnqvist, *Xlebnikov and Carnival. An Analysis of the Poem 'Poet'*, Stockholm: Almqvist & Wiksell (Stockholm Studies in Russian Literature 9), 1979, p. 26.

29 "Na lestnitsakh" ("On the Stairs", 1928).

30 From the long poem "Poet" (1919).

31 Compare these lines from Aleksei Gastev's "Vykhodi" ("Come Out"): "Okeany zaliazgaiut, bryzgnut k zvezdam./Missisipi obnimetsia s Volgoi." ("The oceans will begin to clang and splash to the stars./The Mississippi will embrace the Volga.") (A.K. Gastev, *Poeziia rabochego udara* [*Poetry of the Worker's Stroke*], Moscow: Khudozhestvennaia literatura, 1971, p. 211.) Of course, in contrast to Khlebnikov's vision, Gastev's was highly industrial.

32 See E.F. Kovtun and A.V. Povelikhina, "'Utes iz budushchego.' Arkhitekturnye idei Velimira Khlebnikova" ("'A Cliff From the Future'. Velimir Khlebnikov's Architectural Ideas"), *Tekhnich-*

eskaia estetika (*Technical Aesthetics*), Moscow, 1976, no. 5–6, p. 41. The primitiveness of Muscovite architecture in the post-Civil War years no doubt influenced Khlebnikov's architectural writings.

33 Ibid., p. 42.

34 Kharms jotted down notes for this poem in his diary sometime before October 1, 1933. These notes have been published in Zabolotskii, *Sobranie sochinenii*, vol. 3, p. 388.

35 Letter of 16 October 1933 to Klavdiya Vasilyevna Pugachova. Kharms went on to say in the letter: "But I also know that this poem is bad, it is good only in some of its parts, as if by accident."

36 Abram Tertz (Andrei Sinyavsky), *A Voice from the Chorus*, New York: Farrar Straus Giroux, 1976, p. 20. Sinyavsky's translators render "Golubinaia kniga" as "The Book of the Dove." See note 4, chapter 3.

37 See the section entitled "Gorizontal'noe polozhenie i vertikal'noe – smert' i zhizn'" ("The Horizontal Position and the Vertical – Death and Life") in Nikolai Fedorovich Fedorov, *Filosofiia obshchego dela* (*Philosophy of the Common Cause*), ed. by V.A. Kozhevnikov and N.P. Peterson, 2nd ed., Verny 1906/Moscow 1913, rpt. Westmead, England: Gregg International, 1970, vol. 2, pp. 260–270. Subsequently cited as *FOD*.

38 Kovtun, "Utes iz budushchego," p. 42.

39 S.G. Semenova, "Nikolai Fedorovich Fedorov (Zhizn' i uchenie)" ("Nikolai Fyodorovich Fyodorov [His Life and Teachings]"), *Prometei* 11 (*Prometheus* 11), Moscow, 1977, p. 87. Fyodorov also was known as the "Socrates of Moscow."

40 At least three biographers of Fyodorov have suggested this connection. See Stephen Lukashevich, *N.F. Fedorov. A Study in Russian Eupsychian and Utopian Thought*, Newark, Del.: University of Delaware Press, 1977, p. 26; S.G. Semenova, "Nikolai Fedorovich Fedorov," p. 89; and George M. Young, Jr., *Nikolai Fedorov. An Introduction*, Belmont, Mass.: Nordland Publishing Company, 1979, p. 181.

In addition, the critic N. Skatov unequivocally states that Fyodorov influenced Zabolotsky as he had Mayakovsky (Skatov, *Dalekoe i blizkoe* [*The Far and the Near*]), Moscow: Sovremennik, 1981, p. 196. Finally, Mikhail Geller writes in his monograph on Andrei Platonov that Fyodorov's ideas had a "very strong influence on Zabolotsky." (Geller, *Andrei Platonov v poiskakh schast'ia* [*Andrei Platonov in Pursuit of Happiness*], Paris: YMCA-Press, 1982, pp. 54–55.) Geller believes that Zabolotsky came to Fyodorov's ideas through Tsiolkovsky, but this is doubtful, since

Zabolotsky had already completed his "Triumph of Agriculture" with its Fyodorovian episodes before learning of Tsiolkovsky's work.
41 Young, *Nikolai Fedorov*, p. 185.
42 G. Petrov is referring to 1924 in his "Leningradskii Peterburg," *Grani (Borders)*, 1953, vol. 18, p. 40.
43 E.F. Kovtun, "Varvara Stepanova's Anti-Book," p. 60. Fyodorov's comments on these manuscripts are in *FOD*, vol. 1, pp. 23–24.
44 Viktor Shklovsky has suggested Mayakovsky's familiarity with Fyodorov. See E.J. Brown, *Mayakovsky. A Poet in the Revolution*, Princeton: Princeton University Press, 1973, pp. 253–254. Roman Jakobson also connected Mayakovsky's poetry and Fyodorov's philosophy ("O pokolenii, rastrativshem svoikh poetov," p. 20). See too Lukashevich, *N.F. Fedorov*, p. 25; and Young, *Nikolai Fedorov*, p. 192. S.G. Semyonova states that Mayakovsky knew of Fyodorov through the graphic artist V.N. Chekrygin, several of whose works were inspired by Fyodorov's ideas (Semenova, "Nikolai Fedorovich Fedorov," p. 90).
45 From a manifesto issued in 1920 and reproduced in part in *Vselenskoe delo (The Universal Cause)*, sbornik II, Riga, 1934, pp. 113–115; cited in S. Frederick Starr, *Melnikov. Solo Architect in a Mass Society*, Princeton: Princeton University Press, 1978, p. 248.
46 Young, *Nikolai Fedorov*, p. 180.
47 G.P. Georgievskii, "L.N. Tolstoi i N.F. Fedorov. Iz lichnykh vospominanii" ("Tolstoy and Fyodorov. Personal Reminiscences"), *Novyi zhurnal*, vol. 143, pp. 91–109.
48 Nikita Zabolotskii, "Put' k 'Slovu'," p. 213. As early as 1931 Zabolotsky wrote a children's tale about an expedition to the holy city of Lhasa in Tibet. He published this story under the pseudonym of Ya. Miller. See *Tainstvennyi gorod (The Secret City)*, Moscow-Leningrad: Gosudarstvennoe izdatel'stvo, 1931.
49 *FOD*, vol. 1, p. 421.
50 See Pushkin's "Andre Shen'e" ("André Chenier"), especially the following lines: "Ia skoro ves' umru, no, ten' moiu liubia,/ Khranite rukopis', o drugi, dlia sebia!" ("Soon I shall utterly die, but, cherishing my shadow,/Preserve my manuscript, oh friends, for yourselves!"). Cf. too Pushkin's "Ia pamiatnik sebe vozdvig nerukotvornyi" ("I Raised a Monument to Myself Not Made by Human Hands") and Boratynsky's "Moi dar ubog, i golos moi ne gromok ..." ("My talent is meager, and my voice is not loud ...").
51 *FOD*, vol. 2, p. 410.

52 Irene Masing-Delic terms the decomposing dead in Zabolotsky's poetry the "orphaned dead": "To the cemetery-complex [in 'Queen of the Flies'] belongs the word 'orphan' used to characterize the moss. Clearly the word is here not used in its ordinary meaning. 'Orphaned' are here not the living, but the decomposing dead, who have been forgotten by the living. Being in a state of putrefaction they are frightening to the living who shun them and their abodes; the dead are saddened by this neglect. Oblivion is a severing factor which counteracts the basic unity of the natural realm." Irene Masing-Delic, "Zabolockij's Occult Poem 'Carica Much'," *Svantevit. Dansk Tidsskrift for Slavistik*, Årgang III, nr. 2, Århus, 1977, p. 28.

53 Compare Ovid's story of Daphne's metamorphosis into a laurel tree.

54 Fyodorov addressed the problem of rearranging particles to reconstitute life: "It may be said that death is anaesthesia, during which complete disintegration of the corpse, decomposition and dispersal of matter take place. The retrieval of the scattered particles is a question of cosmotelluric science and art; hence, it is men's work. But the putting together of the particles once they are gathered is a physiological, histological question; thus the question of suturing, so to speak, the tissues of the human body – of the bodies of one's fathers and mothers – is women's work. Of course, it would be strange if the physiological and histological science were limited only to cross-sectioning and did not end in [complete] restoration." See *FOD*, vol. 1, p. 329. This passage incidentally reveals Fyodorov's strong anti-feminist bias.

55 See Irene Masing-Delic, "Some Themes and Motifs in N. Zabolockij's 'Stolbcy'," *Scando-Slavica*, Tomus XX, Munksgaard, Copenhagen, 1974, pp. 13–25.

56 See Nikolai Chukovskii, "Vstrechi s Zabolotskim," p. 228.

57 *FOD*, vol. 1, p. 419.

58 Semenova, "Nikolai Fedorovich Fedorov," p. 89.

59 For Fyodorov's ideas on progress, see *FOD*, vol. 1, pp. 18–23.

60 *FOD*, vol. 1, p. 276.

61 At the end of his life Zabolotsky changed this final line to read: "Chto schast'e chelovechestva – bessmertno" ("That Human Happiness is Undying"). Interestingly, this was one of the poems (along with "Woodland Lake," "Metamorphoses," and others) that Aleksandr Fadeyev criticized for its assumption of equality between humans and animals. In a 1948 letter to the director of "Soviet Writer" publishing house, Fadeyev wrote: "Everywhere you must remove or ask the author to rewrite the passages where

animals, insects, and others are assigned a place equal to man ..." Quoted in Nikita Zabolotskii, "Moskovskoe desiatiletie," p. 260

62 Mihajlo Mihajlov heard this story from Viktor Shklovsky. See Mihajlov, *Moscow Summer*, New York: Farrar Straus Giroux, 1965, pp. 102–103.

63 For Shklovsky's memoirs of Tsiolkovsky see his *Zhili-byli* (*Once Upon a Time*), Moscow: Sovetskii pisatel', 1966, pp. 448–460.

64 Charlotte Douglas, "Beyond Reason: Malevich, Matiushin and Their Circles," in *The Spiritual in Art. Abstract Painting 1890–1985*, p. 191.

65 See John Milner, *Vladimir Tatlin and the Russian Avant-Garde*, New Haven: Yale University Press, 1983, pp. 178–179.

66 Ibid., p. 244, note 41.

67 Letter of 7 January 1932, in *Izbrannoe*, vol. 2, p. 235.

68 Cf. Tsiolkovsky's *Nirvana*, Kaluga, 1914.

69 "Volia vselennoi. Neizvestnye razumnye sily" ("The Will of the Universe. Unknown Rational Forces"), Kaluga, 1928, p. 5.

70 Here it is interesting to compare the poet Osip Mandelstam's view of universal happiness as described by his wife: "... he did not see universal happiness as the goal of history. He felt the same way about universal happiness as he did about personal happiness: 'Why do you think that you must be happy?' The theory of universal happiness seemed to him the most bourgeois of all that we inherited from the nineteenth century." In Osip Mandel'-shtam, *Sobranie sochinenii*, v. 2, p. 599.

71 In retrospect, with our historical knowledge of such theories as Mengele's on building a supreme race, Tsiolkovsky's ideas seem rather horrifying. It must be stressed that he intended no evil and was convinced of his crusade for the good of all mankind. In this context see also Aleksei Tolstoy's *Giperboloid Inzhenera Garina* (*Engineer Garin's Hyperboloid*) (1925–26) with its ideas on extermination and selective procreation, and Sergei Tretyakov's play *Khochu rebenka* (*I Want a Child*) (1927), where the creation of a new world calls for physically and ideologically perfect people.

72 "Stat'i 'Pravdy' otkryvaiut nam glaza."

73 "Volia vselennoi," pp. 1–2.

74 Letter of 18 January 1932, in *Izbrannoe*, pp. 236–239.

75 "Monizm vselennoi" ("The Monism of the Universe"), p. 12.

76 Cf. Yevgeny Zamyatin's *My* (*We*): "We walked again – a million-headed body: in each one of us resided that humble joyfulness with which in all probability molecules, atoms, and phagocytes live." (From *Record Twenty-Two*; quoted here in the English

translation by Gregory Zilboorg [New York: E.P. Dutton, 1952]).
The State in *We* shares many of the attributes of Tsiolkovsky's
utopia.

77 "Monizm vselennoi," p. 16. Cf. also Valery Bryusov's poem
"Mir elektrona" ("The World of the Electron," 1924): "Byt′
mozhet, eti elektrony –/Miry, gde piat′ materikov .../Eshche,
byt′ mozhet, kazhdyi atom –/Vselennaia, gde sto planet .../Ikh
mery maly, no vse ta zhe/Ikh beskonechnost′, kak i zdes′;/Tam
skorb′ i strast′, kak zdes′, i dazhe/Tam ta zhe mirovaia spes′."
("Perhaps these electrons/Are worlds with five continents
.../And perhaps every atom is /A universe with one hundred
planets .../Their proportions are small, but their/Infiniteness is
as great as ours;/They have our passion and grief,/Even the same
worldly conceit.").

78 Letter of 18 January 1932, *Izbrannoe*, p. 236.

79 In other poems, such as "The Trees," Zabolotsky takes an
opposite point of departure. See the discussion of dissection and
construction in chapter 1, p. 54.

80 Ibid.

81 See F.T. Marinetti, "Manifesto del Futurismo" (1909), in *Archivi
de Futurismo*, ed. Gambillo, Maria Drudi and Teresa Fiori, Roma:
de luca editore, vol. 1, 1958, p. 19.

82 Zabolotsky's dream of harmony, even if preternatural, is consistent with his utopian ideal, and in the context of his vision of
universal transformation it is interesting to note the curious
affinities between "The Triumph of Agriculture" and another
long poem, V.S. Pecherin's "The Triumph of Death." ("Torzhestvo smerti," written in 1833–34. The complete text of the
poem is in M. Gershenzon, *Zhizn′ V.S. Pecherina* (*The Life of V.S.
Pecherin*), Moscow: Put′, 1910, pp. 71–90. I am grateful to Nina
Perlina for directing me to Pecherin's work.)
   Both works are dramatic long poems in which not only
humans, but animals and spirits also speak. In both poems,
shortly after spirits from the past enter, great storms blow in, and
when the storms subside, the sun rises (in Zabolotsky, a "red
atom of resurrection"; in Pecherin, an "eternal sun"). Both works
are universal and cosmic, offering a vision of nature transformed.
In "The Triumph of Agriculture," a tractor initiates the process:

> И загремела даль лесная
> Глухим раскатом буквы 'А',
> И вылез трактор, громыхая,
> Прорезав мордою века.
> И толпы немощных животных,

Упав во прахе и пыли,
Смотрели взором первородных
На обновленный лик земли.

The distant forest began to thunder
With the dull peal of the letter 'A',
And a tractor rolled out, rumbling,
Having cut through the centuries with its snout.
Throngs of helpless animals,
Tumbling into ashes and dust,
Looked with primeval gaze
Upon the renewed face of the earth.

In the final section of "The Triumph of Death," Pecherin presents his triumphant vision of a universe restored, in language remarkably similar to Zabolotsky's. Here Death itself is the source of universal renewal:

Смерть

Обновляйся, лик природы!
Ветхий мир, пади во прах!
Вспряньте, юные народы,
В свежих вольности венках!

Death

Renew yourself, face of nature!
Old world, fall into dust!
Arise, young peoples,
In the fresh wreaths of liberty!

Many aspects of Zabolotsky's conception of metamorphosis are present in Pecherin's poem, only where Pecherin focusses on death as the initiator of the transformation process, and thereby the great liberator, Zabolotsky sees an inverse process.

4 MAD WISDOM: THE LONG POEMS

1 Quoted in Nikita Zabolotskii, "Kratkie vospominaniia ob ottse i o nashei zhizni" ("Brief Reminiscences of my Father and of our Life"), *Vospominaniia*, p. 203.
2 Specifically, Part 3, "The Exile," which deals with the kulak and his alienation from society, was greatly shortened and retitled "The Enemy" ("Vrag"). Only a few copies of the original printing survived. See notes to the poem by B.A. Filippov in *Stikhotvoreniia*, p. 328.

3 On the relationship between satire and utopia see Robert C. Elliott, *The Shape of Utopia*, Chicago: The University of Chicago Press, 1970 (particularly Chapter One).

4 See Michael André Bernstein, " 'O Totiens Servus': Saturnalia and Servitude in Augustan Rome," in Robert von Hallberg, ed., *Politics & Poetic Value*, Chicago: University of Chicago Press, 1987, p. 39.

5 See the reviews by E. Usievich, "Pod maskoi iurodstva" ("Under the Mask of Foolishness"), *Literaturnyi kritik* (*The Literary Critic*), 1933, no. 4, pp. 78–91; Mikhail Golodnyi, "Poetu iurodivykh" ("To the Poet of Fools" [a parody of "The Triumph of Agriculture"]), *Krasnaia nov'*, 1933, no. 9, pp. 85–86; and Ermilov, "Iurodstvuiushchaia poeziia i poeziia millionov/O 'Torzhestve zemledeliia' N. Zabolotskogo."

6 There is also a darker side to Saturn's reign, since he victimized his children.

7 Yury Lotman and Boris Uspensky have written that in early Russian culture, "change takes place as the radical rejection of the preceding stage. The natural result of this was that the new emerged not from the structurally 'unexploited' reserve, but as a result of the transformation of the old, as it were, of its being turned inside out. In this way repeated changes could in fact lead to the *regeneration* of archaic forms." This formulation provides a useful way of looking at Zabolotsky's poem. See Iu. M. Lotman and B.A. Uspenskij, "The Role of Dual Models in the Dynamics of Russian Culture (Up to the End of the Eighteenth Century)," in Ann Shukman, ed., *The Semiotics of Russian Culture*, Ann Arbor: The Department of Slavic Languages and Literatures/The University of Michigan (Michigan Slavic Contributions, No. 11), 1984, p. 5.

8 Zabolotsky employs a number of striking images to show the dynamics of change and frequently uses grotesque imagery to represent the regenerating power so crucial to the transformation process. In fact, the grotesque becomes the ruling aesthetic force of his poetic world. The grotesque serves as an important catalyst for change in Zabolotsky's poem because it is always in a state of flux, representing a metamorphosis of sorts in which disparate realms of being are confounded, the human approaching the animal, the animal mingling with the plant. The grotesque expresses the ambivalence of these mergings: they are both beginning and end, birth and death, new and old in one. Because of its generic confusions, the grotesque acts as a liberating force from all that is routine and universally accepted (see Wolfgang

Kayser, *The Grotesque in Art and Literature*, Gloucester, Mass.: Peter Smith, 1968.)

In its capacity as a liberating force, the grotesque has been related to laughter and carnival, specifically by Mikhail Bakhtin. The kinship of grotesque with carnival is evident in the ritual uncrowning of kings, the mockery of sacred institutions during carnival time, and traditional mummery. Bakhtin regards carnival as the second life of the people, organized on the basis of laughter (Mikhail Bakhtin, *Rabelais and His World*, trans. Hélène Iswolsky, Cambridge, Mass.: The MIT Press, 1968, p. 8 [English translation of Bakhtin's 1965 publication, *Tvorchestvo Fransua Rable i narodnaia kul'tura srednevekov'ia i Renessansa*]). This laughter is liberating, for it frees the people from fear. Carnival expresses a utopia where all are equal and where a sense of community prevails. The participants are temporarily liberated from the humdrum routine of their daily lives as the golden age of Saturn returns. Thus carnival involves a process of change and renewal, one which is never closed or stagnant and which is opposed to all pretense at immutability (Bakhtin, *Rabelais*, p. 11). In essence, carnival exemplifies that which is being formed and becoming.

In "The Triumph of Agriculture" the continually shifting narrative voices and the intentionally pluralistic worldview can be readily interpreted as representing a carnival stance. But Zabolotsky's use of carnival differs significantly from Bakhtin's description of it. First, carnival is not as liberating as Bakhtin implies: while it can invert the given order, it never finally liberates (only the grotesque can do that). Second, and more important for "The Triumph of Agiculture," although Zabolotsky introduces images from a "culture of laughter" including carnival to advance his vision of a world renewed, his laughter imagery involves a strong sense of the diabolical or demonic, in contrast to Bakhtin's portrayal of laughter as joyful and positive.

9 Evgenii Zamiatin, "Herbert Wells," in *Litsa (People)*, New York: izd-vo imeni Chekhova, 1955, p. 141.

10 Cf. Robert C. Elliott's characterization of utopia as "Janus-faced," easily slipping into a satirical mode. Elliott, *The Shape of Utopia*, p. 22.

11 Yury Lotman considers laughter in the Russian tradition to be demonic and in this regard refutes the theories of Mikhail Bakhtin. See Iu. M. Lotman and B.A. Uspenskij, "New Aspects in the Study of Early Russian Culture," in Shukman, *The Semiotics of Russian Culture*, p. 40.

12 For more on the comic and demonic see ibid., p. 42.

13 Many years after writing "The Triumph of Agriculture" Zabolotsky stated that the theme of the poem was "the triumph of collectivization." See Lunin, "Nikolai Zabolotskii," p. 126.

14 This image recalls an old Russian riddle about death and resurrection. When the priest arrives after someone dies, he finds the deceased peeking out the window. The riddle asks, "Who is it?" The answer is: "Grain." Grain pushing up through the earth signifies resurrection from burial, the metamorphosis from death into life. In alluding to this riddle, Zabolotsky's line "Skvoz' okoshko khleb gliadel" ("Grain peeked through the window") sets the poem's major theme of new life resulting from old.

15 Irene Masing-Delic, "Zabolockij's Occult Poem 'Carica much,' " p. 35, note 10.

16 In the twenties Zabolotsky saw an album of Bruegel's paintings and often spoke of his interest in the artist (Sinel'nikov, "Molodoi Zabolotskii," *Vospominaniia*, 2nd ed., p. 109). V.N. Al'fonsov proposes a correspondence between Zabolotsky and Bruegel in his *Slova i kraski*. On carnival imagery in Bruegel see N.M. Gershenzon-Chegodaeva, *Breigel*, Moscow: Iskusstvo, 1983.

17 Kim Vasin, "Zhar-ptitsa" ("The Firebird"), in *Kuznets pesen (The Farrier of Songs)*, Ioshkar-Ola: Mariiskoe knizhnoe izdatel'stvo, 1976, p. 176.

18 Hesiod, *The Works and Days*, trans. by Richmond Lattimore, Ann Arbor: The University of Michigan Press, 1973, p. 71.

19 Cf. these lines from Kharms' 1930 poem "On i mel'nitsa" ("He and the Mill"): "[On]: A nyne vash otets zdorov? [Mel'nitsa]: O da, on uchit azbuke korov." ("[He]: Is your father well these days? [Mill] Oh yes, he's teaching cows the alphabet.") In Kharms, *Sobranie proizvedenii*, vol. 2, p. 83.

20 We might also interpret the soldier's dream as an attempt to create new myths for mankind based on the constellations in the sky: the cows in the dream could belong to the Pleiades and Hyades that constitute Taurus (*telets*); the gushing milk could represent the Milky Way. Long ago man created symbols and legends to describe the stars in an effort to understand them; in "The Triumph of Agriculture," Zabolotsky creates a modern mythology for his age. In this regard, his handling of the constellation Aquarius (*Vodolei*) is of particular interest. From Lipavsky's notes we know that Zabolotsky was interested in astrology. His choice of Aquarius – and his later excision of all three references to it – suggests that he understood the connotations of this sign. According to popular belief, the Age of Aquarius was to begin in March, 1948. Even if Zabolotsky

remained unaware of the specific date, it is likely that he internalized the idea of Aquarius as harbinger of a new age characterized by scientific advancement, reason, and greater freedom. (As J.E. Cirlot defines it, "Aquarius symbolizes the dissolution and decomposition of the forms existing within any process, cycle or period; the loosening of bonds; the imminence of liberation through the destruction of the world of phenomena." [*A Dictionary of Symbols*, London: Routledge and Kegan Paul, 1962, p. 15]). Under Aquarius, conflicting forces were to come into balance. Significantly, in Khlebnikov's "Ladomir," the revolt of the slaves is connected with Aquarius; in Zabolotsky's poem, this new age arrives with the tractor, as the soldier proclaims: "Slav'sia, slav'sia, Zemledel'ie,/Ravnodeistvie mashin!" ("Glory, glory, Agriculture,/The equilibrium of machines!"

21 V.P. Shestakova, ed., *Russkaia literaturnaia utopiia* (*Russian Literary Utopia*), Moskva: izd. Moskovskogo universiteta, 1986, p. 13. In Russia, the dream historically has offered a means of avoiding censorship, since what the hero unconsciously sees cannot necessarily be blamed on the author's conscious intent. This point is noteworthy because Russian utopias have tended to carry social criticism that must be transmitted obliquely. "The Triumph of Agriculture" can be seen in this regard as perpetuating popular utopian traditions.

22 Barbara Lönnqvist, *Xlebnikov and Carnival*, Stockholm: Almqvist & Wiksell, 1979, p. 109.

23 The final scene of "The Triumph of Agriculture" also fits Bakhtin's characterization of carnival as a "utopian realm of community, freedom, equality and abundance." See Bakhtin, *Rabelais*, p. 9.

24 See Lotman and Uspenskij, "New Aspects in the Study of Early Russian Culture," p. 42.

25 E. Usievich, "Pod maskoi iurodstva," p. 80.

26 Vladimir Propp, *Theory and History of Folklore*, trans. by Ariadna Y. and Richard P. Martin, Minneapolis: University of Minnesota Press, 1984 (Theory and History of Literature, vol. 5), p. 138.

27 See ibid., p. 133.

28 This creative feature of Zabolotsky's work aligns him not only with Filonov, but also with the filmmaker Aleksandr Dovzhenko. Dovzhenko's film "Earth" ("Zemlia"), released in 1929, provides a striking visual parallel to Zabolotsky's scene of the tractor thundering into the village, a symbol of the new life about to

ensue. (From the poet's son, we know that Zabolotsky saw "Earth" in 1930 or 1931 and liked it immensely. By that time he had already begun work on "The Triumph of Agriculture" and perhaps even finished a draft of the poem. [Nikita Zabolotsky, letter of 4 February 1987 to this writer])

Both Zabolotsky and Dovzhenko focus on the heightened emotions of the villagers as they await the arrival of the first tractor. Considering the common atmosphere in which Zabolotsky and Dovzhenko worked, the similarities between the poem and the film are not entirely surprising; but it is notable that both works go well beyond their ostensible theme of collectivization to embrace symbolically the issues of life and death (the treatment of what happens to the soul after death is particularly striking). The critics were harsh to Dovzhenko as they soon would be to Zabolotsky, branding "Earth" a distortion of reality and a misguided "biological solution to a social conflict." (See L. Varpakhovskii, "'Zemlia' A. Dovzhenko" ("A. Dovzhenko's 'Earth'"), *Pechat' i revoliutsiia*, 1930, no. 3, p. 71.)

29 On the basis of a passage Zabolotsky once underlined from the diary of Eugène Delacroix, it would seem that he considered finalization as stifling to art as to life. The extract is revealing for Zabolotsky's own work: "He [Campbell] was never content with what he had achieved; he ruined his best things by excessive finishing; the whole brilliance of his first creative burst disappeared. This is every bit as true for poems as for paintings; they should not be too finished." (Quoted in Nikita Zabolotskii, "K tvorcheskoi biografii Nikolaia Zabolotskogo" ["Toward a Creative Biography of Nikolai Zabolotsky"], *Voprosy literatury*, 1979, no. 11, p. 235.)

30 This community also meets many of the requirements for Soviet society: automation has replaced manual labor; a *kolkhoz* (collective farm) has been organized; the populace is newly literate. It should be stressed that nowhere does "The Triumph of Agriculture" actually conflict with Soviet ideology; rather, it was the general tone of the poem that displeased the critics, who found it too flip for its subject. They also judged Zabolotsky too sympathetic toward his "ridiculous" characters.

31 Khlebnikov, *Sobranie sochinenii*, vol. 2, p. 30.

32 See "Sokha-kormilitsa" ("The Wet-Nurse Plough") in *Krasnaia gazeta*, vechernii vypusk, 2 January 1928.

33 This was Zabolotsky's dismayed response when his early poems were compared to those of Dostoyevsky's Captain Lebyadkin. See chapter 1, note 86.

34 Quoted in J.T. Fraser, *Of Time, Passion, and Knowledge*, New York: George Braziller, 1975, p. 502.
35 For a broad discussion of NTR and Soviet poetry, see A.V. Makedonov, "O nekotorykh aspektakh otrazheniia NTR v sovetskoi poezii" ("On Some Aspects of the NTR as Reflected in Soviet Poetry"), *NTR i razvitie khudozhestvennogo tvorchestva* (*NTR and the Development of Artistic Creation*), Leningrad, 1980, pp. 97–117. While the term generally is applied to the mid-twentieth century, Makedonov loosely dates the beginning of the NTR as 1905 when Einstein's theory of relativity was published. I am using the term in its broader application here.
36 Zabolotsky wrote several other poems in dialogue form. Especially interesting is his "Disciplina clericalis" (1926), a three-way conversation among the poet, his intellect, and his spontaneous self.
37 In *Stikhotvoreniia i poemy*, Moscow, 1965.
38 Quoted from a conversation in 1933 or 1934 in T. Lipavskaia, "Vstrechi s Nikolaem Alekseevichem i ego druz'iami," p. 52.
39 As a child Zabolotsky assimilated the legends of the pagan Mari among whom he grew up. (The Mari, previously called Cheremis, settled around the Vyatka River in the fifteenth century.) The special appeal of Mari folklore for Zabolotsky and its potential as a source of inspiration for "The Mad Wolf" can be deduced from several documents. From accounts by Zabolotsky's family, we know that the poet encountered Mari tales and religious beliefs when still a child. He was entranced by the rituals he saw when accompanying his father on agricultural visits to Mari villages in the environs of Sernur. Many of these villages still relied on shamans; in fact, the Mari sacred grove was only a gully away from the Zabolotsky home. The poet's sister recalls how "in the spring, when everything was turning green and the birches were putting out leaves, Mari from the two neighboring villages ... would conduct their prayers." An animistic component akin to Mari belief is apparent in the Mad Wolf's investigations of the kinships among all living things, which affirm the deep commonality between man and the natural world. (See Nikita Zabolotskii, "N.A. Zabolotskii i kniga," p. 272; Kim Vasin, "Sernur pesennyi" ["Sernur of Songs"], *Sled na zemle* [*Traces on the Earth*], Ioshkar-Ola: Mariiskoe knizhnoe izdatel'stvo, 1964, p. 49; and L. D'iakonov, "Nikolai Zabolotskii v Urzhume" ["Nikolai Zabolotsky in Urzhum"], *Viatka*, Kirov, 1961, pp. 60–61. For a description of the Mari rituals as Zabolotsky might have witnessed them, see Kim Vasin, "Zhar-ptitsa," p. 162.)

Although the transformations in Zabolotsky's poem have much in common with pagan conceptions of the world, it would be mistaken to find in "The Mad Wolf" only new renderings of ancient tales. Pagan legends may account for the magical underpinnings of the poem, but the intellectual basis of "The Mad Wolf" results from the conscious and deliberate application of a literary text, namely Goethe's *Faust*. Unfortunately, space limitations in the present study preclude an examination of the extensive correspondences between the two poems.

40 Ovid, *Metamorphoses*, trans. Rolfe Humphries, Bloomington: Indiana University Press, 1955, p. 3.

41 I have translated "dushevnaia sila" as "spiritual strength," even though "dusha" properly refers to the soul, not the spirit. In the Russian religious and philosophical traditions the two are not synonymous.

42 This strange simile also appears in "Poema dozhdia" ("Poem of the Rain"), written in the same year. This shorter poem, with its questing wolf and skeptical snake, expresses in more rudimentary form many of the ideas developed in "The Mad Wolf."

43 For a retelling of this legend see N. Teleshev, "Zhivoi kamen'" ("The Living Rock"), in *Zhivoi kamen'* (*The Living Rock*), Ioshkar-Ola: Mariiskoe knizhnoe izdatel'stvo, 1970, pp. 179–181.

44 According to one source, the worship of the warrior-hero Chumbulat "was at one time connected with a huge stone which was located along the Nemda River near the town of Chembula-tova. The stone, also called *čembulat*, was about thirty-five feet high and one hundred and ten feet wide. It was broken up by Russian missionaries in 1830 in order to destroy the Cheremis beliefs in pagan spirits." See Thomas A. Sebeok and Frances J. Ingemann, *Studies in Cheremis: The Supernatural*, New York: Wenner-Gren Foundation for Anthropological Research, 1956, p. 58.

45 The idea of a "living rock" was particularly attractive to Zabolotsky. In "Yesterday, Pondering Death," the philosopher Grigory Skovoroda's face shines forth from a rock.

46 See, for example, the section on "The Fusion of Animals and New Life Forms" in N.S. Melik-Pashaev's article "Chelovek budushchego" ("The Man of the Future") in *Zhizn' i tekhnika budushchego. Sotsial'nye i nauchno-tekhnicheskie utopii* (*The Life and Technology of the Future. Social and Techno-Scientific Utopias*), ed. N.N. Zhordaniia, Moscow: Moskovskii rabochii, 1928, pp. 409ff. On Melnikov see S. Frederick Starr, *Melnikov. Solo Architect in a Mass Society*, Princeton: Princeton University Press, 1978, p. 180.

47 Zabolotsky also may be making a veiled allusion to the increasing number of distorted biological experiments conducted under Stalin's approval. For more on these scandals in Soviet science see David Joravsky, *The Lysenko Affair*, Cambridge: Harvard University Press, 1970; and Raissa L. Berg, *Acquired Traits. Memoirs of a Geneticist from the Soviet Union*, New York: Viking, 1988.

48 For more on Zabolotsky's early reading see Nikita Zabolotskii, "N.A. Zabolotskii i kniga."

49 Due to space limitations, only a few other examples can be cited here. As the poem begins, the verse structure is reminiscent of *raeshnyi stikh*, a form of folk poetry popular in the seventeenth and eighteenth centuries and characterized by uncomplicated rhyming couplets. The aphoristic couplets spoken by the bear characterize him as a primitive, yet he does not turn out to be the monolithic figure the reader is led to expect. In his rejoinder to the wolf, the bear's language – perhaps inspired by the wolf's own lofty words – is already more elegant than the folksy couplets he initially uttered. His description of the wolf in the forest ("Ona [figurka] plyla, podobno rybam,/Tuda, gde neba plamena" ["It [the figure] was floating, like fish,/Toward the flames of the sky"]) evokes the poetry of Fyodor Tyutchev, Russia's foremost nineteenth-century metaphysical poet. According to a concordance of Tyutchev's works, the word *nebo* "sky" occurs one hundred twenty times in his poetry, while the various forms of the root *plam* – "flame" are encountered hardly less frequently. (Borys Bilokur, *A Concordance to the Russian Poetry of Fedor I. Tiutchev*, Providence: Brown University Press, 1975, pp. 325ff.) And the image of the floating wolf straining to see the stars echoes lines from Tyutchev's "Kak okean ob″emlet shar zemnoi" ("As the Ocean Covers the Earth"). Significantly, it is the backward bear who speaks in a Tyutchevian mode. Zabolotsky twists the poetic stance of apprehension before the gaping abyss by associating the bear, with his primordial fear of chaos, with Tyutchev's lines. Furthermore, he cannot resist distorting Tyutchev – even as the bear imitates him – by using the simile "like fish." While obviously "learning from the classics" (as the critic Tarasenkov put it), Zabolotsky does not fail to give his wit full rein, invariably making the poetry his own.

Further on in the poem, the bear becomes enraged at the wolf's dreams and cries: "S dorogi proch'! Idu na vy!" ("Out of my way! I'm coming against you!"). Here, the literary associations are lofty indeed. "Idu na vy!" is the battle cry from the *Povest'*

vremennykh let (*Russian Chronicles*), a message sent by Prince
Svyatoslav to Constantinople warning of his imminent attack.
Svyatoslav's words were repeated many centuries later by Khlebnikov in both his early poem "My zhelaem zvezdam tykat'"
("We want to be on familiar terms with the stars," *c.* 1908) and
his later "Kubok pechenezhskii" ("The Pecheneg Goblet,"
1916). Zabolotsky's use of this line is thus many-layered.

50 Compare Pimen's lines "Bezumnye potekhi iunykh let" and "Ia
dolgo zhil i mnogim nasladilsia" ("The mad amusements of
young years" and "I've lived long and enjoyed a lot") with the
Mad Wolf's "Vse eto shutki prezhnikh let" and "Ia mnogikh sam
perekusal" ("But those are all pranks of bygone years" and "I
myself bit my fair share"). Although other echoes from Pushkin
occur throughout the poem, they are too numerous to include in
this overview.

51 Cf. these lines from Khlebnikov's "Pochemu" ("Why," 1921–22):
"Lisan'ka ... vzobralas'/I razmyshliala o budushchem .../Razve
sobakoiu stat'?" ("The fox ... clambered up/and pondered the
future .../Could she really become a dog?").

52 The pertinent lines read: "Vol'chei zhizni reformator,/Ia, khotia
i nekrasiv,/Budu zhit', kak imperator,/Chast' nauki otkusiv."
("The reformer of wolves' lives,/I, albeit ugly,/Will live like an
emperor,/Having tasted of science." The colorful Russian
expression *gryzt' nauku* (literally, "to gnaw science") means "to
study hard"; here, not only will the Mad Wolf gnaw at science, he
will actually bite off a bit of it (*otkusit'*). In a complicated trope,
Zabolotsky emphasizes the basically carnivorous nature of the
wolf by playing on a standard phrase that expresses the attain-
ment of knowledge. As one image elides with the next, he is able to
depict the wolf as both reformer and savage beast.

53 Although Zabolotsky is content for the most part merely to
amplify Derzhavin's style, at the end of Part Two he imitates him
openly. In Derzhavin's 1784 ode "Bog" ("God") we find: "Ia
tsar' – ia rab – ia cherv' – ia bog!" ("I'm an emperor – a slave – a
worm – a god!") Zabolotsky's Mad Wolf cries: "Ia – tsar' zemli!
Ia – gladiator dukha!/Ia – Garpagon, pod"iatyi v nebesa!" ("I
am the ruler of the earth! The gladiator of the spirit!/I am
Harpagon, raised up to the heavens!") (The allusion to Harpagon from Molière's *L'Avare* underscores the Wolf's obsession, but
whereas Harpagon sacrificed everything to his greed, the Mad
Wolf makes his sacrifice to science.) In these lines, Zabolotsky
preserves Derzhavin's hyperbole and use of contradictions for

effect, but instead of employing the eighteenth-century odic four-foot iamb, he uses the elegiac iambic pentameter, a mode appropriate to this tale of imminent tragedy.

54 This relationship has often been noted. Wolfgang Kayser, for one, writes: "... from an early date, insanity, quasi-insanity and dreams were used to define the source of creativity." Kayser, *The Grotesque in Art and Literature*, p. 184.

55 In his 1913 study, Hieromonk Aleksei defines *iurodstvo* as "the separateness of certain individuals from society and their conscious renunciation of society for certain aims of salvation." See his *Iurodstvo i stolpnichestvo. Religiozno-psikhologicheskoe issledovanie (Fools in God and Stylites. A Religio-psychological Study)*, St. Petersburg, 1913, p. 58.

56 In this respect Zabolotsky, like many artists of the avant-garde, may be seen as participating in Russia's neovitalist movement. See Charlotte Douglas, "Evolution and the Biological Metaphor in Modern Russian Art," *Art Journal*, vol. 44, 1984, pp. 153–161.

57 Zabolotsky's idea is akin to Kandinsky's dictum that "form alone, even though totally abstract and geometrical, has a power of inner suggestion." (Wassily Kandinsky, *Concerning the Spiritual in Art*, New York: Dover Publications, 1977, p. 28).

58 Cf. William Blake: "And every Generated Body in its inward form/Is a garden of delight & a building in magnificence ..." (*Milton*, Book the First, Boulder: Shambhala and New York: Random House, 1978, p. 105.)

59 For an earlier image of nature as a stove of life see Zabolotsky's 1928 "Pekarnia" ("The Bakery"), in which the bakery oven is likened to a woman giving birth.

60 The pertinent lines read: "A pechka zhizni vse pylaet,/Gorit, treshchit elemental,/I chelovek ladon'iu podsypaet/V miasnoe varevo siiaiushchii kristall." ("The stove of life still blazes,/The elemental spirit burns and crackles/And with his palm man sprinkles/Sparkling crystal in the meaty broth.") Zabolotsky also uses alchemistic imagery, including the *elemental*, in "Queen of the Flies." See Irene Masing-Delic, "Zabolockij's Occult Poem 'Carica Much'," pp. 21–38.

61 Zabolotsky's idea that nature is capable of continual self-perfection is distinctly Lamarckian, a poetic stance politically unwise for the Thirties (in 1930 Soviet geneticists had declared that "Lamarckist teleology conflicted with the Marxist outlook." See Joravsky, *The Lysenko Affair*, p. 234). Mandelstam also praised Lamarck in his 1932 poem "Lamark" ("Lamarck").

62 The concept of verticality is particularly important to the poem.

The vertical posture of the animals, with their eyes fixed on the "vertical stars" above, reflects not only their spiritual progression, but also the Fyodorovian concept of verticality as *samosozdanie* or "self-creation." See Lukashevich, *N.F. Fedorov*, p. 48.

63 Zabolotskii, *Izbrannoe*, vol. 1, p. 381.

64 Vladimir Ivanovich Vernadskii, "Biosfera v kosmose" ("The Biosphere in the Cosmos"), *Biosfera. Izbrannye trudy po biogeokhimii (The Biosphere. Selected Works in Biogeochemistry)*, Moscow: Mysl', 1967, p. 260. The limiting factor that Vernadsky fails to mention is the availability of the resources (food) for the growth of these organisms. They do not create this mass, but merely convert it from one form to another.

65 Grigorii Savvich Skovoroda, "Razgovor piati putnikov ob istinnom schastii v zhizni (Razgovor druzheskii o dushevnom mire)" ("A Conversation Among Five Travellers About True Happiness in Life [A Friendly Conversation About the Spiritual World]"), *Sochineniia v dvukh tomakh (Works in Two Volumes)*, Moscow: Mysl', 1973, vol. 1, pp. 337–338.

66 For more on Skovoroda's philosophy, including a useful bibliography, see Joseph T. Fuhrmann, "The First Russian Philosopher's Search for the Kingdom of God," *Essays on Russian Intellectual History*, Austin: University of Texas Press, 1971, pp. 33–72.

67 Raisa Berg affirms that "Questions of symmetry interested Vernadsky. He linked the moment when life originated on Earth with the origination of asymmetry in the structure of albuminous molecules." (Berg, "Palachi i rytsari sovetskoi nauki ["Butchers and Knights of Soviet Science"], *Vremia i my [Time and Us]*, New York, 1982, no. 65, p. 175.)

68 In this respect Vernadsky followed Fyodorov. In terms of theory, too, Fyodorov may be seen as Vernadsky's precursor for his ideas on the regulation of nature. It is not surprising that Vernadsky chaired the Fyodorovian Commission for the Study of the Natural Productive Forces of Russia (see Young, *Nikolai Fedorov*, p. 183).

69 Metchnikoff (1845–1916), a professor at the Pasteur Institute, was considered an expert in the science of life. For an explication of his ideas see *The Nature of Man. Studies in Optimistic Philosophy*, New York: G.P. Putnam's Sons, 1910 (rpt. 1977).

70 I.A. Kozikov, *Filosofskie vozzreniia V.I. Vernadskogo (The Philosophical Views of V.I. Vernadsky)*, Moscow: Izdatel'stvo moskovskogo universiteta, 1963, p. 48.

71 Ibid., pp. 33–34.

72 Vernadsky did not fully work out his theory of the noosphere until the late 1930s; hence Zabolotsky independently developed his

idea of a new "plane of existence" brought about in large part by reason.

73 This passage is quoted in chapter 1, pp. 47–49.

74 See John E. Bowlt, "Esoteric Culture and Russian Society," p. 176.

75 Kozikov, *Filosofskie vozzreniia V.I. Vernadskogo*, p. 54.

76 For a very different representation of the properties of the sphere, see Kharms' poem "Mne vse protivno" ("Everything Offends Me"), written in the same year. (In Kharms, *Sobranie proizvedenii*, vol. 3, p. 64.)

77 Kozikov, *Filosofskie vozzreniia V.I. Vernadskogo*, p. 59.

78 Wassily Kandinsky, in a letter to Will Grohmann of 12 October 1930, quoted in Rose-Carol Washton Long, "Expressionism, Abstraction, and the Search for Utopia in Germany," *The Spiritual in Art: Abstract Painting 1890–1985*, p. 214.

79 This is Kazimir Malevich's characterization of his Black Square.

80 The Russian word for autumn is *osen'*. Thus "O" is a graphic representation of the season. The Russian *khorda* refers to a mathematical chord, i.e., a straight line joining two points on a curve.

81 Grigorii Skovoroda, "Razgovor o tom: znai sebe" ("A Conversation About Knowing Oneself"), *Sochineniia v stikhakh i proze* (*Works in Verse and Prose*), St. Petersburg, 1861, pp. 55–138.

82 Skovoroda, "Razgovor o tom: znai sebe," p. 138.

83 A.I. Pavlovskii, "Filosofskaia lirika" ("Philosophical Lyrics"), *Problemy russkoi sovetskoi literatury. 50–70e gody* (*Problems of Russian Soviet Literature. The '50s to the '70s*), Leningrad: Nauka, 1976, p. 216.

84 For commentary on Skovoroda in relation to Zabolotsky's late poetry see ibid., pp. 216–218.

85 Quoted in Rostovtseva, *Nikolai Zabolotskii. Opyt khudozhestvennogo poznaniia*, p. 97.

86 Skovoroda, *Sochineniia v stikhakh i proze*, p. 87.

87 Ibid., p. 67.

88 Cf. the use of "head" in both Russian (in its Church Slavonic form) and English to express power or, at the very least, prominence.

89 Skovoroda, *Sochineniia v stikhakh i proze*, p. 60.

90 In writing about utopias, Gary Saul Morson has stated: "A key point I would like to make is that utopias insist on that familiar paradox: the "real" world is an illusion and the imagined world is the higher Reality." (Morson, *The Boundaries of Genre*, Austin: University of Texas Press, 1981, p. 86.) This is certainly true for Zabolotsky's poem.

5 AUTUMNAL OBSERVATION

1 See Helen Vendler, "Second Thoughts," *The New York Review of Books*, April 28, 1988, p. 41.

2 Stanislav Kuniaev, "Ogon', mertsaiushchii v sosude," pp. 95–122. In this essay Kuniaev cites with approval an appalling poem about Zabolotsky by Anatolii Peredreev, one stanza of which reads: "Ty zaplatil v svoem nachale dan'/Nabegu razrushitel'nykh glagolov,/I lish' polei netronutaia dal'/Tebia spasla ot nikh, kak ot mongolov." ("You began by paying tribute/To the forays of destructive verbs,/And only the distant virgin fields/Saved you from them, as from the Mongols.").

3 Renato Poggioli, *The Poets of Russia*, Cambridge, Mass.: Harvard University Press, 1960, p. 339.

4 Aleksis Rannit, "Zabolotskii: A Visionary at a Crossroads of Expressionism and Classicism," in *Stikhotvoreniia*, p. XXII.

5 Letter to M.I. Kas'ianov, 7 November 1921, in *Izbrannoe*, p. 231.

6 According to the poet's son, this was Zabolotsky's favorite poem. Along with "The Nightingale" it is the only serious poem Zabolotsky composed during the eight years of his imprisonment and exile. He did, however, write a number of humorous poems or *stishki* during those years. See Nikita Zabolotskii, "Ob otse i o nashei zhizni" ("About Father and about our Life"), *Vospominaniia*, 2nd edn, p. 264.

7 In the first variant of the poem the sick man's eye is "ustremlennoe k miru inomu" ("fixed on another world"). See *Sobranie sochinenii*, vol. 1, p. 620.

8 See, for example, Zabolotsky's letter of 19 April 1941, quoted in chapter 2.

9 Zabolotsky's response to nature was not unique. Varlam Shalamov has written of a similar experience, as has Andrei Sinyavsky, for whom nature gave "so much food for heart and eye even in [prison] that one wants constantly to thank it." (See Abram Tertz, *A Voice from the Chorus*, p. 123.)

10 Aleksandr Blok associated birds with artistic creation in his 1913 poem "Khudozhnik" ("The Artist").

11 Butterflies held mixed appeal for Zabolotsky. Nikolai Chukovsky relates that he once tried to win Zabolotsky's admiration for the poet Fet by reading him Fet's description of a butterfly. Zabolotsky replied: "Have you ever examined a butterfly carefully, up close? Didn't you ever notice what a terrifying snout (*morda*) it has, and what a disgusting body?" (Quoted in Chukovskii, "Vstrechi s Zabolotskim," p. 225.) In this context cf. Mandel-

stam's 1933 poem "O, babochka, o, musul'manka" ("O, Butter-fly, o Moslem").

12 Zabolotsky could also have a sense of humor about his situation, however, as evidenced by the *stishok* "Pishmashinka i avtor" ("An Author and His Typewriter") he composed for Nikolai Stepanov in 1949 or 1950. The verse ends with the author chastising his typewriter for complaining about so much work: "Ty, dura, nichego ne ponimaesh', – /Ty lish' stat'i moi perebeliaesh',/A mne za nikh vletaet po spine." ("You don't understand a thing, you fool –/You only make clean copies of my articles,/But I catch hell for them.") Published in *Sobranie sochinenii*, vol. 1, p. 471.

13 Apart from political considerations, Zabolotsky may have dis-carded this version for artistic reasons. The word *gorlyshko* in Russian is not only the diminutive for "throat" but also means the "neck" of a bottle. Perhaps Zabolotsky deemed the implied conjunction of *pet'* "to sing" and *gorlyshko* too close to the phrase *pit' iz gorlyshka*, "to drink from the bottle."

14 One example of many will suffice. The following lines from "The Ivanovs" are written in iambic tetrameter, with alternating masculine/feminine rhymes and ending in a couplet (ababcc):

> Стоят чиновные деревья,
> Почти влезая в каждый дом.
> Давно их кончено кочевье,
> Они в решетках, под замком.
> Шумит бульваров теснота,
> Домами плотно заперта.

15 For a detailed analysis of this poem, see E.G. Etkind, "N. Zabolotskii. 'Proshchanie s druz'iami'" ("N. Zabolotsky. 'A Farewell to Friends'"), *Poeticheskii stroi russkoi liriki* (*The Poetic Structure of Russian Lyrics*), Leningrad: Nauka, 1973, pp. 298–310.

16 Zabolotsky's desire to find this unity was constant throughout his career: the philosopher in "Disciplina clericalis" (1926) draws similar parallels, comparing inanimate objects to "sisters" and "brothers"; and Bombeev in "The Trees" vows to "seek, in defiance of fate/My fathers, brothers, and my sisters."

17 Zabolotsky also evinces social concerns in many of the poems from *Scrolls* and in the long poems.

18 See also Zabolotsky's 1957 essay, "Pochemu ia ne pessimist" ("Why I am not a Pessimist"), where he writes of "the majestic buildings of thought, unseen to the eye, which . . . rise above the life of the human world." In *Sobranie sochinenii*, vol. 1, p. 592.

19 Nikita Zabolotskii, "K tvorcheskoi biografii N. Zabolotskogo," p. 221.

20 Nikita Zabolotskii, "Ob otse i o nashei zhizni," p. 270. *Russkaia starina* was published from 1870 to 1918.

21 Aleksei Agafonovich founded the Urzhum Museum of Local History and later donated these artifacts to it. See Nikita Zabolotskii, "Put' k 'Slovu'," p. 212.

22 The seminar was taught by Professor D.V. Bubrikh. See ibid.

23 "Osada Kozel'ska" has been lost, although the poetic fragment "Sobor, kak drevnii kazemat" is presumed to belong to the projected third part of the poem. (See *Sobranie sochinenii*, vol. 1, p. 630.)

24 Nikolai Zabolotskii, "O neobkhodimosti obrabotki russkikh bylin" ("On the Need to Rework the Russian *Byliny*"), *Sobranie sochinenii*, vol. 1, pp. 557–9.

25 Nikita Zabolotskii, "N.A. Zabolotskii i kniga," p. 285. For an excellent English translation of Rubruck's report of his travels, see *The Mission of Friar William of Rubruck. His Journey to the Court of the Great Khan Möngke 1253–1255*, trans. Peter Jackson, London: The Hakluyt Society, 1990.

26 Nikita Zabolotskii refers to "Rubruck in Mongolia" as a "cycle of poems" ("tsikl stikhotvorenii"). See Nikita Zabolotskii, "N.A. Zabolotskii i kniga," p. 286.

27 It is also possible that Zabolotsky had been thinking about this theme for nearly thirty years, since Rubruck figures in the 1929 novel *Trudy i dni Svistonova* (*The Works and Days of Svistonov*) by the Oberiut Konstantin Vaginov.

28 S.V. Poliakova has demonstrated convincingly that Zabolotsky used as his source for "Shepherds" the medieval drama "Komediia na Rozhdestvo Khristovo" ("Christmas Comedy") by Dimitri Rostovsky. See her article "'Komediia na Rozhdestvo Khristovo' Dimitriia Rostovskogo – istochnik 'Pastukhov' N.A. Zabolotskogo" ("Dimitri Rostovskii's 'Christmas Comedy' – the Source of N.A. Zabolotskii's 'Shepherds'"), *Trudy otdela drevnerusskoi literatury akademii nauk SSSR* (*Proceedings of the Division of Old Russian Literature of the Soviet Academy of Sciences*), vol. 33, 1979, pp. 385–387.

29 Zabolotskii, *Sobranie sochinenii*, v. 1, p. 636.

30 Pasternak has said of Zabolotsky's late poetry: "When he read his poems here, it seemed as if he had hung on the walls a multitude of framed pictures, which did not disappear but continued to hang ..." (In Zoia Maslenikova, "Portret poeta," p. 291.)

31 See Tyutchev's "Osennii vecher" ("Autumn Evening", 1830) and "Est' v oseni pervonachal'noi" ("In the Beginning of Autumn there is ...", 1857), as well as Pushkin's "Osen'" ("Autumn", 1835), particularly Stanzas V and VII.

32 Osip Mandel'shtam, "Barsuch'ia nora" ("The Badger's Lair"),
    Sobranie sochinenii, vol. 2, p. 270.
33 Quoted in Roskina, *Chetyre glavy*, p. 77.
34 Interview in Stanford, California, May, 1982. Elsewhere Brodsky
    has said: "[Zabolotsky] is an absolutely wonderful poet
    ("sovershenno zamechatel'nyi poet"). The early as well as the
    late." Asked whether he prefers the early or late Zabolotsky,
    Brodsky replied: "I don't know. Both are equally valuable to
    me." (Unpublished interview with Tomas Venclova, February
    16, 1988).

Select bibliography

This bibliography lists all the major editions of Zabolotsky's poetry as well as other pertinent works. It is not intended to be exhaustive. The listing does not, for instance, enumerate Zabolotsky's uncollected poems and articles, and while the major editions of Zabolotsky's translations for adults are included, his books and translations for children are not. For an extensive bibliography of works by and about Zabolotsky up to the mid-1980s, the reader should refer to *Russkie sovetskie pisateli. Poety. Bibliograficheskii ukazatel'*, vol. 9. Moscow, 1986, 192–256. See also the bibliography in Zabolotskii, *Stikhotvoreniia*, ed. G.P. Struve and B.A. Filippov. Washington, 1965, 271–299; and Filippov, G., "Bibliografiia literatury o N. A. Zabolotskom," *Sovetskaia poeziia dvadtsatykh godov*. Leningrad, 1971, 181–202.

This bibliography consists of three sections: major editions of Zabolotsky's work; works about Zabolotsky; and works of general interest. In this latter category are listed books and articles that deal with the artistic influences that helped shape Zabolotsky's vision, as well as works treating the Russian political and cultural milieus of the 1920s and 1930s. Further references are included in the Notes to the Text.

I. MAJOR EDITIONS OF ZABOLOTSKY'S WORK

Collected Works (listed chronologically, beginning with the most recent edition)

Stolbtsy i poemy. Stikhotvoreniia. Moscow, 1989.

Stikhotvoreniia i poemy. Moscow, 1985.

Sobranie sochinenii v trekh tomax. Moscow, 1983–1984. [This is the most complete edition of Zabolotsky's work to date]

Stikhotvoreniia i poemy. Moscow, 1981.

Izbrannye proizvedeniia v dvukh tomax. Moscow, 1972.

Stikhotvoreniia i poemy (Biblioteka poeta, Bol'shaia seriia). Moscow–
Leningrad, 1965.
Stikhotvoreniia, ed. G. Struve and B.A. Filippov. Washington, D.C.
and New York, 1965.
Izbrannoe. Moscow, 1960.
Separate volumes of verse (listed chronologically)
Stolbtsy. Leningrad, 1929. rpt. Ann Arbor, 1980; English trans. by
Daniel Weissbort. *Scrolls,* London, 1971.
Vtoraia kniga. Leningrad, 1937.
Stikhotvoreniia. Moscow, 1948.
Stikhotvoreniia. Moscow, 1957.
Veshnikh dnei laboratoriia (*Stikhotvoreniia 1926–1937 gody*), ed. N.N.
Zabolotskii. Moscow, 1987.

Memoirs and uncollected letters
"The Story of My Imprisonment." trans. Robin Milner-Gulland.
Times Literary Supplement, 9 October 1981, 1179–1181; rpt. in Russian
in *Minuvshee* 2 (1986) and *Novoe Russkoe Slovo,* 21 November 1986.
"Dusha obiazana trudit'sia: Pis'ma Nikolaia Zabolotskogo."
ed. N.N. Zabolotskii and E.V. Zabolotskaia. *Literaturnoe obozrenie*
5 (1983), 106–112.
"Zhivaia dusha cheloveka" [letters to family from exile]. ed.
N.N. Zabolotskii. *Sobesednik,* vyp. 4, Moscow, 1983, 293–301.
"Iz pisem N. Zabolotskogo zhene iz zakliucheniia. 1938–1944 gody."
ed. N.N. Zabolotskii and E.V. Zabolotskaia. *Znamia* 1 (1989),
96–127.

Major editions of poetry translations (listed alphabetically)
Gruzinskaia klassicheskaia poeziia v perevodakh N. Zabolotskogo (v dvukh
tomakh). Tbilisi, 1958.
Guramishvili, David. *Davitiani: Stikhotvoreniia i poemy.* Translated
from the Georgian. Moscow, 1953.
Na dvukh Aragvakh peli solov'i. Stikhi o Gruzii. Gruzinskie poety. Perevody.
Tbilisi, 1975.
Pshavela, Vazha. *Stikhotvoreniia i poemy* (Biblioteka poeta, Bol'shaia
seriia). Translated from the Georgian. Leningrad, 1957.
Rustaveli, Shota. *Vitiaz' v tigrovoi shkure.* Translated from the Georg-
ian. Moscow, 1957. rpt. 1962, 1966, 1969, 1977, 1982.
Slovo o polku Igoreve. Translated from the Old Russian. Moscow, 1983.

II. WORKS ABOUT ZABOLOTSKY (LISTED ALPHABETICALLY)

Al'fonsov, V.N. *Slova i kraski.* Moscow, 1966, 177–230.

Aleksandrov, A.A. "Oberiu. Predvaritel'nye zametki." Česko-slovenska Rusistika 5 (1968), 296–303.
"Stikhotvorenie Nikolaia Zabolotskogo 'Vosstanie.'" *Russkaia literatura* 3 (1966), 190–193.
Amsterdam, A. "Bolotnoe i Zabolotskii." *Rezets* 4 (1930), 12–14.
Antokol'skii, Pavel. "Oborval sebia na poluslove …" *Nedelia* 20 (1973).
Berggol'ts, Ol'ga. "Novyi put'. Na vechere N. Zabolotskogo v Dome pisatelia." *Literaturnyi Leningrad*, 23 December 1936.
Beskin, Osip. "O poezii Zabolotskogo, o zhizni i o skvoreshnikakh." *Literaturnaia gazeta*, 11 July 1933.
Björling, Fiona. *Stolbcy by Nikolaj Zabolockij. Analyses.* Stockholm, 1973.
"'Ofort' by Nikolaj Zabolockij. The Poem and the Title." *Scando-Slavica.* Tomus 23 (1977), 7–16.
Chikovani, Simon. "Vernyi drug gruzinskoi poezii (Pamiati N. Zabolotskogo)." *Literaturnaia Gruziia* 6 (1958), 61–68.
Denisova, E.L. "Struktura tsikla N. Zabolotskogo 'Posledniaia liubov' (k voprosu o tiutchevskoi traditsii)." *Traditsii i novatorstvo v sovetskoi literature. Sbornik trudov.* Moscow, 1977, 145–153.
D'iakonov, L.V. "Nikolai Zabolotskii v Urzhume." *Viatka*, Kirov, 1961, 60–61.
"Viatskie gody N.A. Zabolotskogo. *Kirovskaia pravda*, 8 May 1978.
Dozorets, Zh.A. "'Mozhzhevelovyi kust' N.A. Zabolotskogo (opyt kompleksnogo analiza)." *Filologicheskie nauki* 6 (1979), 51–58.
Dymshits, A. "O dvukh Zabolotskikh." *Literaturnaia gazeta*, 15 December 1937.
Ermilov, V. "Iurodstvuiushchaia poeziia i poeziia millionov" [review of "The Triumph of Agriculture"]. *Pravda*, 21 June 1933.
Ermolinskii, Sergei. "Nikolai Zabolotskii. Saguramo." In Ermo-linskii, *Iz zapisok raznykh let. Mikhail Bulgakov. Nikolai Zabolotskii.* Moscow, 1990, 234–255.
Etkind, Efim. "N. Zabolotskii. 'Proshchanie s druz'iami.'" *Poeti-cheskii stroi russkoi liriki*, Leningrad, 1973, 298–310.
"Slovesnaia analogiia muzikal'no-simfonicheskomu tsiklu. Poema N. Zabolotskogo 'Gorod v stepi.'" *Materiia stikha.* Paris, 1978, 479–490.
Filippov, G.B. "O 'Lodeinikove' N. Zabolotskogo (K probleme evoliutsii tvorcheskikh printsipov." *Sovetskaia literatura. Problemy masterstva.* Leningrad, 1968, 167–181.
"Poeticheskii mir Nikolaia Zabolotskogo." *Zvezda* 5 (1973), 182–189.

Ginzburg, Lidiia. "Zabolotskii kontsa dvadtsatykh godov." In Ginzburg, *O starom i novom*. Leningrad, 1982, 339–350.
Gitovich, Sil'va. "Arest N.A. Zabolotskogo." *Pamiat'*, Paris, 1982, 336–353.
Golodnyi, Mikhail. "Poetu iurodivykh" [parody of "The Triumph of Agriculture"]. *Krasnaia nov'* 9 (1933), 85–86.
Gorelov, Anatolii. "Raspad soznaniia" [review of *Scrolls* and "The Triumph of Agriculture"]. *Stroika* 1 (1930).
Grishchinskii, K. and G. Filippov. "Tak oni nachinali ... O studencheskom zhurnale 'Mysl',' o N. Braune i N. Zabolotskom." *Zvezda* 11 (1978), 182–189.
Ierardi, Vera. "L'Ordine nel Disordine: Costruzione di un'utopia." *Annali. Sezione Slava.* Napoli, 1979, 225–243.
Karlinsky, Simon. "Surrealism in Twentieth-Century Russian Poetry: Churilin, Zabolotskii, Poplavskii." *Slavic Review*, vol. 26, Dec. 1967, 605–617.
Kaverin, V. "Za rabochim stolom." *Novyi mir* 9 (1965), 163–168.
Kievskii, M.I. "Neizdannaia kniga N. Zabolotskogo." *Russkaia literatura* 2 (1971), 163–164.
Kuniaev, Stanislav. "Ogon', mertsaiushchii v sosude." In Kuniaev, *Svobodnaia stikhiia*, Moscow, 1979, 95–122.
Likhachev, D. and N. Stepanov. "Rabota N. Zabolotskogo nad perevodom 'Slova o polku Igoreve.'" *Voprosy literatury* 1 (1969), 164–176.
Ljunggren, Anna. "Oblich'ia smerti: k interpretatsii stikhotvoreniia N. Zabolotskogo 'Ofort.'" *Scando-Slavica*, Tomus 27 (1981).
Lunin, Evgenii. "Nikolai Zabolotskii: 'Ia nashel v sebe silu ostat'sia v zhivykh.'" *Avrora* 8 (1990), 125–133.
Makedonov, A.V. *Nikolai Zabolotskii: Zhizn'. Tvorchestvo. Metamorfozy.* Leningrad, 1968. 2nd. ed. 1987.
"Puti i pereput'ia N. Zabolotskogo." *Ocherki sovetskoi poezii.* Smolensk, 1960.
Masing-Delic, Irene. "Some Themes and Motifs in N. Zabolockij's 'Stolbcy.'" *Scando-Slavica*, Tomus XX, 1974, 13–25.
"The Chickens Also Want to Live': A Motif in Zabolockij's *Columns*." *Slavic and East European Journal* 3 (1987), 356–369.
"Zabolockij's Occult Poem 'Carica Much.'" *Svantevit. Dansk Tidsskrift for Slavistik*, Årgang III, nr. 2, 1977, 21–38.
"Zabolotsky's 'The Triumph of Agriculture': Satire or Utopia?" *Russian Review* 42 (1983), 360–376.
Milner-Gulland, Robin. "Grandsons of Kozma Prutkov: Reflections on Zabolotsky, Oleynikov and their Circle." *Russian and Slavic Literature*, Columbus, Ohio, 1976, 313–327.

"Left Art in Leningrad; the OBERIU Declaration." Oxford Slavonic Papers, N.S. III, Oxford, 1970, 65–75.

"Zabolotsky and the Reader: Problems of Approach." *Russian Literature Triquarterly* 8, 385–392.

"Zabolotsky: Philosopher-poet." *Soviet Studies* 22 (1971), 595–608.

"Zabolotsky's *Vremia*." *Essays in Poetics*, vol. no. 1 (1981), 86–95.

Neznamov, P. "Sistema devok" [review of *Scrolls*]. *Pechat' i revoliutsiia* 3 (1930), 77–80.

Pavlovskii, A. "Nikolai Zabolotskii." In Pavlovskii, *Poety-sovremenniki*. Moscow–Leningrad, 1966, 167–228.

"Nikolai Zabolotskii. Filosofskii mir. Poetika. Traditsii." *Russkaia literatura* 2 (1965), 34–58.

Poliakova, S. "'Komediia na Rozhdestvo Khristovo' Dmitriia Rostovskogo – istochnik 'Pastukhov' N.A. Zabolotskogo." *Trudy otdela drevnerusskoi literatury akademii nauk SSSR*, v. 33 (1979), 385–387.

Popov, Iu. "Nikolai Zabolotskii v Karagande." *Prostor* 4 (1984), 202.

Pratt, Sarah. "Antithesis and Completion: Zabolockij Responds to Tiutcev." *Slavic and East European Journal* 2 (1983), 211–227.

Rodnianskaia, I. "Poeziia N. Zabolotskogo." *Voprosy literatury* 1 (1959), 121–137.

Roskina, Natal'ia. *Chetyre glavy*. Paris, 1980, 61–98.

Rostovtseva, I. *Nikolai Zabolotskii: Literaturnyi portret*. Moscow, 1976. rpt. as *Nikolai Zabolotskii: Opyt khudozhestvennogo poznaniia*. Moscow, 1984.

Sarnov, V. "Vosstavshii iz pepla. Poeticheskaia sud'ba N. Zabolotskogo," *Oktiabr'* 2 (1987), 188–202.

Savchenko, T. "Khlebnikov i Zabolotskii (k probleme metricheskogo svoeobraziia)." *Russkaia i zarubezhnaia literatura*, vyp. 11. Alma-Ata, 1971, 55–61.

Selivanovskii, A. "Sistema koshek" [review of *Scrolls*]. *Na literaturnom postu* 15 (1929), 31–35.

Shilova, K.A. "O siuzhete v lirike N. Zabolotskogo." *Problemy russkogo romantizma i realizma*. Kemerovo, 1973, 154–175.

Silina, E.V. "Tema prirody v poezii V. Khlebnikova i N. Zabolotskogo." *Voprosy metodiki i istorii literatury*. Pskov, 1970, 42–57.

Sinel'nikov, I. "Molodoi Zabolotskii," *Pamir* 1 (1982), 59–69.

Smirnov, I. "Zabolotskii i Derzhavin." *XVIII vek*. Leningrad, 1969, sb. 8, 144–161.

Stepanian, Elena. "Khudozhnik svoei zhizni. Zametki o lirike Nikolaia Zabolotskogo." *Literaturnoe Obozrenie* 5 (1988), 27–31.

Stepanov, Nikolai. "Nikolai Zabolotskii. Stolbtsy" [review]. *Zvezda* 3 (1929), 190–191.

"Novye stikhi N. Zabolotskogo." *Literaturnyi sovremennik* 3 (1937), 210–218.
Tarasenkov, Anatolii. "Pokhvala Zabolotskomu" [review of *Scrolls* and "The Triumph of Agriculture"]. *Krasnaia nov'* (1933), 177–181.
Turkov, A. *Nikolai Zabolotskii*. Moscow, 1966.
Nikolai Zabolotskii: Zhizn' i tvorchestvo. Posobie dlia uchitelei. Moscow, 1981.
Usievich, E. "Pod maskoi iurodstva." *Literaturnyi kritik* 4 (1933), 78–91; rpt. in *Tri stat'i*, Moscow, 1934, 325–348.
Vasin, Kim. "Russkii poet Mariiskogo kraia." In Zabolotskii, *Stikhotvoreniia i poemy*. Ioshkar-Ola, 1985, 137–141.
Zabolotskaia, E.V. and A.V. Makedonov. "Stikhi Nikolaia Zabolotskogo." *Literaturnaia Gruziia* 4 (1969), 185–188.
eds. *Vospominaniia o Zabolotskom*. Moscow, 1977. 2nd. ed. 1984.
Zabolotskii, N.N. "K tvorcheskoi biografii Nikolaia Zabolotskogo." *Voprosy literatury* 11 (1979), 220–237.
"Moskovskoe desiatiletie" [chapter from a forthcoming biography]. *Moskovskii vestnik* 1, 1991, 253–313.
"N.A. Zabolotskii i kniga." *Vstrechi s knigoi*, vyp. 2, Moscow, 1984, 271–291.
"Ob otse." *Daugava* 3 (1988), 105–116.
"Put' k 'Slovu.'" *Almanakh bibliofila*, vyp. Moscow, 1986, 211–230.
"Vzaimootnosheniia cheloveka i prirody v poezii N.A. Zabolotskogo." *Voprosy literatury* 2 (1984), 34–52.
"Zabolotskii pishet 'Stolbtsy'" [chapter from forthcoming biography]. *Avrora* 3 (1992), 80–91.
Zoshchenko, M. "O stikhakh N. Zabolotskogo." *Rasskazy, povesti, fel'etony, teatr, kritika 1935–1937*. Leningrad, 1937, 381–387.
Zuev, Nikolai. "'Dusha obiazana trudit'sia.' Nikolai Zabolotskii." *Zhizn' i poeziia – odno*. Moscow, 1990, 228–246.

III. WORKS OF GENERAL INTEREST (LISTED ALPHABETICALLY)

Afishi doma pechati 2 (1928), 11–12.
Aleksandrov, A.A. "Materialy D.I. Kharmsa v rukopisnom otdele Pushkinskogo doma." *Ezhegodnik rukopisnogo otdela Pushkinskogo doma na 1978 god*. Leningrad, 1980, 64–79.
Bakhterev, I. and A. Razumovskii. "O Nikolae Oleinikove." *Den' Poezii*. Leningrad, 1964, 154–160.
Bakhtin, Mikhail. *Rabelais and His World*. Cambridge, Mass., 1968.
Barron, Stephanie and Maurice Tuchman. *The Avant-Garde in Russia 1910–1930*. Los Angeles, 1980.

Berg, Raisa. "Palachi i rytsari sovetskoi nauki." *Vremia i my* (1982), 160–231.

Bondarev, T.M. "Trudoliubie i tuneiadstvo, ili torzhestvo zemledel'tsa." In G.I. Uspenskii, "Trudami ruk svoikh." *Polnoe sobranie sochinenii* 9, Leningrad, 1949, 91–118.

Brown, Edward J. *Russian Literature Since the Revolution.* New York, 1963. rpt. Cambridge, Mass., 1982.

Cohen, Stephen F. *Bukharin and the Bolshevik Revolution.* New York, 1973.

Cornwell, Neil, ed. *Daniil Kharms and the Poetics of the Absurd: Essays and Materials.* New York, 1991.

"Dnevniki Filonova v vospominaniiakh ego sestry Glebovoi." V. Chalidze, ed. *SSSR: Vnutrennie protivorechiia* 10. Benson, Vt., 1984, 129–273.

Douglas, Charlotte. "Evolution and the Biological Metaphor in Modern Russian Art." *Art Journal,* vol. 44, 1984, 153–161.

Elliott, Robert C. *The Shape of Utopia.* Chicago, 1970.

Engels, Frederick. *Dialectics of Nature.* trans. Clemens Dutt. New York, 1940.

Fedorov, N.F. *Filosofiia obshchego dela.* ed. V.A. Kozhevnikov and N.P. Peterson, 2nd ed. Verny 1906/Moscow 1913, rpt. Westmead, England, 1970.

Flaker, Aleksandar. "Avangard i erotika." *Russkaia literatura* XXXII (1992), 41–52.

Fleishman, Lazar. *Boris Pasternak v tridtsatye gody.* Jerusalem, 1984.

Forsh, Ol'ga. *Sumasshedshii korabl'.* Leningrad, 1931; rpt. Washington, 1964.

Fuhrmann, Joseph T. "The First Russian Philosopher's Search for the Kingdom of God." *Essays on Russian Intellectual History.* Austin, 1971, 33–72.

Gasparov, Boris M. "Poema A. Bloka 'Dvenadtsat'' i nekotorye problemy karnavalizatsii v iskusstve nachala XX veka." *Slavica Hierosolymitana.* Jerusalem, 1977, 109–131.

Gibian, George, ed. *Russia's Lost Literature of the Absurd. A Literary Discovery.* Ithaca, New York, 1971; rpt. as *The Man in the Black Coat: Russia's Literature of the Absurd.* Evanston, Ill., 1987.

Gleason, Abbott. et al. *Bolshevik Culture. Experiment and Order in the Russian Revolution.* Bloomington, Ind., 1985.

Iudina, M.V. *Stat'i, vospominaniia, materialy.* Moscow, 1978, esp. 262–268.

Jaccard, Jean-Phillipe. *Daniil Harms et la fin de l'avant-garde russe* [Slavica Helvetica 39]. Bern, 1991.

Jakobson, Roman. *Noveishaia russkaia poeziia.* Prague, 1921.

K istorii russkogo avangarda/The Russian Avant-Garde. Stockholm, 1976.

Kayser, Wolfgang. *The Grotesque in Art and Literature.* Gloucester, Mass., 1968.

Kharms, Daniil. *Sobranie proizvedenii* [v 4-kh tomakh]. Bremen, 1978–1988.

Khlebnikov, Velimir. *Sobranie sochinenii,* München, 1968–1972.

Khodasevich, Vladislav, "Dom iskusstv." *Literaturnye stat'i i vospominaniia,* New York, 1954.

Kiselev, A. "Uchenie N.F. Fedorova v svete sovremennosti (o Filosofii Obshchego Dela)." *Grani,* vol. 81 (1971), 122–153.

Kovtun, E.F. "Iz istorii russkogo avangarda (P.N. Filonov)." *Ezhegodnik rukopisnogo otdela Pushkinskogo doma na 1977.* Leningrad, 1979, 216–235.

Kovtun, E.F. and A.V. Povelikhina. "'Utes iz budushchego.' Arkhitekturnye idei Velimira Khlebnikova." *Tekhnicheskaia estetika* 5–6 (1976), 40–42.

Kozikov, I.A. *Filosofskie vozzreniia V.I. Vernadskogo.* Moscow, 1963.

Kříž, Jan. *Pavel Nikolajevič Filonov.* Prague, 1966.

Lesnaia, Lidiia. "Utuerebo" [review of OBERIU performance]. *Krasnaia gazeta,* vech. vyp., 25 January 1928.

Levin, Ilya. "The Fifth Meaning of the Motor Car: Malevich and the Oberiuty." *Soviet Union/Union Sovietique* 5, pt. 2 (1978), 287–295.

Likhachev, D.S. and A.M. Panchenko. *"Smekhovoi mir" drevnej Rusi.* Leningrad, 1976.

Lodder, Christina. *Russian Constructivism.* New Haven, 1983.

Lönnqvist, Barbara. *Xlebnikov and Carnival. An Analysis of the Poem 'Poet'* [Stockholm Studies in Russian literature 9]. Stockholm, 1979.

Lotman, Iurii. *Analiz poeticheskogo teksta: Struktura stikha.* Leningrad, 1972, esp. 256–270.

Lukashevich, Stephen. *N.F. Fedorov. A Study in Russian Eupsychian and Utopian Thought.* Newark, Del., 1977.

Maguire, Robert. *Red Virgin Soil.* Princeton, 1968.

Mandelstam, Nadezhda. *Hope Against Hope.* New York, 1976.

Mandelstam, Osip. *Sobranie sochinenii v trekh tomakh.* New York, 1971.

Markov, Vladimir. "Mysli o russkoi futurizme." *Novyi zhurnal* 38 (1954), 169–181.

Medvedev, Roy. *Nikolai Bukharin. The Last Years.* New York, 1980.

Men'shutin, A. and A. Siniavskii. *Poeziia pervykh let revoliutsii. 1917–1920.* Moscow, 1964.

Misler, Nicoletta. "Pavel Nikolaevich Filonov. Slovo i znak." *Russian Literature* XI (1982), 237–308.

and John E. Bowlt. *Pavel Filonov: A Hero and His Fate*. Austin, 1983.
My znali Evgeniia Shvartsa. Moscow, 1966.
Oleinikov, Nikolai. *Ironicheskie stikhi*. New York, 1982.
Puchina strastei. Leningrad, 1991.
Pecherin, V.S. "Torzhestvo smerti." In M. Gershenzon, *Zhizn' V.S. Pecherina*, Moscow, 1910, 71–90.
Poret, Alisa. "Vospominaniia o Kharmse." *Panorama iskusstv* 3, Moscow, 1980, 345–359.
Postupal'skii, I. "K voprosu o nauchnoi poezii." *Pechat' i revoliutsiia* 2–3 (1929), 51–68.
Rakhtanov, I.A. *Rasskazy po pamiati*. Moscow, 1966.
Semenova, S.G. "Nikolai Fedorovich Fedorov (Zhizn' i uchenie)." *Prometei* 11, Moscow, 1977, 87–105.
Shklovskii, Viktor. *Sentimental'noe puteshestvie. Vospominaniia 1917–1922*. Moscow, 1923.
Shukman, Ann, ed. Lotman, Ju. M. and B.A. Uspenskij, *The Semiotics of Russian Culture* [Michigan Slavic Contributions 11]. Ann Arbor, 1984.
Skovoroda, Grigorii Savvich. *Sochineniia v dvukh tomakh*. Moscow, 1973.
Sokol, Elena. *Russian Poetry for Children*. Knoxville, 1984.
Starr, S. Frederick. *Melnikov. Solo Architect in a Mass Society*. Princeton, 1978.
Stepanov, N. "V zashchitu izobretatel'stva. Makalaturnyi potok." *Zvezda* 6 (1929), 182–192.
Stites, Richard. *Revolutionary Dreams. Utopian Vision and Experimental Life in the Russian Revolution*. New York, 1989.
Struve, Gleb. *Russian Literature under Lenin and Stalin*. Norman, Ok., 1971.
The Spiritual in Art: Abstract Painting 1890–1985. Los Angeles and New York, 1986.
Thomson, Philip. *The Grotesque*. London, 1972.
Tsiolkovskii, Konstantin. *Budushchee zemli i chelovechestvo*. Kaluga, 1928.
Monizm vselennoi. Kaluga, 1925.
Rastenie budushchego. Zhivotnoe kosmosa. Samozarozhdenie. Kaluga, 1929.
Volia vselennoi. Neizvestnye razumnye sily. Kaluga, 1928.
Vernadskii, V.I. *Biosfera. Izbrannye trudy po biogeokhimii*. Moscow, 1967.
Vvedenskii, Aleksandr. *Polnoe sobranie sochinenii*. Ann Arbor, 1980.
Weststeijn, Willem G. *Velimir Chlebnikov (1885–1992): Myth and Reality* [Amsterdam symposium on the centenary of Velimir Chlebnikov]. Amsterdam, 1986, esp. 543–572.

Wiles, Peter. "On Physical Immortality. Materialism and Transcendence." *Survey* 56 (1965), 125–143; Pt. II, *Survey* 57 (1965), 142–161.

Young, George M., Jr. *Nikolai Fedorov. An Introduction.* Belmont, Mass., 1979.

Zhordaniia, N.N., ed. *Zhizn' i tekhnika budushchego. Sotsial'nye i nauchnotekhnicheskie utopii.* Moscow, 1928.

Index

Titles of works are listed under the names of the authors

CAMBRIDGE STUDIES IN RUSSIAN LITERATURE

General editor MALCOLM JONES

Editorial board: ANTHONY CROSS, CARYL EMERSON,
HENRY GIFFORD, BARBARA HELDT, G. S. SMITH,
VICTOR TERRAS